Dad,

I thought these would remind
you of your Sierra experience.

Happy Birthday

Love,

Lisa

August 16th — no, um, is
it August 18th? Nope
that's not right either.
Oh yeah, I remember,
August 19, 1997

THE NATURE OF NATURE

SOS

THE NATURE OF NATURE

NEW ESSAYS FROM
AMERICA'S FINEST
WRITERS ON NATURE

EDITED BY

WILLIAM H. SHORE

A HARVEST BOOK
HARCOURT BRACE & COMPANY
San Diego   New York   London

CONTENTS

———————— ～ ————————

CONTENTS

CONTENTS

PREFACE

⌒

AL GORE

John Muir, America's foremost conservationist, once wrote: "This grand show is eternal. It is always sunrise somewhere; the dew is never all dried at once; a shower is forever falling; vapor is ever rising. Eternal sunrise, eternal sunset, eternal dawn and gloaming, on sea and continents and islands, each in its turn, as the round earth rolls."

This collection of new essays invites a fresh and closer look at the beauty and mystery of that grand show. An appreciation of nature is a prerequisite for saving our endangered planet. From local crises of air and water pollution to global phenomena like the destruction of the rain forests, global warming, and the diminished diversity of plant and animal species, our relationship to nature is undergoing profound change, and not for the better. A burgeoning worldwide population and our natural environment are on a collision course with potentially catastrophic consequences.

I learned in the course of researching and writing my own book, *Earth in the Balance,* that the challenge of saving our planet and creating a sustainable lifestyle is one too large for government alone. Each of us must find a way to make a difference, a way to contribute. As I wrote at the time, I have come to believe that the world's ecological balance depends on more than just our ability to restore a balance between civilization's appetite for resources and the fragile equilibrium of our environment. It depends on more, even, than our ability to restore a balance between ourselves as individuals and the civilization we aspire to create and sustain. In the end, we must restore a balance within ourselves, between who we are and what we are doing.

These essays inspire a reverence for nature's beauty and our place in it, as well as that sense of inner balance upon which we all ultimately depend. Each of these essays will take you on a journey to a world of which we are of course a part—but can never fully know. Ideally, when you return you will keep a small part of that mysterious new world with you—to learn from, to cherish, and to revisit for further exploration. If just one of these essays instills a sense of greater curiosity, protectiveness, and commitment toward our natural resources, then this book will have succeeded on at least one level.

This collection helps us renew ourselves in a second way as well, as a model of how creative people can use their talent to make a broader contribution to the world around them. For this book is at once a celebration of nature and also a celebration of creative individuals, individuals who have found a unique way to give something back to their community.

Each of the contributing writers to this anthology donated their work so that the proceeds could be used by Share Our Strength, an organization committed to leading the fight against hunger here in the United States and around the world. So whether the authors are musing upon the closely observed habits of moths and millipedes, or exploring terrain ranging from the Adirondacks to northern India, through this book they are using their talent to help others in need.

Let us all follow the lead of these authors. Let us all take more responsibility for our friends and our families, and for our communities and our world. With service to community and a new appreciation for nature, we can renew our environment and help alleviate poverty—and we can renew our spirits and ourselves.

INTRODUCTION

WILLIAM H. SHORE

It should not be surprising that nature writing, at its best, so often reaches the level of fine literature. All of the elements of great literary drama are there for us to discover in the natural world: life and death, growth and the struggle for survival, beauty and mystery, evolutionary patterns and the randomness of fate.

No act is more natural, more synonymous with nature, than the simple act of growing. But there are children in America today who are not growing the way they should be, because they are hungry and malnourished. They are under height, underweight, often neurologically and developmentally impaired. We know this from surveys, from medical research, and from what doctors and teachers and social workers see with their own eyes.

Fortunately, hunger in America has not reached a point at which children starve and die in the streets or fields, as is the case in some impoverished developing countries. But as a result, its severity is often hidden or disguised or ignored. More than 10 percent of the entire population of the United States, somewhere between twenty-five million and thirty million people, depend upon public or private food assistance for their survival. The funds that Share Our Strength raises and distributes are specifically aimed at reaching and helping these people.

The funds provide emergency food assistance to children and their families and also go beyond that, supporting not only clinical efforts aimed at treating the most severe victims of malnutrition but also long-term educational and advocacy efforts designed to prevent hunger in the first place. The funds raised from books like this one help provide revenue necessary to fund such programs.

This book exists because the generosity of the contributing writers has been matched by a commitment from Harcourt Brace to benefit the broader public interest. No one's commitment has been greater than that of Alane Mason, our editor there. Her skill, judgment, and dedication helped to bring out the best in this book. Her assistant Celia Wren, and SOS's editorial assistants Meg Russell and Marie Nash, also were instrumental in fitting together the many pieces that make an anthology whole. Finally, Flip Brophy, our agent at Sterling Lord Literistic, who has donated her time on behalf of this cause, is the member of the SOS family who unfailingly brings all of our ideas for books to fruition.

One's relationship to nature is a deeply personal experience. To some it's best represented by a walk in the park, or along the river, or under a summer night's sky. To others it reaches its pinnacle in the study of a smell, a sound, the sight of a bird's egg, a gray whale, or lodgepole pine. And while all of nature is laid out before us to appreciate, not all is understood, known, or even knowable. But about human nature we do know at least one thing, which is that it embodies an irrepressible and infinite ability to create, to express, to give, and to share. This fine collection of essays is ample testimony to that. I hope that you will take not only enjoyment but inspiration from this work.

THE NATURE OF NATURE

A CAREFULLY
CONTROLLED EXPERIMENT

———— ⌒ ————

BILL McKIBBEN

June 29—It is a warm, close afternoon, and I am stringing twine around a small patch of the forest behind my home.

Why am I stringing twine around a small patch of forest? Because, by God, I am through with being a dilettante. This morning I finished writing a magazine article on the oldest trees in the eastern United States—seventeen-hundred-year-old bald cypresses in North Carolina swamps, Massachusetts hemlocks nearly half a milennium old, the magnificent tulip poplars of the Smokies. I spent most of my time in these groves peering up slack-jawed and thinking my usual liberal-arts-type thoughts: "Cathedral grandeur," say, or "That's *tall,*" or "Whoa!"

As I wrote the article, however, I noticed, and not for the first time, that the best interviews I conducted were with the field biologists, the people who were down on the ground carefully studying the life of these places, finding reasons to save them. A Mr. Duffy had demonstrated that even after a century clear-cut areas lacked the wildflowers of the ancient forest; a Mr. Petranka had patiently proved that large-scale logging could cut salamander populations 80 percent. And Stephen Selva, a biologist I met in Maine whose license plate read "LICHEN," had discovered a species that seemed to exist in only two places in the world: eastern old-growth forests and someplace in New Zealand. "It's sort of the spotted owl of the East," he explained. "Unfortunately, it's a lichen."

Thus the string. Because of my admiration for these people, I have pledged to be more systematic in my study of the natural world. No longer will I indulge in those daily hikes where I stride as quickly as possible to the top of something in order to gaze out enraptured on an Adirondack vista. Instead I will study my backyard plot. The time has come to develop the left—or is it the right?—side of my brain, whichever one it is that science lives in.

I intended to build a ten-foot-square research plot, but an old white pine has turned it into a slight rhomboid. First observation: my plot has a lot of mosquitos today. I estimated density: thick. Question for further research: what brand of mosquito repellent do real biologists use? To-morrow will be a good time to actually start an inventory of the flora and fauna of my stand.

July 5—The mosquitos have been joined by the most intense heat wave since the 1940s. Day after day it tops ninety degrees, even here at fifteen hundred feet. My plot is within sight of my pond, a flawed research design.

July 9—There's a maple tree on one corner of this plot. It's fourteen and a half inches around at breast height. Its leaves appear healthy.

About six feet up the trunk, however, a piece of rusting fence wire sticks jaggedly out. The rest of the fence has disappeared. Here is a puzzle common in the eastern forest. What can be logically deduced from this rusting piece of wire?

What can be deduced is pasture. It is easy enough to imagine the man who strung the fence. He must have arrived here late in the nine-teenth century and cut down the big hemlocks so their bark could be used by the local tannery. Perhaps he found enough spruce to justify borrowing a team of horses and hauling it out. And then he decided to farm, as his parents had farmed in Massachusetts or in Ireland, not com-pletely aware of how thin the soil was, perhaps hoping that the first ninety-day growing season was a fluke. But the second? And the third? Day after day, pulling stones from the field—the biggest heap is ten yards east of my plot—all the time wondering if he was throwing good labor after bad.

I can see that farmer's son deciding to leave, to take his chances in the cities to the south or the fields to the west, and the farmer growing older, unable to maintain his spread. The forest sidling back in on his field—the pines daring to rise a few inches and then exulting in their sunny freedom and shooting up with the spreading shape of a field tree. Is this a hard thing or a sweet one?

A woman grew up in this tiny valley in those days. Jeanne Robert Foster was so beautiful that she managed to get to New York City, where she became a Gibson girl, and then a poet, a friend of Pound and Picasso and Joyce. She wrote about the mountain poverty of those farms where she had grown up, places redeemed only by hardscrabble religion and the beauty of the hills. One poem tells of walking such a field, three miles from my plot with an old farmer, who had grown desperate at the decay. "I must find a man who still loves the soil," he says,

> Walk by his side unseen, put in his mind
> What I loved when I lived until he builds
> Sows, reaps, and covers these hill pastures here
> With sheep and cattle, mows the meadowland
> Grafts the old orchard again, makes it bear again
> Knowing that we are lost if the land does not yield.

There is true human sadness at the work of a generation dissolving. I know old men in my town who will not drive out this way; it pains them too much to see the fields they cleared grown back in. Yet there is, at my feet, the remains of a trillium that bloomed a month ago, nourished by the sun that filters into this woods before summer closes the canopy, an old occupant who has reclaimed her home.

The fence has rusted away, leaving this one small strand of wire as a memorial to the momentary and (in the larger scheme of things) gentle touch of a particular human being on this particular landscape. A testimony to the recuperative power of any spot where it rains. This quadrant of mine has sojourned briefly in civilization, but it has not been civilized.

July 14—I am tired, and in sitting down to rest against the maple tree on the southeast corner of my plot I fear I have crushed several maple saplings. There are twenty-three of them spread around me, and a couple of hemlocks that have been browsed so thoroughly by white-tailed deer that they have pretty much given up. Is the destruction caused by my rear end on the maple saplings philosophically comparable to the damage done by hungry deer?

I have pretty much given up on the word "wild." Here in this one small place, the quality of the sunlight is affected by the thinning ozone, the temperature reflects our industrial society's emissions of CO_2, the rain falls with a noticeably acid taint. And the deer—they've been nurtured for years by a state conservation department eager to please hunters, their predators largely exterminated save for the rifle and the Ford. Are they wild anymore, or are they a human creation? We need a more honest word to describe places where people are not in total control yet have their thumb on the scale.

July 20—Still, the idea of "wild" haunts this place. Due east of my plot, clearly visible today through the leaves, is a small mountain—not one of the hundred highest even in New York State, but the dominant peak in this area, a mountain that I love. And I am not alone in that love. A man whose name should be more widely known, Howard Zahniser, had a summer cabin not far from here, with a view of the same angle of this mountain as my plot affords. From there, he wrote many of his telling speeches on behalf of wilderness, and planned the two decades of lobbying that culminated in the federal wilderness statute finally enacted in 1964. The law—the most progressive and the most philosophical that Congress has ever passed—sets aside "untrammeled" land where man is "only a visitor." His son, Ed, maintains that the choice of words was careful, and paid off in the 1970s, when eastern lands were added to the national wilderness system. "Most of those lands were not pristine, but had re-covered from human use to the extent that Congress found them now untrammeled," he writes.

So it is with my study site. There is no denying that most of the Nikon-triggering grandeur in this country is west of the Mississippi, in tracts more nearly virgin than these Adirondacks. But there is something about this plot, standing for all the other recovering places, that speaks well for human humility. People have taken a step back here, and the land has responded.

August 8—Some unscientific animal has stolen the string demarcating my research area. By now, however, I know it well enough not to mind.

Any one piece of ground exists in many different dimensions. When my dog visits me here, she concentrates on the dimension of smell, and doubtless has made many valuable observations to which I am not privy. I am working today on sound, trying to separate the noises that filter back to this spot. There is the sound of Mill Creek falling over the lip of a beaver dam, a spectacular piece of engineering that has built for us a new wetland in recent years. An occasional fish jumps in that swampy pond, slipping back into the water with a gurgle. Once, in response to some alarm, a beaver slaps hard, and the sound echoes lazily; only once, on this humid afternoon does some bird let go a snatch of song.

Most of the sound is constant, more flowing—a ceaseless pulse of insect warble that I normally tune out with ease, but now, listening hard, find deeply reassuring. Trills, occasional tiny buzz-saw riffs, oscillating chirps blended together into high-pitched waves. It is life, pure and simple—life without the stories that come attached to the beaver slap or the birdcall or the gears grinding every so often on the nearest road. It is life on automatic, the deep life that our lives emerge from and skate across and subside back into.

August 26—The moon is working back toward full tonight, bleaching my study site in its soft wash of light. There's an old birch tree here, and I like to rub its trunk—the smoothness of the paper, the random weave of bumps and gashes, the peelings that it sheds as it grows. It is like holding a cast-off snakeskin—like holding time.

September 5—Most of the leaves in my plot are still green, the deep leathery green of old age. A few have turned, scarlet premonitions of the approaching explosion. It's still summer, but it feels like 3:00 A.M. in the city, the last moment when it's still night, when it's maybe fifteen minutes from becoming morning, right at the point where "out late" turns into "up early." Everything inside this plot—and all that I can see outside it—has moved further along on its journey these past couple of months. The saplings are a little taller, the birch somewhat shaggier, the dead maple a bit more rotted, the old rot a little more like dirt and nearly ready to nurse the next round of seeds.

This morning over breakfast, I read an article in the paper about an economist who figures that most Americans will change careers eight times in their lives to keep up with the rapid pace of technology. And they may move to new towns or new parts of the country that often, probably trading in a husband or wife along the way. The last century has been an experiment in how much we can speed up society before the strains prove unbearable. The next century, if the scientists are right about phenomena like climate change, will test whether nature can manage a similar acceleration, whether systems geared toward repetition can handle enormous variability. Will beech trees still survive on this spot if the temperature increases three or four degrees? Probably not. Autumn starts to take on a different meaning—not just one spot along the endless cycle of natural time, but perhaps a metaphor for the slow expiration of the natural when it is forced into linear, human time. Autumn, implying May, is bittersweet; this new fall would be simply bitter.

September 12—A chipmunk, working without visible grant support on a careful study of nut production, has taken over my quadrant and is angered when I come to visit. Time for me to leave, to take down my corner posts and resume my meandering—I'm not cut out for the cutthroat world of science.

Without the string, with the poles gone, my study site blends back into the anonymous woods. But the scientific method has appealed to me greatly. Look low, look carefully. And know globally—the small and the subtle refer constantly to the overarching, the huge issues of the moment are reflected in the duff and the mushroom and the sapling. The war (and the courtship) between humans and the land can be read on this ten-foot-by-ten-foot (give or take) patch of grown-in pasture, and the chances for truce (or for marriage) assessed. I should close, I know, with questions for future research, suggestions for these scientists who will probe more deeply. How do we want to live? What matters to us? What does a tree say as it stands in the forest?

NATURAL DISASTERS

NATALIE ANGIER

For a girl who grows up in a fierce neighborhood of the Bronx, dodging cars while frolicking in the middle of the street, or watching race riots break out between the neighborhood black and Irish boys, or being slammed down onto the sidewalk and beaten into a slobbering pulp by bigger and surlier children, what else is there left to be afraid of but nature?

As a child, I spent fifty weeks every year in New York City and the other two weeks somewhere in the country, on the annual family vacation: up in the Catskills, out at Cape Cod, up by a lake near the Canadian border. The exact location didn't matter—country was country, and the country terrified me. It was too green, too bushy, too alive, and it succored dangerous things I couldn't see. Everything had a sinister purpose, and that purpose was directed against me. Insects wanted to sting me, plants wanted to brush against me and make me break out in a rash, colorful toadstools wanted to tempt me to eat them until I toppled over, poisoned, like Babar the Elephant's father.

Because I never learned to swim well, lakes were an assured threat, even if I simply splashed around in shallow water by the shore. After all, you never know when you'll hit a sudden drop-off in the lake bottom and find yourself in completely over your head. Nor did the terra seem much firmer. I'd read about quicksand, and I was always on the lookout for a spot of ground that would suck me into extinction. And to feet reared on concrete, every dirt path has a suspicious give to it.

The countryside was so unsentimental, so starkly didactic. I hardly ever saw wild animals when they were alive; most of my transphylogenetic encounters were with corpses—a dead deer, a dead raccoon, a dead robin, all of them stiff, smelly warnings against excessive merriment or youthful smugness. Once I watched a hawk scoop up a field mouse in its talons and then flap away triumphantly, the mouse's little feet and tail dangling down pitifully, like untied shoelaces. All the rest of the afternoon, I kept feeling things brushing against my hair, and though I hated mice when they came into our cabin, that day I was in trembling solidarity with rodents everywhere.

My fear of nature began with bees. Somewhere around the age of four, I picked up the deep-seated conviction that were I to be stung by a bee I would not be able to bear the pain. I imagined that a bee sting would be far worse than being punched or scratched or any of the other injuries I was accustomed to—worse because of the legend of the angry bee. In my view, any creature willing to sacrifice its life to punish a human surely must deal a parting blow that is itself nearly fatal. People always told me, "If you don't bother bees, they won't bother you," but I didn't believe it. Bees to me were fuzzy pellets of unpredictable malice. Step near a bee without realizing it and *wham!* it turns dogface, no questions asked, no prisoners taken. Sniff a flower that just happens to conceal a foraging bee and *zing!* there goes the nose.

My fear of bees dominated several of my summers in the country. Every shape in the grass began to resemble a bee, and every buzz was an oncoming bee. If there were bees or hornets around a picnic table, I would take my food and go indoors to eat, even though that meant I would be eating alone. I remember going butterfly catching with an older friend. The boy put down his net over a butterfly and then wandered off for a moment. I noticed that besides the butterfly there was a bee trapped beneath the net. It was buzzing and it was *mad*. Unwilling to see how it would respond once liberated, I abandoned my friend and fled back to my mother. The bee in the net remains my most vividly terrifying childhood memory, exceeding the alarm I felt at age six when I visited Niagara Falls with an uncle and he jokingly said he was going to throw me over in a barrel.

My pathological fear of stinging insects kept me unstung until the age of fifteen, when I stepped on a yellow jacket while I was walking barefoot on the beach. The pain eclipsed my worst expectations. I thought I had caught fire; I thought I had been shot. I cried, I screamed, I hopped. My lower leg swelled up as though I were a float in a Macy's parade. And the sole consolation for my suffering was the knowledge that my lifelong phobia had been justified.

Most of my memories of leaving New York are memories of confronting new threats of nature. When we visited relatives in Arizona, I was perfectly delighted with the heat, the saguaros, and the horizon, but then my aunt mentioned rattlesnakes. There were a lot of rattlesnakes outdoors, she said matter-of-factly. Because my only experience with snakes had been in the Bronx Zoo, where we could pester them mercilessly by tapping on their glass enclosures and *ha! ha!* they couldn't get out, I thought it almost a certainty that the snakes would take their revenge on me now that I was on their turf. When I looked out my aunt's window at the unceasing expanse of sand, I was sure the sand was moving, swaying, rattling, waiting. The entire desert had become a mouth agape. I spent most of the visit indoors.

When I was eleven, another aunt and uncle invited me to spend a year in Zambia with them and their three young children. I was a sophisticated girl, and I knew that the international experience would make me a more interesting person. Then I learned about the tsetse fly. The tsetse fly transmits sleeping sickness, I discovered—a disease for which there was and is no cure. The idea of a stupor overtaking you, and your spirit and personality seeping out of you, struck me as the most awful fate imaginable. No, I told them. I can't go to Africa. I might get bitten by a tsetse fly.

I think about these early fears often, now that I'm an adult who loves nature, who is practically a card-carrying pantheist, who borders on fascism in her belief that wilderness must be preserved at all costs. (Forced sterilization after your second child? Sure, why not?) I think about it, because I worry that my love may be more theoretical than real, and in the end almost useless. I've had plenty of epiphanous experiences in nature. I have hiked and backpacked and canoed and rafted. I've nibbled on mud and leaves in the Olympic rain forest in Washington, seeking a visceral connection with Mother Gaia. I've taken my tree-, bird-, and flower-identification books on walks and learned to name names. I have stood still in the woods and and just breathed and breathed, annoyed with my lungs for their short-term memory and wondering why somebody couldn't just bottle this air and sell it in the city.

I have seen bears and coyotes and monkeys and whales and dolphins, and every time it has been more exhilarating than catching a glimpse of Al Pacino or Mikhail Baryshnikov on the streets of Manhattan. You feel privileged when you see a creature flash across your path unexpectedly. It's a momentary state of grace.

Yet through it all, I am still, at bottom, scared of nature. The trees, the bushes, the symphonies of thousands of chattering birds at dawn, the raw efflorescence of renewal and decay, continue to confuse me, and confusion, of course, is the midwife to cowardice. I can walk the streets of New York late at night and feel cocky about my toughness, but when I'm in a dense forest I'm as skittish as a gerbil. Once, I went hiking in the woods of upstate New York with the Cornell biologist Thomas Eisner, who was the subject of a story I was working on. He was showing various insects to me, overturning rocks to reveal millipedes, picking up and gently squeezing beetles until they secreted a defensive chemical that smelled like the menthol you rub on aching muscles. All of a sudden I noticed a big, hairy, multilegged insect on my sleeve, probably a caterpillar. Without bothering to temper my reaction in front of a man whose life had been spent extolling the splendor of arthropods, I shrieked like a child and frantically brushed the creepy thing off me. Eisner frowned at me in irritation and disappointment. "You still don't take insects seriously, do you?" he said.

At the time, I vigorously denied the accusation, but Eisner had a point. In the abstract, and from a distance, I find insects fascinating; but if to take something seriously is to respect it up close and on its own terms, then the truth is no, I don't get the point of insects. I feel queasy when they're around, and I probably wouldn't mind—maybe I wouldn't even notice—if I never saw another representative of the class again.

The same might be said of so many other things I supposedly love about nature. I love hiking and camping, but only in short bites, and only because I know I can put an end to my wilderness experience at pretty much any time I choose. A girlfriend whom I think of as a genuinely woodsy sort of woman once observed how little time humans in the Western world spend outdoors, and I thought, Gee, she's right. We work indoors, we sleep indoors, we spend time with the family at the end of the day indoors, we commute in closed vehicles. If I had to guess, I'd say that most adults spend less than an hour each day outdoors. Realizing this simple fact, my friend and I shook our heads and agreed how awful it was that we cut ourselves off from fresh air, sun, nature's rhythms. But again, I was lying. In fact, I prefer being indoors most of the time. For me, indoors is the default mode, the place where I will end up if I don't have a pep talk with myself on all the great virtues of going outside, or if my husband and I haven't planned some sporty outdoor activity.

When I have been on assignment in seriously outdoor places, like the tropical forests of Central and South America, I have felt schizoid. On the one hand, I'm always elated to be the receiving end of large sensations, images that are at once ancient and fresh: to see a flock of parrots sweeping in emerald arcs through the sky, or a capybara, the world's largest and laziest rodent, snuffling through the forest under-growth like a sack of butter perched atop four web-footed limbs.

On the other hand, the rain forest is merciless. You trudge through mud as high as your kneecaps and feel it slip over the top of your rubber boots, gather at your feet, and ooze around your toes, hour after hour. You wear an oil slick of insect repellent and still every mosquito in the district finds the dime-size patch of skin behind your right ear that you neglected to slather over. You think of how desirable you are to so many bloodsucking species around you, how much you look to them like a lunch cart. You think of how you can't wait to get back to the campsite, douse yourself in cold water, and zip up the tent.

Whenever I have been in the tropics, I have understood why it is that human beings throughout history have sought to put a barrier between themselves and nature, to beat off its relentless hunger, to domesticate it, to pave it over. This is always a depressing realization to me—one that works against my gauzy fantasies and shapeless ecopolitics. Many people talk, have always talked, of how humans should learn to live in pragmatic rapport with nature, to see that we are all cut of the same fabric, to stay within our means and the means of the planet that supports us. But I don't know if humans will ever be able to live in the vicinity of nature and not muck it up.

For a long time, I've had a notion that is anathema to my biophiliac friends and to the part of myself that hikes and camps and canoes: if we really want to save nature and its stupendous diversity, we should draw a line down the center of the planet. One half of the world will be for people, in a great linked metropolis, while the other half will be set aside for everything else. Forget about harmony, evolutionary fraternity, and the great challenge of intelligent stewardship. Humans clearly are capable of wreaking spectacular havoc on nature, and they have yet to demonstrate that they are capable of anything else. Maybe that's because there are too many others like me around, and nothing is more dangerous than a bunch of scared people.

THE EXPLORER'S JOURNEY

A REPORT FROM THE FRONTIER[1]

DAVID G. CAMPBELL

When I was a teenager, I crashed the biggest party in the world. It was a party for the astronauts who were going to the moon. To think that fellow humans would touch with their gloved hands the face of another planet so exalted me that it kept me awake at night. While my friends collected baseball cards and recited statistics about athletes, I learned the jargon of space travel and memorized the dimensions and statistics of the vehicles. I found it auspicious that the rockets used for the early exploration of space were plowshares that had been beaten from swords. These accomplishments, I thought (perhaps naïvely), were the pyramids and cathedrals of my time and culture. I watched the secondhand reports on television, distilled of detail and of what must have been the astounding *feel* of spaceflight or—yet more incomprehensible—of *moon* walking, and wanted more. The astronauts, by any measure, were the Magellans of our day. But they weren't discoverers. They didn't craft the interplanetary vehicle. They didn't plot its trajectory from Earth to moon. They didn't distill the laws of physics from all the clutter of natural things. In many

---

[1] This essay was presented at a Scholars' Convocation at Grinnell College, January 30, 1992. Some of this material appeared in slightly different form in *The Crystal Desert*, by David G. Campbell (Boston: Houghton Mifflin, 1992).

ways, these heros of the moment were interchangeable parts, and perhaps there's a certain democracy in that. The discoverers—the teams of controllers, the geologists, physicists, engineers, mathematicians, physiologists, all the full panoply of science—were invisible. But collectively they made Apollo possible.

I searched the televised faces of the astronauts for any sign of epiphany but found none. *How is it possible,* I wondered, *for mortals to go into space and not be changed?*

I wanted to be present at the moment that comes only once in the history of a planet—when its life-forms leave their natal sphere. Nothing of this magnitude had occurred since the middle Ordovician period, four hundred and fifty million years ago, when the first marine animal—arachnid, crab, lungfish, or amphibian—crawled from the sea onto the shore of a continent that has long since vanished. And so I decided to join the press corps, the easiest way I knew to get a ringside seat for the launch. I figured that it would be like being at the quayside when the *Niña,* the *Pinta,* and the *Santa Maria* departed from Palos, almost five hundred years earlier.

A friend's father, who was the editor of a weekly newspaper in minuscule Rotan, Texas, requested a press pass from NASA for me. NASA didn't blink, and the authorization came in time for *Apollo 11,* the first moon landing. I sneaked away from the summer quarter at college, and caught a plane from Detroit to Orlando, joining all the pasty mobs seeking UV-B. I was too young to rent a car, and so I hitchhiked down the Bee-Line Highway toward Titusville. I found cheap accommodations at the Lone Cabbage, a fishing camp on the St. John's River. In the evenings, I sat with gray-stubbled bass fishermen on creaky lawn furniture under the slash pines in the still Florida air, eating pickled sausages, watching the scrub jays flicker through the woods, and talking about fish.

Cape Canaveral is a spit of sand that was trussed up from the sea during the Pleistocene. The rambling buildings and gantries of the Cape—the launch sites of *Explorer I* (which discovered the Van Allen radiation belts), of Alan Shepard, of John Glenn, of the Surveyors (which made the first soft landing on the moon)—were scattered along the beach like the toys of a careless and spoiled child. The wind tumbled off the sea, and the salt spray slowly dissolved the structures. But to me it seemed as if a solar wind blew across this beach. This was one of two places (the other was Baikonur, in Kazakhstan) where earthly life was leaving its natal planet.

On the nights before the launch, there were "photo opportunities" in a field across a still bayou from Pad 39A, where the moon rocket stood. Although I had no camera, I bluffed my way aboard the photographers' bus by carrying an empty suitcase and pretending it was a camera bag. Across the bayou, the white Saturn V, 363 feet high, was pinned in the crossed beams of arc lights, inconstant in the sea wind. The rocket seemed to be as insubstantial as light. Michael Collins, the command-module pilot, would later write that as he lay atop the fully fueled rocket he could feel it sway in the wind and hear it shift and groan under the weight of its own fuel. Some of that fuel was kerosene—the corpses of plants in Carboniferous forests a third of a billion years old—and the oxidant was liquid oxygen, also the product of life, of photosynthesis.

On one such evening, while the photographers arranged their tripods all in a row as if they were a firing squad, all snapping the same scene (which has now become quite famous, a photographic cliché), I walked down to the edge of the bayou with a veteran reporter—a man who had covered many historic events in his time. I was making my first voyage to the edge of history; he was making his last. The water was pocked with concentric rings made by pilchards that came to the surface in the safety of night to feed on gnats and mosquitos. Now and then, a mullet would splash in the shallows. And on the small sand beach in front of us, bathed in the reflected light of *Apollo 11*, a female horseshoe crab was crawling ashore with a coterie of males clasped to her stiff tail, in love's embrace. Timing her exodus according to the moon-drawn tides, this ancient relative of the spiders was leaving the sea to deposit her eggs on the land, just as our ancestor had done for the first time five-and-a-half billion lunar cycles ago. She left her tracings in the alien sand: the rosettes of her feet, the long mark of her tail. The reporter and I didn't speak. It was one of those moments when everything seemed to murmur of beauty and purpose, when Earth made a spontaneous and eloquent gesture that transcended even language—a moment that, once experienced, is never forgotten and becomes part of you. We were transfixed, literally and figuratively mired in the life-endowing muck of this planet, just as three men, strapped on top of a tower of enormous potential energy, were about to leave it for a sterile and deadly orb in the sky.

Finally, the old reporter spoke from the darkness. "I never imagined that I would see this," he said. "It's so unexpected and lovely. We are on the edge, you know. This is a moment when human beings are peering over the rim of everything into the void. Of all the wonderful and awful things that I have seen in my life—the South Pole, the invasion of Normandy, the test of a hydrogen bomb on Bikini, Gandhi's funeral, with its ululating masses—this is the most memorable."

"You've witnessed the great events of this century," I said. "How satisfying that must be."

"Oh, no," he replied. "As reporters, we sit on the sidelines and watch. Professional vicariants, we discover nothing. I'd trade it all to be on the other side of that bayou."

I don't know whether I decided to become a scientist that night on the edge of the bayou. But from that moment, I knew that vicariance wouldn't be enough. I wanted to be an explorer—a discoverer. I wanted to be a participant in knowing. Biology seemed the clear choice. The virtue of this planet, which distinguishes it from most, if not all, of the rest of the cold, indifferent universe, is life. Earth would be better named Vita. As a biologist, I celebrate life—such obvious employment, given where I live. I chose to work in the wilderness, but I suppose I could as well have become a bench-top biologist. Today biology—like astronomy, physics, and planetary exploration—is experiencing a renaissance. We have cracked the genetic code and used it to manufacture new and unexpected compounds. We are beginning to understand that most complex of all ecosystems, the tropical forest. We are beginning to understand patterns of species diversity—and extinction. We are beginning to realize that living things have transformed the face of Earth, mantling it with plants and animals, converting carbon dioxide to rocks, adding oxygen to the atmosphere.

My research has chiefly been in the rain forest of the Amazon, the most diverse and complex biome to have evolved during the three-and-a-half-billion-year history of life on Earth. There, steeped in life's exuberance, a small group of colleagues and I try to decipher the reasons for that diversity—how so many species came into being and have managed to coexist over the millennia. I also conduct research in the Antarctic. Antarctica—at least, terrestrial Antarctica—is the antithesis of the Amazon (there are no trees, the largest animal is a flightless midge), which may be why it so appeals to me. It is like the silence between movements of a symphony. But Antarctica is also an ocean wilderness, and the invertebrate life that coats the seafloor at the bottom of the world may be as diverse as life anyplace on Earth.

Not all of today's discovery is high tech. In this age of molecular biology and genetic engineering, the description of new species is still going on, and it is still as pioneering a science as it was during the time of—for example—Mark Catesby, who in 1725 was the first to describe many American plants and animals. Today, 213 years after the death of Carolus Linnaeus, the founder of modern taxonomy, biologists don't know—even to the nearest order of magnitude—how many species of plants and animals there are on Earth. Estimates range from five million to a hundred million. About half these species occur in the tropics—in particular, tropical forests. Yet as of today, only about one-and-a-half million species of plants and animals the world over have been formally described by taxonomists.

I once had the privilege of being the first botanist to collect plants along a newly opened stretch of the TransAmazon Highway. The highway ran straight through the forest, indifferent to rivers and terrain, and the trees grew right to the edge of the road. We slept in a truck, because at night jaguars visited our camp. Six percent of the plants we collected on that expedition turned out to be new to science. Since we collected thirty or forty plants a day, that's two or three new species a day. Alas, botanical exploration is not a profession for those who desire immediate gratification. It took five years for the specialists working on our collections to determine that the species were new. And just last year I collected orchids on the mist-fed summit of Tepequém, a steep-sided sandstone mountain that rises a thousand meters above the tropical forest and savannah of northern Brazil. We were only the third team of botanists to visit the summit, and I'm sure that we found some new species. But we won't know for years.

In tropical Central America, South America, and the West Indies, it is estimated that there are approximately ninety thousand species of flowering plants. No one knows the exact number, because botanical exploration is not complete. As of 1988, only 4,254 species, 4.7 percent of the estimated total, had been formally described in *Flora Neotropica,* the definitive series of scientific monographs for the region. Since 1988, an average of 236 species per year have been added to *Flora Neotropica;* at this rate, it will take 381 years to complete the inventory of the region's flowering plants. The situation is even worse for fungi, of which about fifty thousand species are believed to occur in the tropical Americas. As of 1988, only 949 species, 1.8 percent of the total, had been described in *Flora Neotropica,* and it is estimated that it will take 948 years to finish the inventory of fungi. We obviously have a long way to go in exploring Earth's life-forms. Most of life on Earth has yet to be discovered. Let me repeat that extraordinary statement: most of life on Earth—this planet that would better be named Vita—has yet to be discovered.

Of course, most of the tropical forests of the Americas won't be around for 381 more years, let alone for another 948 years. Just as we are on the threshold of comprehending life's wonderful diversity, we are on the verge of destroying a large part of it. Hundreds of thousands, perhaps millions, of species will become extinct at the hands of our species during the next several decades. Most will be tropical. Already, about 20 percent of the Amazon forest has been destroyed, and at the present rates of destruction almost none will be left in fifty years. The tropical forests of western Ecuador have been cut back to a few small reserves of several acres. The countries of El Salvador and Haiti are totally deforested.

It is therefore inevitable that, in the decades to come, thousands of species of flowering plants will become extinct in the American tropics before they are ever inventoried by humans. Their value to us in terms of new foods, fibers, and medicines will never be known, let alone the value of their genes as templates for genetic engineering.

I should point out that there is nothing new about extinction, which is the necessary requisite of evolution. Extinction has been with us as long as there has been life. What is new are the current, human-accelerated rates of extinction, which are from a thousand to ten thousand times Earth's normal background rate. Seldom if ever before has Earth lost so many species so fast.

These problems may at first seem unimportant and remote to Americans. In contrast to the tropical forested areas of the world, the inventory of flora in the United States has been completed right down to the last species, and although some of them may go extinct in the years to come, probably none will go extinct anonymously. Since their homeland is botanically well understood, why should Americans care about extinctions in other countries? There are many evocative reasons, not the least of which are esthetic and moral. But there are economic reasons as well. Did you know that 43 percent of prescription drugs are manufactured from natural products? Did you know that the National Cancer Institute is today screening thousands of species of tropical plants for activity against cancer cells and against the AIDS virus? Did you know that the best treatment for certain childhood leukemias is a product manufactured from the periwinkle, a tropical herb from Madagascar? We are entering an age when much engineering will be genetic—when cells can be made to manufacture just about any product, *if* they are provided with the genetic blueprint. This, of course, is another aspect of our renaissance time. But just as we attain that technological level, we are losing the very blueprints the technology will need.

These days, ecologists must devote long years, even decades, of their careers to conservation. In a way, we feel like professional mourners, going to wakes for our livelihood. We shall never share the unalloyed joy of the astronomers, our fellow explorers in the physical sciences. And we wonder, as we are beginning to peer into distant parts of the universe and also to read the book of life itself, why we must at the same time destroy the living inheritance of our home planet.

All of this leads to the overwhelming question for my generation of tropical biologists: How did this extraordinary species richness evolve? One theory, worked out jointly by ornithologists, entomologists, and botanists, comes to the surprising conclusion that species richness may be due to disruption and catastrophe. Ironically, Antarctica may have played the key role in the evolution of the extravagant diversity of the Amazon. Consider this: eighteen thousand years ago, Earth was locked in the Wisconsin Ice Age, the most recent of at least four episodes of glaciation during the past million years. At the peak of those Pleistocene glaciations, one-fifth of Earth's water was frozen, and sea level fell more than three hundred feet. Today, 5 percent of Antarctica is ice-free, but during the Ice Ages the entire continent was suffocated by ice. The glaciers extended far out to sea, which was covered by pack ice for hundreds of miles farther from shore. Near-freezing ocean currents plied north from Antarctica along the western shores of South America and Africa, changing patterns of atmospheric circulation. The result may have been the desiccation of both continents. In each cycle, the pampas and coastal deserts of the southern third of South America crept north, and the Amazon forest retreated into a dozen or so small refuges surrounded by arid savannah. In Africa, the Kalahari Desert edged as far north as the Congo River valley, and here, too, the forest withered into a few isolated pockets. The patches of tropical forest became virtual islands, having little or no genetic exchange with each other. Species that had once been widespread were broken up. The particular genetic traits of the isolated individuals, and the particular selective pressures of each forest island, fostered the divergence of daughter species from their common ancestor. When the glaciers melted, humidity returned to the Amazon and the Congo River valleys. The forest once again became continuous, and the ranges of the sibling species overlapped.

There were three possible scenarios at this point. If little evolutionary divergence took place between taxa, then they might still be sufficiently related to hybridize. If they were genetically incompatible and could not hybridize yet still made similar demands on their environments—for food, a place to grow, or light, for example—then one sibling species, over time, would competitively exclude the other. But if they were sufficiently different so that competition was slight or nil, then they might manage to coexist, and what had once been a single species would become several. Moreover, the process was potentially exponential, because each of the sibling taxa could split into as many new taxa as there were refuges during the next cycle of glaciation. The episodic dissection and merging of the two great zones of continuous tropical forest, choreographed by climatic events on the Antarctic continent, may be the explanation for their extraordinary richness of species. It's a small world, indeed.

I have played a role, however slight, in this discovery, by helping to catalog the number of species in plots of Brazilian tropical forest and, later, small areas of the seafloor off Antarctica. Like Apollo, it was a collective endeavor—one that spanned generations.

My research has taken me repeatedly to the margin of the Rio Xingu, a vast southeastern tributary of the Amazon. I stay in the homestead of Dona Margarita, an Arara Indian matriarch who seems ageless. Dona Margarita, who cannot read and whose father hunted with a bow and arrow, was born on this spot. Her husband, Lopreo, is a rubber tapper and a collector of Brazil nuts, a debilitating profession that keeps him in perpetual debt to itinerant river traders. Theirs is a marginal and dangerous life, threatened by malaria, tuberculosis, bandits, and snakes. But Dona Margarita and Lopreo stay by their beloved river. She once told me that the Xingu was a singing river. You could hear the song, she said, just before dawn, when the nocturnal din of the crickets and frogs was diminished and before the first diurnal birds and howler monkeys awakened. For weeks, I listened in vain, but one still morning I discerned a barely perceptible metallic hum—like a distant tuning fork—that seemed to come from all directions at once. Now that I know how to listen, I hear it all the time. Nobody knows the source of the sound, but I believe it to be due to the peculiar harmonics of billions of sand grains as they tumble down the nearby rapids.

Dona Margarita worries about me. At first she thought that I was prospecting for gold, like other outsiders who journey to the Xingu. But now she's convinced that I'm just an eccentric—harmless but confused. "You're too tall to walk in the forest," she once admonished me. "You blunder into wasp nests and step on snakes without seeing them. Walk slowly, observe. But most important," she said, taking my hand as if I were one of her children, "get out of the forest when it's windy. Stay in the safety of the clearings when the wind blows. I've lost more friends to treefalls than to snakes or wasps."

I usually travel to the Xingu in November, which marks the beginning of the rainy season, the annual renewal of life in the forest. It is a widely held misconception that the Amazon forest is an ever-humid place of torrential and perpetual rains. In fact, these conditions occur only in elevated Andean areas, fifteen hundred miles west of the Xingu. Indeed, most of the Amazon valley—and especially the eastern Amazon—experiences an extended period of relative drought during the summer. And like their counterparts in the temperate zones, many Amazonian trees are deciduous, an adaptation to the season of adversity. The dry season is also the flowering season: the production of seeds is timed to coincide with the return of the nourishing rains, which bring everything back to life. The trees are refoliated with fresh green leaves. The slow-legged reptiles emerge from their summer dormancy. Red-footed tortoises leave their burrows to congregate expectantly under the orange-fruiting *abiu* trees, waiting for the morsels to drop. The local people know this and wait for the tortoises, which they consider a delicacy.

And the snakes, hungry from their period of estivation, are on the hunt. At other times of the year, one may go for months without seeing a snake in the Amazon, but during the first days of the rainy season they seem ubiquitous. Last year, I came within inches of encountering a venomous eyelash viper. It lay coiled on a bough at about chest level, perfectly camouflaged, as green as the foliage on which it rested. Even the edges of its triangular head were curled like leaves. I was measuring the tree on which it rested, when my alert companion noticed it before it struck. It was just luck that saved me from being bitten. It was just luck that I didn't die. We managed to measure the tree anyway, and to leave the snake in peace.

I first journeyed to the forest on the edge of the Xingu in 1980. There were sixteen of us on the expedition: Brazilian, British, and American; botanists, river pilots, cooks, tree climbers, technicians. I was the ecologist. We spent three weeks there, identifying, mapping, and measuring every tree on three hectares of tropical forest: 1,997 trees in all. Three hectares is just a mote in the vast Amazon valley, but it seemed a universe to us. Those three hectares contained 265 species of trees— almost half as many as there are in all of North America. And each tree was an ecosystem, bearing mosses, ferns, philodendrons, lianas, and legions of insects. We collected a herbarium specimen of foliage, flowers, or fruit from every tree. The vouchers were a necessity in a region where many species are new to science and for which there were no field guides. Inevitably, several of the species turned out to have never before been described by scientists.

My colleagues and I mapped every tree on a system of Cartesian coördinates. This facilitates important analyses, such as patterns of distribution, nearest neighbors, niche width in terms of soil, hydrology, light, and terrain. Dona Margarita thinks I'm crazy to try to *measure* a forest. Such an inept tool, a tape measure, to try to describe a patently polydimensional thing.

Yet it was while conducting this detailed and painstaking research that I first appreciated the astounding complexity of tropical forests. Not only did I gain a sense of the species richness of the forest as a whole but I came to know each tree on the three hectares as an individual. Suddenly the forest trees had voices; they were no longer an anonymous chaos of inscrutable green. I learned the architecture of every tree: how it ramified, how it presented its leaves to the filtered sun, how its bark attracted or repelled climbers, how the epiphytes festooned its boughs, whether the leaf morphology changed relative to height. I noted the fresh yellow-pink xanthophyll of the new leaves, the termite nests, the wood-pecker holes (which are visited repeatedly and harvested of grubs), the shimmering inflorescences in the far-flung canopy. A few of these trees offered shelter during the rain or comfortable roots on which to sit and eat lunch. Others were of magnificent dimensions, such as the silk cotton tree, fifty meters tall, spreading its boughs just as wide above the canopy. Some, such as *Rinorea juruana* (it has no colloquial name), were noncon-formists, blooming in the wet season and making the forest redolent with their scents. A few were dangerous, such as the *tachí* tree, which harbored entire colonies of stinging ants, offering them shelter in return for pro-tection from predators. The stings feel like red-hot wires. I once brushed my neck and face against a *tachí* and blacked out from the pain. These are the trees that I will always remember. But most of the trees were nondescript and rare. Forty-five percent of the species on the three hec-tares were represented by only one individual.

Over the years, I became curious about the fates of those trees that I had recorded in such detail. How many had survived? How fast had they grown? Was the species composition of the forest changing? These simple questions, so basic to our understanding of the Amazon, had no answers. Time is an invisible thing, yet it is the key to understanding the tropical forest. You learn very little by taking a walk through the forest. It's like looking at a photograph or a still life. The trees seem immortal to us, and by comparison with them we seem as transient as ants. But a forest moving through time is not static. Individuals disappear and are replaced by others. Whole plant communities transmute into others. And so I returned to the Xingu in 1985, and again in 1990, in order to measure the dynamics of the little patch of forest and to learn the fate of each of the trees I first encountered there five and ten years before. Some, like the silk cotton tree, would stand long after I vanished. Others had died, after a long struggle in the lethal shade of light-greedy canopy species, and survive only as numbers in my data book. Juvenile palms had consolidated their leaves into sturdy adult trunks and invested in strength. Saplings had lurched into a light gap created by the death of a forest giant and directed all their energies in growing toward the sun. The Xingu study site was the most dynamic tropical forest ever measured, with 3.65 percent of its trees dying every year. At this rate, half the trees of the Xingu would turn over in less than twenty years. *Voila!* Discovery. So much for the myth of the unchanging, eternal tropical forest.

But most surprising, I learned that 59 percent of these mortalities were due to just plain bad luck: being clobbered, snapped, or broken by a tipsy neighbor. The windstorms of the rainy season caused most of this mortality. Death, it seemed, was indifferent to the complex adaptations, the billions of bits of information engineered into the genes of these trees—something that Dona Margarita had known and had tried to teach me. This may have been my most important discovery. But its significance was not clear to me until I went to the Antarctic.

My work in the Antarctic was similar to that in the Amazon: the measurement of the species richness of small samples. The study site was a plot on the ocean floor, which I visited by diving. Scuba diving in the Antarctic is the closest thing on Earth to walking in space. The water temperature is a few tenths of a degree below freezing: exposure causes death in about four minutes. And so I climbed into an inflatable dry suit, ballasted by thirty-eight pounds of lead and insulated by two layers of woolen underwear. Bearing this burden, I walked as awkwardly as a crab.

Only a handful of people have ever dived there, and, as in the Amazon, discovery was commonplace. In the shallow Antarctic sea, there may be as many species of bottom-dwelling invertebrates per unit area as on the Great Barrier Reef. There are more species of sponges, especially glass sponges, on the continental shelf of Antarctica than anywhere else on Earth—in fact, more species than have existed anywhere in all of geological time. The diversity of bryozoans ("moss animals"), sea spiders, giant isopods (which are related to the pill "bugs" in your garden), and other invertebrates is just as unexpectedly high. What could possibly account for this?

It turns out that, through a striking similarity of process, Pleistocene refuges may also explain the diversity of the Antarctic seas. As the Pleistocene glaciers obliterated terrestrial Antarctica and slid out to sea, crushing the continental shelf, shallow-water marine forms had to retreat beyond their reach, or perish. In most areas, their only escape was into submarine canyons that tumbled onto the abyssal plains to the north. Like the forest refugia six thousand kilometers away, these canyons became virtual islands, and their benthic faunas became isolated. Species that had once been circumpolar were broken into many small populations. When the glaciers retreated, the sibling taxa recolonized the empty shallows. The same three postglacial scenarios ensued in the Antarctic as in the Amazon. And, as in the tropics, diversity multiplied exponentially with each succeeding Ice Age.

While the Pleistocene refuge theory may explain, at least partly, the evolution of the enormous species richness of the tropical forests and the Antarctic continental shelf, it cannot explain why that diversity is sustained. One way that species richness could be maintained is by prolonging the competition between one species and another. This prolongation occurs when the chance that an individual (of either competing species) will succumb to some indiscriminate outside force is greater than the chance that it will die because of the competition. In tropical forests, a toppling tree destroys many trees that grow beneath it, and also those that are woven into its canopy by vines, and in the Xingu forest, as we have seen, up to 59 percent of tree deaths are due to the bad luck of being involved in one of these disasters. Such a high rate of competition-independent mortality has a profound effect on the forest ecosystem: it lengthens the time it would take for one closely related species to drive another to extinction. On the Antarctic continental shelf, competition-independent mortality is caused by rocks—from pebbles to massive boulders—carried from land and then dropped by passing glaciers. The falling rocks create a pattern of destruction very similar to that of treefalls in a tropical forest, and may foster species richness in the same way.

Both in the Amazon and the Antarctic, adversity—glacial catastrophes, killer trees and rocks—has spawned and maintained new species. The discovery was there in front of me, and since I'm the only person I know who worked in both places, it was, for a little while, all mine.

A discovery like this one sneaks up on you. The connection between the Amazon and Antarctica was proved in the most empirical manner possible: the patient sampling of the seafloor, the tedious enumeration of the plants in a plot of tropical forest, and the work of generations of scientists before me. Most people believe that an esthetic understanding of nature, a sense of place, can be achieved only through emotional, often subliminal, channels. But quantitative science also leads us to the esthetic, even the sublime: that dying leads to genesis, that catastrophe fosters diversity. Every scientist's journey is different, as well it should be. But the bond we share is discovery. We are the adventurers and explorers of our time. And no discovery is ever trivial. Basic science always leads down interesting new paths. When I discover something, I carry the knowledge around for a few days and savor it, without telling a soul. For a while, I am the only person in the history of this planet to embrace that morsel of information. It's a wonderful feeling.

The lament of the veteran reporter served me well. I'm glad that I didn't become a vicariant. I have, however briefly, dwelled on the edge of knowing—that place he so coveted. My life has been woven into the tapestry of exploration, a heritage that goes back to our first terrestrial ancestor.

In four years, I'll return to the Xingu. Dona Margarita will be there, as ever, ageless. She doesn't understand when I talk about discovery. She already knows more about this forest than I'll ever learn. She knows more species of tree—at least, by her system of classification—than I. She can identify the birds by their call. She understands time, and patience. She still finds it bizarre that I measure the forest in numbers.

One evening during my last visit to the Xingu, I walked on the riverbank with Dona Margarita. During her long life, this woman had never journeyed very far from the banks of the river. It was her universe. When we came to the sandy beach, we looked skyward. A horizon is such a privilege there, in the closed forest, and like the seedlings waiting hopefully for a light gap, one takes advantage of every chance to view the sky. We paused for a long moment. "When I was a girl," Dona Margarita said, "I stood on this spot and noticed a comet in the eastern sky above the river." Dona Margarita may well be in her nineties, and she may have seen Halley's Comet, but she doesn't know her own age, and there is no way of knowing which comet she saw. "The comet stretched across half the sky, and night after night I came to the edge of the river and watched. Now *that* was discovery!" Dona Margarita gestured excitedly to the sky. "I looked up, and it was there, just for me."

THE EMUS

SY MONTGOMERY

Squatting amid barbed, low-growing *Bassia*, sticky clover burrs, spiky stipa grass, and a sea of other angry-looking ground cover, I nonetheless wielded my knife gently. Even as their toxin-tipped spines festered in my fingers, I respected these plants, even admired them, for the patient trickery with which they steal life from the red desert soil. I lopped off more plants with my case knife, stuffing them into thrice-reused paper lunch bags labeled in black Magic Marker with the species name.

The most challenging part of my task that winter July day was to keep my equipment from blowing away. If I didn't anchor the lunch bags with rocks, knees, or the edge of the metal ring that marked off an area of one square meter for my plant sampling, the wind would carry the bags and their contents across the outback until they lodged in a wombat warren. My work at Brookfield Conservation Park was part of an experiment run by Sandy Tartowski, the only other person in camp at the moment, who was going to dry the plants I collected and weigh them as part of a study on the nitrogen cycle in this section of arid South Australia.

The stillness of the outback is punctuated with bounding arcs of kangaroos, spotted on the way to and from the plant-sampling sites in the morning and evening, and the spectacular flights of roseate cockatoos flocking overhead in noisy bursts of gray and pink. Generally, however, the larger animals are reclusive in the desert, and most of the action takes place unseen. *Exocarpos,* sometimes called the native cherry, steals moisture from the roots of its neighbors through special root structures called hostoria. *Spinifex,* growing in the sandiest corner of the park, spreads itself from rounded tufts into ever-widening rings of needle-sharp grass. Plants battle with drought and salt; some plants here store so much salt that an animal will sicken if it eats them.

Mostly, though, changes in the weather were the only activity I could observe. Sometimes I would look up after a light rain to see a rainbow spreading itself across the sky, or great piles of fat gray clouds gliding over one another. I would rather have been studying animals than plants.

I don't recall having heard a sound, but something twisted my mind sharply away from my work. I looked up and felt a shock spring from the top of my head down to my neck. Three birds taller than a man strolled through the brown grass twenty-five yards away from me. Emus.

It is alarming to know that emus exist; it is yet more alarming to watch them. The emu (*Dromaius novae hollandiae*) is stranger even than the ostrich, that long-suffering victim of cartoons and of metaphors about shortsighted planning. Slightly shorter than the ostrich, the six-foot, seventy-five-pound emu looks even less birdlike: unlike the voluptuous ostrich plumes that once decorated ladies' hats, the emu's feathers are primitive, stringy, and twin-shafted, hanging on its rounded body like hair. From this bushy brown body sprout two eight-inch wing stumps and a long black neck with a periscope head and gooselike beak.

Its legs are magnificent. Most birds' legs are easy to ignore, as people generally do; birds' legs are disturbing. Out from the softest tufts of bright feathers, parrot or chickadee, poke these scaly, reptilian appendages, a throwback to embarrassing ancestors like archaeopteryx. And the legs are on backward. Instead of bending forward where you'd expect the knees to be, birds' legs bend back.

But the legs are the apex of the emu's evolution; they are too spectacular to ignore. Thick, long, and muscular, armored with flesh-toned scales, they enable this flightless animal to run forty miles per hour and sever fence wire with one kick.

Backward-bending, the emus' legs lifted with the grace and fluidity of a double-jointed ballerina on a careless stroll; their necks dipped downward into an S-shape as they picked at grass. If they saw me, they didn't care. They strolled over the ridge casually, until their haystack bodies blended into the round brown forms of wintering bushes, and were gone.

The emu stands beside the kangaroo on Australia's coat of arms, symbolic of the otherwordly creatures that evolved on this stranded continent. The forms crafted by the salt-strewn, drought-ravaged land outpace our imagination: pouched antelopes that leap on two feet instead of running on four; spine-covered, egg-laying mammals with whiplike ribbons of sticky tongue; and man-size flightless birds are all certainly of a more bizarre invention than angels. That's how I felt when I saw the emus—as if I had been visited by angels: they came upon my consciousness like a vision, a glimpse into the corner of the mind of God. I realized I was sweating in the forty-degree cold.

This was no good at all. If you sweat out here in the winter, the moisture stays in your clothing and then you freeze at night, unless you depart radically from routine and change clothes. The cold was only one reason why I didn't change clothes much. The last fourteen nights, I'd curled into my sleeping bag in a fist-tight ball, head buried with the drawstring tight in order to warm my body with my own breath. In the morning, I would wake to three inches of ice in the teakettle. The other reason I avoided changing clothes was lice; I wanted to restrict their habitat. I kept hoping that any day now they'd discover they were on the wrong host and vanish in search of a kangaroo, or else some more appropriate mammal.

I didn't tell Sandy Tartowski about the lice. I feared she would then want to study them. On a field project in Costa Rica, she and her colleagues had become infested with botfly larvae. These are grublike animals that live under your skin. They breathe through little tubes that poke out through the wound they entered, and if you grasp the tube at just the right moment you can pull them out, Sandy told me. But some people, she said, let a few remain embedded in their flesh, just to see what they will do. In the interest of ecological science, Sandy had hosted several through their life cycle, until they grew nearly two inches long. At this stage, they drop out through a hole in the skin, fall to the ground, and pupate. "Quite a neat little evolutionary trick they pull," Sandy commented.

Everything both in and out of camp was game for study, which was one of the purposes of the fourteen-thousand-acre park, as well as being a preserve for wombats. Especially after the other scientists began to arrive, every flat surface in camp was littered with discoveries and experiments. Empty mayonnaise jars housed fist-size lycosid spiders; olive jars restrained two-inch cockroaches. Plastic bags containing fox scat and wombat, kangaroo, and rabbit fecal pellets gathered on the tables under the tin-roofed shed that sheltered our supplies; tagged plant specimens awaited enshrinement in our moldy herbarium, actually a photo album. Even the tiny, gas-powered refrigerator served the demands of ecology; you had to select your lunch carefully, or you might end up with the bait mixture for capturing field mice and fat-tailed dunnarts.

Sandy came to pick me up at dusk in the Jeep. Carrying seventy-eight bags of plants the four kilometers back to camp would have been unwieldy. Also, I would have gotten lost. It's hard to navigate a landscape painted in the colors of camouflage: winter's olive-drab leaves, red earth, brown bark. The landscape here is mostly savannah, part mixed woodland and part scrub—an endless expanse of bare earth, grasses, wombat warrens, bushes, and mallee, a stunted type of eucalyptus. On a different project in the park, I had managed to stretch an afternoon walk home from a nearby claypan into a six-hour hike through the darkness, four kilometers past the dirt driveway to camp. I'd still be walking, nearing the border of Western Australia, if a schoolteacher who happened to be leaving a camping trip with his class hadn't spotted me straggling along the track leading to the highway. On top of the obvious difficulty of navigating with few landmarks, I have no sense of direction.

Like a prophet reporting a dream, I told Sandy about the emus. She was excited. No one, not even Stephanie Williams, the ornithologist who had lived here at the park long enough to finish her doctoral thesis, had seen emus on the reserve since December.

Sandy, at twenty-seven, was a big, brawny woman who looked like she could beat up your father. When she screwed the lids on jars or closed the valve to the LP burner, you had to use pliers to open them again. She had lived here at Brookfield for two years, sleeping in a low blue tent, writing in a spacious orange office tent under a tree where the roseate cockatoos, also called galahs, nested. The pink-breasted parrots recognized her and didn't even squawk when she approached.

Sandy was working on her Ph.D. thesis for Cornell. Before entering academia, she led a top-flight female wilderness rescue team in Minnesota; shipped out on freighters as an able-bodied seaman; hacked through South American jungles to study howler monkeys; and alarmed all her bosses and professors by calling them by their first names on first meeting. Sandy could do that; she was their equal, and she knew this without conceit. She could pilot a plane, fix a broken Jeep (or a broken arm); she could even juggle. And everyone who was familiar with her ecological work referred to it as brilliant.

Her competence drained my confidence. I was only a year younger, and I'd spent the past five years in New Jersey, sitting in an office swivel chair. I had no formal scientific background. I had few camping skills. I'd only recently figured out how a woman can take a leak in the woods without peeing on her shoe. I couldn't use a compass, and some nights I would spend half an hour trying to find my tent. I was scrawny—five-foot-five and only a hundred and ten pounds. But Sandy liked me. She liked anything living, as long as it wasn't Republican.

Sandy seldom stayed under the shed to talk after dinner but went to her orange tent to write up her reports. Until the other scientists and volunteers began to arrive, nights were solitary.

Particularly at night, the land and the sky can produce an engulfing loneliness in a soul whose family and friends are half a world away, living in a different season and in a day you passed yesterday. When I hugged my best friend Caroline good-bye in a restaurant parking lot back in New

Jersey, she looked up at the night sky and said, "At least we'll still be under the same stars." But that is not true. In the Southern Hemipshere, instead of the Big Dipper, there's the Southern Cross, and Orion stands on his head.

But the loneliness eventually becomes a sort of freedom, a sort of comfort. Absent from the friends and work that define and reflect identity, selfhood becomes transient. The land does not encircle you like a clique of friends; it simply stretches out and out, and you're not "in the middle of it," you're simply there, somewhere, an infinitesimal blot of temporary protoplasm. My twenty-six years of life meant nothing here, in this land still seeded with salt from a Miocene ocean. The stunted mallee, the ephemeral grasses, the orange-red soil, the twisted acacia all testify to the millennia of fierce, silent violence this land has endured. Through drought and fire and day after day of searing sun, the land faces pain without fear, the seasons of struggle forming a rhythm like the prose of the Old Testament, like the sound of the sea, like the ebb of the vanilla moonlight over the mallee. To be lonely, but to abandon that selfish pain, is to stand powerless, minuscule, and jubilant, as the memories in the land overwhelm the self. It is a feeling as peaceful as sleep, as comfortable as death.

I lay in my tent that night listening to the bats squeak, feeling the cold, and thinking of the emus. I wondered where they slept.

The other scientists and volunteers began to arrive a week after I saw the emus. First to appear was Dr. Pamela Parker, a researcher with the Chicago Zoological Society, and Brookfield's heart and soul; she had helped the zoological society establish the park, a former sheep station, as a reserve for the study and preservation of the endangered southern hairy-nosed wombat and the creatures and land that form its world. Petite, lively, and always smiling, this forty-year-old woman seemed still surprised with life after two and a half decades of research, and was given to exclaiming "Fantastic!" in a childlike voice just a step away from laughter. Pearl Yusuf, a twenty-one-year-old veterinary assistant, flew in from Chicago. A tall muscular black woman from the city's infamous South Side, she arrived with her Sony Walkman, hip-hop-era sunglasses, and a new tent she had tried out on her first camping trip a month before. She was going to study the effect of fox predation on rabbits—which have existed in Australia in plague proportions almost since the day they were introduced by Europeans in 1886. Carol Berkhower, who memorized operas and played championship chess, was a math major at the University of Chicago; she would help with the fossil dig at Victoria Cave at Naracoorte, in the adjacent state of Victoria. The cave, one of the richest boneyards on the continent, had been discovered in 1969 by Dr. Rod Wells, the Brookfield project codirector. I hadn't decided on a specific study project, to my mounting horror.

I had worked with Rod and Pamela a year earlier. That two-week visit had been arranged through Earthwatch, of Watertown, Massachusetts, an organization that matches up scientists with interested laymen who volunteer to help with fieldwork. I'd helped to observe wombat warrens (although I never saw a wombat emerge from one), counted and sorted the fecal pellets of wombats, kangaroos, and rabbits (from which one can estimate population size), observed and recorded bird behavior at artificial watering points. This year, Pamela had invited me back, confident that I could devise my own research project. Although I had always wanted to study animals, I really had no idea what I would study, or how. But her invitation was compelling enough for me to quit the newspaper job I'd held for five years, pack up my books in liquor boxes, and move all the socks and thermal underwear and sweaters I owned into my new green Timberline tent.

Our initial "fieldwork" together—Pearl, Carol, and I—was tearing down barbed-wire fences. Pamela needed the metal fenceposts to mark wombat warrens. We were taking down a fence near the center of the park when I saw the emus again.

They arrived noiselessly, five hundred yards away from us; they appeared to be taking turns picking at a low, bird's-nest-like clot in a eucalyptus tree. Again, the shock leaped down from the top of my head; but now I was with other people, and I blushed, as if I'd caught myself having an erotic thought during an English lecture. We approached them with cameras and binoculars, ducking foolishly behind bushes, then proceeding when we imagined they weren't looking (but emus are always looking), until they were only a hundred yards from us. Then one of the emus pulled itself up to its full height, neck upstreched, and advanced straight toward us. The other two emus stood still, watching us. About fifty yards away now, the upstart bird turned to the right, defecated meaningfully, and ran in that direction for twenty-five yards. After that the emus ignored us, and finally strolled off over a ridge toward the east.

I found the emu's dropping, a discarded fuel tank from an alien's spaceship landing. Embedded in the bile-colored ooze were hundreds of round green quarter-inch seeds. They were striated like a basketball. I went to the matted section of the tree where the emus had been feeding and spotted the red fleshy berries of mistletoe. I picked one and peeled off the mushy covering. Inside was the round green basketball.

I had decided what I would study.

As young girls cherish their first boyfriend's high-school ring, as Victorians saved locks of their loved ones' hair, I collected emu droppings. There were stories in these seven-inch greenish-black wet pancakes on the ground: how digestion was proceeding, how much moisture was in the food, what seeds had been eaten. I had read, on a foray into Adelaide's scientific libraries, that a Western Australian researcher named S. J. Davies was one of only two men to have studied emus in any detail. Davies had discovered that some seeds germinated up to five times more quickly in emu "pies," making the birds important disseminators, gardeners in the desert. I was going to try this experiment with the mistletoe seeds.

Collecting the pies was a logistical nightmare. I wanted fresh pies, and they are largely liquid. I tried scooping them up with a spoon, but I couldn't capture the entire pie that way. I tried digging up a bit of the soil under the pies, but this filled the specimen with dirt and rocks and possibly seeds the emu didn't eat. For a while, I scooped them up as best I could and carried them in my backpack in a plastic bag; occasionally I'd forget to take them out, and the next day I'd find them in the same pocket as my lunch. Eventually Dean Newell, the park ranger whose warm house and family was a human refuge in the park, figured out the best way to transport the droppings: we would dig out a divot of the earth underneath each one with a shovel, place the whole thing on a stiff cardboard, and transport it back to camp by truck. Once I got the pies back to camp, I would pick through the ooze with tweezers, counting and identifying each seed. Sometimes there were more than five hundred seeds in a single pie. I then replaced half the seeds in the pie they had come from and spread the other half on a moist paper towel, and waited to see which set germinated better.

This was the usual way humans studied animals in the park, examining the fringes of their lives with cardboard and shovels, paper bags and string. Another of Sandy's studies made use of rolls of toilet paper; fifty-two rolls were staked out as termite bait, and their decomposition measured the animals' appetites. Pamela seldom saw any wombats (although carcasses, victims of the recent year-long drought, gaped at us from the mouths of abandoned warrens). She and Rod Wells pieced together the details of wombat life mostly by studying the animals' fecal pellets, the plants they ate, and their awesome warrens, earthworks comprised of mounds and holes that would stretch over twenty feet of surface, rise five feet above the surroundings, and bore ten feet beneath the topsoil.

My pie expeditions were really an excuse to search for the emus themselves, although I seriously doubted that I would see them a third time. It was pointless to go looking for three animals by walking two or three miles an hour over a fourteen-thousand-acre park; better to survey the flat land like an Eskimo, looking for movement, change in the land. The rewards were sometimes spectacular, sometimes obscure. At the close of one unusually sunny day, which was bright and warm enough for me to stow my Army jacket in my backpack, I returned to the ridge where I had first seen the emus. I was drawn over the ridge as if by a magnet, and sat on a fallen log for some time, watching meat ants crawl over my boots, feeling unspeakably happy. I faced away from the Stipa Loop, one of the main tracks, along which fenced plant exclosures had been erected to measure grazing impact. In front of me were dozens of gray stumps, stunted mallee, gray-green gigera bushes that smelled of gasoline, haying stipa grass—all so fierce and perfect and stark. I raised my binoculars and suddenly kangaroos were everywhere, bouncing in all directions. Everywhere I swung the binoculars were three or four kangaroos, as if God had just dropped handfuls of them like rubber balls from the sky, scattering them in explosions of perfect arcs. And once one stopped, it was invisible. The outback is full of kangastumps and wombush, betrayed only by motion.

We were returning from an unlikely trip to a camel ranch in Kapunda to make a tape recording. Dean's wife, Florence, was in a play to raise money for the area's elementary school—located in Blanchetown, a tiny town half an hour's drive from camp, where we went for showers—and the script required camel noises. The animals obliged with vocalizations like a plumber wrestling with a clogged drain. Florence, Carol, Pearl, and I had just passed the Newells' house in the truck, headed for camp, when I saw the birds again.

"Stop the car!" I shouted. The three emus were grazing near Dean's shed, in a depression where a shallow lake had formed during a rainstorm nearly a decade ago. Carol crawled out of the car after me.

More from custom than for any practical reason, we hid behind bushes as we watched them. The average bird's eyesight is forty times sharper than a human's; surely they saw us. But it would have seemed too forward just to advance nakedly into their lives. The grace with which they moved was almost painful to me, like music. I imagined the curved patterns their feet and legs and necks left in the air as they strolled and stooped. They were gathering great mouthfuls of a broad, low-growing leaf as they strolled. At first they seemed oblivious to us. Then, one of the animals began walking straight toward me as I crouched sheepishly behind my bush, its black head held high on its periscope neck, until it was within twenty-five yards of my hiding place. Then it ran straight across my line of vision. Each animal did this in turn as my heart pounded. Was this a challenge? An invitation?

It was a test, an experiment. The animals wanted to know whether I was dangerous, I concluded. How fast can that animal run? they must have wondered. Will it run after me? What does it want? They must have decided that I was harmless, for soon I was able to approach within twenty feet of them. I could see their eyes clearly for the first time; brown and gleaming as mahogany, with pupils black as holes. I could see the wind playing with their twin-shafted feathers. I could hear plants being crushed under their huge feet as they moved. I wanted to drink in their every movement, to make it part of my understanding. But to watch them wasn't enough; I wanted to know the meaning of what I saw. I wanted to take back a pattern, like a drawing, of these moments. I would need numbers.

I followed the emus for three hours, rapt, until dark. When I returned to camp, I made a checklist of their behaviors. I would tally these behaviors every thirty seconds with a tic of the pencil. Then, I would total the number of times each behavior was performed. The pattern would emerge.

The next time I went looking for the emus, I found them immediately. A high-school student named Danny, visiting Dean as part of a vocational program, wanted to help with my study. He was considering a career working with animals, perhaps as a park ranger. Just west of the Newells' house, we saw them. I handed Danny a checklist and a pencil.

For the first time, I noticed a scar on the leg of one of them. It was a seven-inch slash, with a strip of black flesh hanging off it. Danny became more and more disconcerted about the wound; he left to get Dean, to see if he could do anything about it. I followed the emus.

It was extremely difficult to remember to glance at my watch every thirty seconds and record the behavior of all three. I decided to record only the behavior of one, but I couldn't identify the individuals yet; even the one with the scar wasn't always easy to pick out at a distance of fifty feet and more. For perhaps an hour, I ticked off the behaviors: stroll, stand, browse, graze. The three stayed close together; never did one get more than three hundred yards from the other two. I followed them as if in a trance; I paid no attention to where we were going, I just kept going there.

Drops of light rain began falling, and the emus moved into an area more densely wooded; the soil was sandier, peopled with spindly mallee saplings. I felt something restful and safe about the place. It felt like home.

Then, in silent agreement, the emus dropped to their knees, as if to pray, one after the other. Then another set of drops, to their chests. It had not occurred to me that they might have two different sitting positions. I made a note on my sheet.

I felt awed to have witnessed this new behavior, yet utterly comfortable. That they would sit with me in attendance seemed an expression of trust. I sat also. They stayed there for perhaps ten minutes, occasionally picking at vegetation. I took out my sandwich from my backpack. We ate lunch together.

Abruptly, one stood—an awkward motion in two steps: first, a jerk with neck and chest to kneeling position, then a sort of squatting leap to stand, like a camel rising. The other two then stood, and they began to stroll calmly in a new direction.

I followed them until the Newells' house came into view. Dean and Danny rolled up the main track in the truck. The emus didn't run. Dean said he didn't think the leg wound was serious. I felt as if I were inside a ring of enchantment. The emus seemed to be waiting for me, maybe twenty-five yards away. I followed them until dark.

For a long time it seemed that finding them was hit-or-miss. Some days I would walk all day without seeing them; several days, when it rained, I was the sole person to leave camp, only to return with an empty data sheet three or four or five hours later, the bottom half of my jeans plastered to my wet calves below the point where my borrowed poncho stopped, my feet turning purple and white inside sopping socks. The days I didn't find them were lovely, though; since I knew no place to go and look for them, I just wandered freely, stopping whenever I liked, to inspect the wombats' awesome earthworks piled two feet above the surroundings and pocked with cavernous holes, or to watch flocks of galahs wheeling in the sky, pink and gray like a sunset. In the early mornings, I would go to the dense mallee north of the east-west track and see the blue-green parrots called mallee ringnecks glittering above my head, and hear the trees creaking, and startle the kangaroos.

I learned how to use a compass. I wanted to map the emus' movements, and I did not want to risk becoming lost. This was the concern that had caused me to leave them that first day when it got dark; I would not have my own ineptitude separate us. Looking for them, even in vain, I became strong and confident; my legs became muscular from striding through the outback, and I was able to walk very fast without tiring, and keep warm in this way. I had a single, clear focus to my life, and my time seemed unbounded without the showers and mirrors and makeup and ingratiating small talk that are woven into the fabric of office life. My needs were pure. I didn't need to be pretty, but strong, not witty, but alert. The days I looked for the emus, wandering expectantly through their stark and staggering world, nose running, hair matted, I felt beautiful for the first time in my life.

The days I did find them were pure bliss. In the beginning, every new behavior was a revelation. I remember the "first times" the way that one remembers special anniversaries: the first time your dad let you drive the car, the first time you made dinner for your husband. I remember the first time I saw them drink: I had not even written "drinking" as a behavior to be checked off on my data sheet. I just thought that they didn't drink—or that they drank so rarely that there would be no chance to record it. Wombats are said to be able to live out their seventeen years of life without having to drink; less than nine inches of rain falls here in an average year, and there are few average years; the weather swings from one staggering extreme to another, turning the desert from billiard-table-bare red soil and rocks to fields of waving grasses and wildflowers.

But this winter was a rainy one, and the tracks were full of puddles. The emus would kneel by one of these puddles and scoop up beakfuls of water, sometimes for up to four minutes. And when they departed, sometimes they walked through the puddle, leaving the imprint of their huge armored feet in the red mud.

Soon I was able to recognize the individuals. The one with the scar I named Knackered Leg ("knackered" is an impolite Australian expression, I later discovered; I had thought it merely meant "messed up," but later someone explained that the expression comes from the word "knackers," which means "testicles.") Knackered Leg tolerated my presence best, and often looked me straight in the eye; I could get closest to him. Black Head seemed to be the most forward of the emus, he took the lead and set the direction for the other two most often. Bald Throat had a whitish patch on his neck, where the black feathers were sparse, and he seemed skittery. When a car approached, he was usually first to run.

I refer to the three as "he's" for no anatomical reason. No one has discovered how to identify the gender of emus without dissecting them—or until someone lays eggs. Although the female, of course, lays them, the male sits on the greenish-black eggs—up to twenty five-inch pointed ovals in a single clutch—until the eggs hatch, when the female, who has been lingering nearby, disappears. The cock stays with the yellow-and-brown-striped chicks until they turn into full-grown emus, up to eighteen months later.

The birds I followed were not adults. They didn't have the turquoise neck patches that characterize the mature animals. They were yearlings, still exploring their world with humor and delight. The wind was a plaything; on gusty days they would dance with it, throwing their necks to the sky and splashing the air with their feet. Bald Throat would usually start this behavior, and then Knackered Leg and Black Head would join in. They discovered teasing, that favorite pastime of children. One day I watched them approach the Newells' dog, a mutt of perhaps fifty pounds, who was often kept chained outside the house. The dog was barking hysterically, but Black Head, neck and shoulders raised as if in quizzical alarm, continued walking toward the straining animal head-on. The other two followed, in similar posture. When Black Head was within twenty feet of the dog, which by now was hurling itself against its chain so violently it nearly choked midbark, he raised his wing stumps forward, hurled his neck upward and leaped into the air with both feet kicking, repeating his head-neck dance for perhaps forty seconds and gleefully inciting the others into similar antics. The dog went absolutely wild, and the emus then raced off across the dog's line of vision at a dead run, until they abruptly stopped three hundred yards away and lay down to preen.

I loved watching them groom themselves. Sometimes the grooming was merely a scratching with beak tip at a fluff of black neck feathers; but when their gooselike beaks would comb roughly through the longer, beige-brown body feathers, I recalled those sunny afternoons as a little girl when my mother would trail her fingers over my feet or my grandmother would brush my hair. The birds groomed leisurely but quickly; each scratchy-sounding beak stroke lasted less than two seconds, but sometimes the grooming sessions went on for half an hour, with frequent stops in between feathers to pick at the vegetation around where they were sitting. I imagined that this activity comforted them.

Unlike other birds, they did not groom one another, but only themselves. But they were quite aware of themselves as a group. Whenever one of them would stray too far from the others, he would look up suddenly, realize the situation, and usually run or trot until the gap was closed. At dusk, quick movements—even quick movements of a fellow emu—could easily cause all to run. Once they began running, I lost them. Even if I could have run after them at forty miles an hour, I would have succeeded only in chasing them farther away. And at dusk, when every bush looks like an emu, they could melt into the mallee like morning's frost.

So on most evenings we would be separated by the time the pink sunset dimmed to purples and blues. Having lost them among the mallee somewhere around the east-west track, which ran perpendicular to the camp driveway, I would return to camp, which by now was full of the new faces and stories of visiting scientists and volunteers. We would huddle by the eucalyptus-scented campfire, over lap-held dinners, and talk; Rod Wells would sometimes come from Adelaide, where he taught biology at the university and tell us about fossil hunting in ancient streambeds; a visiting Chicago biologist told us how to catch wild bats: "grab them by the incisors" (in other words, let the bat bite you). Pamela told us aboriginal legends about Dreamtime, before the world began; a volunteer recited a five-minute poem about an Arctic explorer. There were tales of army ants in the tropics, sea songs from Sandy, worries about nuclear war, snippets of letters from home read aloud. And every night, as I lay inside my tent and let go my consciousness, like a child's balloon grown too taxing to hold, I thought of the emus, and how they slept.

It was possible that they didn't sleep at all. Maybe they simply rested briefly several times during the night, as they did during the day. Did they have to pick a new spot to sleep every night, or did they return to the same site? Or did they stroll and graze some nights and rest others? Did they huddle together for warmth? What position did their necks assume when they slept?

On several mornings, I got up at 4:00 A.M. to explore north of the east-west track, to see if I could find where they slept. On one of the days following such a morning expedition, I spent the day disoriented. I found the emus, but they ran away from me, frightened by a car in the distance. Then I discovered my self-winding watch had stopped during the night, then restarted, telling me it was afternoon all morning. On this day it seemed nothing worked right.

But then, around 5:00 P.M. Pamela drove up to camp and told me that she had seen the emus heading north near the east-west track. She drove me to the site. They had already crossed the barbed-wire fence that bordered the track and were melting into the darkening bush. I followed them, striding vigorously to catch up; they remained calm. It was nearly dark when they sat down, all facing the same direction, under four mallees that formed a kind of canopy against the blue-and-orange-streaked sky. I sat also, and night closed gently around us, like a mother pulling up a quilt around her children.

I sat cross-legged, surrounded by a comforting and exciting intimacy, until I could no longer see them. The moon was waning and dim. I could not tell if they were sleeping.

After many minutes, I realized that I was not doing my job; I was gathering no information. I wanted to know what position their necks were in. I turned on my flashlight, first onto the ground, so as not to startle them too much if they were awake, then swung the light to face them. Their necks were up. If they had been asleep, their necks in a different position, I'd have wakened them. I shut off the light and waited. I heard no sound. I didn't even know if they were still there. I turned the light directly on them, and they leaped to their feet with a rumble of thuds. I extinguished the light, hoping they would calm down, but they were running all around me, their huge feet striking the ground with the full weight of their seventy-five pounds, crashing, frenzied, racing with my heart in the darkness.

I had violated their trust. I had shattered our intimacy.

In the weeks that followed, I had less trouble finding them during the day but always lost them at night. They had switched their diet from large amounts of mistletoe, which ceased to appear in their droppings, almost exclusively to wild mustard, a broad-leaved, dandelionlike plant that appears in late July. There were two particularly lush patches of it only half a kilometer from the Newells' house, and I could usually find the emus there by 9:00 or 10:00 A.M. The emus were so used to me that I could even bring volunteers along one at a time. The volunteers later invariably all bought half a dozen postcards of emus at the general store in Blanchetown.

I could sometimes get within five feet of the emus now—close enough to examine their toenails in detail, close enough to see the veins of the leaves they were eating. But I could not spend all my days with the emus. Pamela had been gathering data for more than five years on fecal-pellet transects, and the rainy weather had delayed the collection of this data. We all had to spend time conducting the five-kilometer transects, using a sighting compass to walk a straight line, stopping every two hundred and fifty meters to count and identify the fecal pellets found within an area of one square meter (measured by setting down a metal ring at these points), marking the results on data sheets. This data determined relative populations of wombats, kangaroos, and rabbits, and had to be collected before Pamela returned to Chicago September 1 and camp dispersed.

Earlier in the winter, I had eagerly committed myself to excavating fossil marsupials with Rod Wells at Victoria Cave. It was the chance of a lifetime, to help explore the richest prehistoric boneyard in Australia. And now, mid-August, Carol and I were going there—in my case, with secret reluctance. Time was running out. In two weeks I would have to leave the park for a writing assignment in New Zealand.

The work was tedious but fascinating. We scratched the dirt with our tiny trowels and paintbrushes, revealing the heel bones of *Procoptodon,* an extinct eleven-foot-high kangaroo, and the vertebrae of tiny reptiles. We drove around with the lower jaw of *Zygomaturus,* a wombat the size of a hippo, in the trunk of our car. But Carol and I persuaded Rod's assistant to drive us back to Brookfield two days early. At first, he thought we wanted to leave because our tent had flooded in a rainstorm, but I told him I worried about all the data I was missing on my emu study.

I shouldn't have worried. I'd left Peggy, a volunteer who had worked at the Philadelphia Zoo, in charge of the study when I left. She had accompanied me with the emus, knew the routine, and was competent, reliable, and self-assured. Peggy had collected thirty sheets of new data. Volunteers had arrived since we left, and they were all calling the birds "Peggy's emus." One volunteer told me excitedly that the emus had even come into camp once, "looking for Peggy." Peggy had made some modifications to my data sheets. One of them was to rename the emus. Knackered Leg, Bald Throat, and Black Head required two letters each to represent them on the sheet; she had renamed Knackered Leg "Scar," to replace "KL" with "S," and Black Head and Bald Throat were renamed Blackie and Whitey, "B" and "W" for short. Peggy called the emus "the 'mus" (pronounced "Mews"). I went to bed early that night, and felt strangely ill, angry at nothing.

The next day, I found the emus out near Stephanie's bird blind. Pearl came with me, as her rabbit study wasn't working out—although she knew where they were, they never seemed to come out for observation, and fox sightings were rare. The minute I saw the emus, I wished Pearl would leave.

The wind was tossing my data sheets around, and the emus were behaving strangely. They were exceptionally jumpy, performing the head-neck dance at each other and bushes, and running frequently. I was annoyed; someone had taken my clipboard while I was away. My hair thrashed at my face and stung my eyes. I kept missing the thirty-second intervals to take the data down.

Around 5:00 P.M., as always, they headed toward the east-west track, this time closely following the main track. It began to rain—small, hard, mean drops that hurt my scalp. The emus were becoming more agitated, their movements jerky, less fluid. They didn't graze along the way. Pearl and I saw Carol along the east-west track, and Pearl and Carol decided to head home for dinner, since the rain was coming down harder. They urged me to come with them. They might as well have asked me if I wanted to rip my head off. Carol offered me her raincoat as she and Pearl walked off; I was annoyed to have to turn my head away from the emus to say no. The two of them called to me—they could have someone pick me up in the car later, didn't I want dinner, I would freeze without a hat. I couldn't have cared less; the rain came harder, colder, and the emus were walking faster, getting farther and farther away in the darkening bush.

We crossed the east-west track, and I held my breath as they stepped over the barbed-wire fence; I was worried, as always, about Knackered Leg's scar. He bumped his good leg on the wire, and I winced. Then a new gust of wind, and they trotted into the bush. It was raining harder, with a cold, bone-chilling wind. My coat and hair were drenched. I didn't care. I wanted only to find them. I wanted to record their behavior in the wind. I wanted to know how they sheltered from the rain. But as I caught sight of them again—far away, deep in the bush, their haystack bodies bouncing as they gathered speed—I realized that it wasn't the data I was after. I just wanted to be with them. And then they disappeared.

The rain was changing to hail. I embedded myself in a gigera bush for shelter and began to cry.

A few days later I went into Adelaide on another library expedition. I told my friend Dennis, a zookeeper at the Adelaide Zoo, about my feelings of the past few days. The unexpected jealousy, the crushing disappointment when they ran away from me that night.

He nodded. "You're in love with them," he said. "You're in love with the emus. Crikey! How do you think I feel about me seals, me otters at the zoo? It's the same thing."

Five days before I was to leave for New Zealand, I found the emus around 10:00 A.M., sitting down near one of the mustard patches near the Newells' house. Knackered Leg looked up as I approached; the other two birds turned their heads and rose in my direction, then craned back to their grooming and feeding. The wind pulled their back feathers straight up in the air with its gusts. When they stood, the wind was strong enough to nearly knock them over. They remained sitting most of the time, and I lay on my belly to minimize the chill of the wind.

By noon, they had moved across the main track, nearer to the Newells' house, to the shallow depression where I had first watched them with Carol. I stood three feet away from Black Head and held his gaze. Staring into that intelligent, shining brown eye, I felt as if I were capable of looking directly into the sun.

Something frightened him. He jumped and ran two steps and glanced past me. I turned and saw Florence fifteen feet behind me. I had a phone call from the states. I went into their house to return the call.

When I returned to the mustard patch, the emus were still there grazing, and shortly they began to stroll north. A student drove by on the main track, and the emus didn't run. Dean's truck passed with a load of volunteers clicking cameras at us. The emus were undisturbed. Never had I seen them so calm. I thought: Tonight?

My gear was still scattered—scavenged by volunteers while I was at Victoria Cave. I had no flashlight in my backpack, no compass, no lighter. This would be a moonless night. That felt right. Light a cigarette and the bus comes; forget your umbrella and it will rain. I wasn't annoyed. It was like Lent; perhaps if I gave up my habitual orientation, I could achieve a higher one.

No one ran, even though it was dusk. We crossed the east-west track into the thick bush. I switched to observing Knackered Leg alone; it was impossible to see all three in the darkening scrub. I stayed close to him, maybe five feet away, beyond which I could see nothing but the looming shapes that were trees and bushes. I heard Black Head and Bald Throat jogging nearby, but Knackered Leg paced steadily.

I could no longer see my data sheet or my watch. If Knackered Leg had stopped moving, he would have been invisible. We were all having trouble with the moonless dark, bumping into low bushes. The sun was gone. There were no stars; it was cloudy.

When they lay down, I had to count the thumps—one, knees; two, chests—to know they had gone all the way down. I couldn't tell what position their necks were in. We were deep in the mallees, the ground under us bare of vegetation.

I recognized their activities by sound: the shifting of the great armored feet under their bodies, the combing of feathers through their beaks, the jump-thud of their getting up to look around, the splatter of wet feces hitting the ground.

The ground was cold. I ate an apple, for the warming calories—I wasn't hungry.

There was a breeze, and somebody stood up. The noise of the breeze rattling the eucalyptus leaves obscured what he was doing. I waited about three minutes, frightened. Had they all gotten up and gone away? The breeze died. I heard no sound. I waited, feeling cold. They've left. I will have to go home. I stood and took three paces forward, and noise exploded around me, thunks and rustles. I'd walked into one of them. I waited and heard them resettle on the ground a few yards away. I went to them.

I heard no sounds after that but an occasional chill breeze. They slept. I thought that if they traveled at all at night, they would not do so tonight. It was dark and safe. I wanted more than anything to be asleep with them, as if our dreams would merge.

But I was really cold. My hands ached like all my fingers had been jammed. My feet felt far away, frozen and alien as Antarctica. I tried to keep warm by blowing my breath up my sleeves, assuming painfully uncomfortable positions so my limbs would shake more from the strain and warm me up. Nothing worked. My legs seemed as bereft of blood as the ground. But I wanted so to stay with them.

If I went to sleep, I would probably freeze to death. I had to go back to camp. I had no idea where it was.

A qualification: I knew the camp was to the west. But I didn't know where the west was. Since we had bumped into each other and moved, I had lost track of where the sun had set. With no stars, no compass, and no flashlight, I had no means of rediscovering directions.

For perhaps thirty minutes, hand stretched out in front of my face to deflect unseen branches, I walked steadily, calmly, through the bush until I came to Carol's tent. I then became completely disoriented and wandered around the camp perhaps another thirty minutes searching vainly for my tent, or the shed, or another tent, until the beam from a flashlight caught my eye. This was another researcher; she was standing less than ten yards from my tent.

That whole day I had walked the boundaries of longing and fulfillment. I had felt a closeness with the emus akin to telepathy: I did not know what they were thinking nor did they know what I thought, but between us was a trust deeper than any I have ever shared with another organism. Trust was no contract guaranteeing my safety; I knew, always, that those great feet could kill me with a single kick—although I doubted this would happen. Certainly I could have been injured or lost when I was with them, but I did not fear either of these things. Simply being with them was worth a great price.

When we were nearing the east-west track that day, as they were leading me on to their sleep, they had stopped to graze on wild mustard in a clearing. Then I thought, I wish I could tell you what you've given to me. How could I express to creatures whose experience of the world was so different from mine what they had allowed me to feel? I thought, You have eased in me a fear more gripping than what you feel when you are separated from the others. You have given me a comfort more soothing than the feel of your feathers passing through your beaks under the warm sun. I can never repay you, but I want you to feel my thanks.

This, of course, was analogous to laying flowers on a grave. The recipient doesn't know or care. But the human species is like that: we have to utter our prayers, even if they go unheard. So while I was sitting there with them in the darkness, deep in the bush, I whispered over and over, "I love you. I love you."

A NATURAL HISTORY OF THE PLASTIC PINK FLAMINGO

JENNIFER PRICE

I hadn't stooped to think about pink flamingos until the fall of 1992, when I rented a shore house in East Haven, Connecticut, despite the two pair on the front lawn. I had just begun to write a book on American attitudes toward nature. The plastic birds were an eyesore, incongruous, and uncalled-for, I told my roommate. "And what," I sneered, "does a pink flamingo say about how we think about nature? If anything." Kathy, a naturalist and avid outdoorsperson, wasn't sure, but told me that she had moved in *because* of the flamingos, and had a friend who had taken a pink flamingo named Eudora backpacking, skiing, and mountain-biking before leaving it behind accidentally in a cabin at Donner Pass.

I recounted Eudora's story to several friends, who told me of taking pink flamingos on spring skiing trips, and stealing them off lawns on drunken late-night outings in high school. Everyone had a pink flamingo story to tell. My neighbor had done a "pink flamingo installation" for her senior show in art school. My agent knew a *New Yorker* editor with a notorious love for pink flamingos. My history professor recalled a National Public Radio feature on a pair of kidnapped flamingos that had sent back postcards from the Eiffel Tower and other tourist sites all over Europe. The plastic bird, I was discovering, was a pervasive icon in American culture. And a compelling one—backpackers do not take on extra cargo without just cause. Why cart pink flamingos into the wilderness? Why put them on lawns? Why snatch them *off* lawns? The questions seemed to merit answers, and I have been thinking about pink flamingos ever since. Why use them as croquet wickets for your bring-your-own-Jell-O lawn party, as Kathy would do in the spring?

The plastic flamingo was invented in the 1950s, but its history is rooted in older traditions of landscape art. In the United States, the bird descends from the bronze and cast-iron animal sculptures that inhabited private estates in the late nineteenth century. Antelope and swans outnumbered the occasional flamingo. But in those American upper-crust yards all lawn ornaments received a lukewarm reception. While European landscape architects favored geometrical designs, emphasizing human control over nature, the leading American designers tended to follow the English "natural" style, pioneered by Andrew Jackson Downing. Human control, Downing believed, should be a means to *re-create* nature, in its "purest" forms of beauty—which at the time generally meant expending vast amounts of other people's labor to make one's estate look like a British landscape painting. Downing cautioned against the overuse of statuary, particularly on the estate's farther reaches, where he believed nature, not human artifice, should reign. In 1881, his student Frank Scott published a do-it-yourself manual for the emerging middle class of suburban homeowners. *The Art of Beautifying Home Grounds of Small Extent* warned against "the attempt . . . glaringly and injudiciously made, to crowd within a confined space the appropriate adornments of the most ample garden."

By the 1920s, Americans in the ever more populous suburbs were making their own cement statues. Scott and Downing notwithstanding, the down-classing of lawn art was well under way. The process culminated (or bottomed out) in the 1950s, with the dual explosions of suburbs and plastics and the ensuing manufacture of plastic lawn ornaments. Like the private estate, the suburban middle-class lawn has been a calculated mix of art and nature. The 1950s yard was a family's private piece of

American nature, a tangible sign of newfound independence, affluence, and leisure. One could design this mini-estate exactly as one wished, and the new suburbanites found ample space for human artifice. Why downplay the reshaping, or human control, of this patch of nature? Why hide the statuary, even if one could? Middle-class homeowners had worked hard for their property, and for their leisure time, and their landscape designs emphasized rather than concealed the money and labor involved. Plastic ducks, frogs, basset hounds, and toadstools took up residence in the subdivisions. Union Products, a lawn-and-garden plastics company outside Boston, manufactured all these figures—along with a two-dimensional flamingo, which sold fairly well. In 1957, Don Featherstone, a young art designer at the company, designed a three-dimensional flamingo, which sold even better. In the decades ahead, it would only rarely outsell the ducks, but it would become far more famous.

Why the flamingo, which in the past had been only a minor figure in the bestiary of garden sculpture? After the War, middle-class tourism had expanded dramatically, and families who flocked to the Florida beaches had been driving back north with abundant flamingo knickknacks. Along with palm trees, the flamingo became a symbol of the Sunshine State. This was a little ironic, since the state's flamingos had been hunted to extinction in the late nineteenth century, for their plumes and meat. But no matter. In New Jersey in the 1950s, Featherstone's flamingo gave the suburban lawn the appropriate cachet of affluence and leisure. And if the pink bird blended even less well into the natural scenery than did the ducks or frogs, so much the better to announce one's esthetic labors. Sears, Roebuck sold the three-dimensional Union Products flamingo in its 1957 catalog. "Place in garden, lawn, to beautify landscape," the catalog suggested. Upper-class estate owners in adjacent counties may have sneered at the bird as a lower-class parody of outdoor sculpture, but for at least some Sears shoppers, to put a plastic flamingo on your lawn was to beautify the rectangle of nature outside your door. And the birds cost only $2.76 a pair.

As pink flamingos and their plastic kin spread across the lawns of America in the late fifties and sixties, they encountered organized resistance. Lawn ornaments ran afoul of the ascendant highbrow critiques of popular culture. And in the debate over lawn ornaments, so far no one had developed a sense of humor. Art critics launched the most direct attacks. In his 1969 book *Kitsch: The World of Bad Taste,* Gillo Dorfles called mass-produced garden and lawn ornaments the archetypal kitsch objects, vulgar mistakes committed by ignorant consumers. The pink flamingo, fast becoming the archetypal lawn ornament, became the epitome of lowbrow art and culture—fake, false, ungenuine, nonunique, and the definition of bad taste. And while cultural critics lambasted the flamingo and its ilk as desecrations of art, a separate group of critics, from the burgeoning environmental movement of the late sixties, faulted the birds as an affront to nature. "You'll not find me putting pink flamingos on my lawn, much less growing a lawn," the nature writer Anne LaBastille would protest. "I want every member of this . . . community to flourish *naturally.*" For a rising number of Americans, the ideal thing to do with nature, even the strip of earth by the driveway, was nothing at all. You shouldn't strive to make your yard look artificial *or* natural—it should just *be* natural. And no matter how strictly you observed this ideal— whether or not you elected to mow the grass—you would find nature's "purest" beauty in the wilderness, far away from human artifice. By the late sixties, whether one preferred art or nature, the plastic pink bird had magnetized widespread upper-middle-class fears about the artificiality of postwar life in America.

And then people began to laugh. John Waters's 1972 movie *Pink Flamingos* opened with a shot of pink flamingos outside the trailer of Divine, a three-hundred-pound transvestite playing "the filthiest person alive." As the pink flamingo rose to prominence as the emblem of bad taste, it became useful for rebellion against the canons of taste and propriety. The flamingos began to cross over into new neighborhoods. To put pink flamingos on a *spacious* lawn was to take a stand against élitism. It was at this time that the flamingos began to accompany people on spring ski trips, to double as croquet wickets at lawn parties thrown by the sort of people who don't throw lawn parties, and to disappear into the hands of teenagers under cover of night. In short, the flamingo became a useful thing to have around when you wanted to do something absurd, outrageous, oxymoronic, funny, or inappropriate. A flamingo was an imaginative way to post a sign (whether you did so consciously or not): "Something subversive happening here." The pink bird also began to show up on top of backpacks. The symbol of artifice was carted into the wilderness, the autonomous domain of nature. Through the 1970s, as the flamingo literally crossed onto new terrain, it became a ubiquitous signpost for crossing the overlapping boundaries of class, taste, propriety, art, and nature.

By the 1980s, the pink flamingo had acquired a fairly complex set of meanings, but things continued to grow more complicated. When the designer-cop TV show *Miami Vice* splashed a glamorous vision of Florida across Reagan-era America, plastic flamingo sales boomed. The birds reclaimed their original connotations of Florida-style leisure and glitz, and the show's cross-class appeal endeared these meanings to its high-income fans. Soon you could buy the birds not only at Kmart and highway pottery shops, but through ads in *Rolling Stone* and at trendy new pop-culture marts, like Archie McPhee's in Seattle, where a pair of flamingos cost two dollars more than at Kmart. Not every new fan, though, was tuning into pink flamingos through *Miami Vice.* As the children of the fifties became the thirty-somethings of the eighties, they were beginning to wax nostalgic about fifties kitsch; and the flamingo, the archetype of kitsch, began to appear in collectibles stores. The pink birds evocatively called up a collective childhood past. Even the name would do, as in a Boston store called Forever Flamingo, and the Manhattan restaurant Flamingo East, with retro decor. How ironic, then, that just as the plastic flamingo found new life as a memorial to kitsch, artists began to feature it in decidedly highbrow photography shows and avant-garde "installations" or "art environments."

Whether by the high road or low road, as the baby-boom generation came of age, the pink flamingo acquired legitimacy among a higher-income crowd. As the children of the 1950s had become the hippies of the 1960s and 70s, they became the yuppies of the 1980s, and rebellion became mainstream. Crossing boundaries had always been cool; now it was safe, too. Like jeans in boardrooms and Jeeps in Short Hills, the flamingo was simultaneously glitz and grunge. It was a piece of highbrow lowbrow. "Here," advertised the catalog for Cat's Pyjamas, a trendy shop specializing in flamingo items, "you'll find just what you need to ruin your neighborhood." By 1985, John Waters, disgusted, had divested himself of every flamingo he'd ever owned. Don Featherstone, who had become the vice-president of Union Products, made the first major alteration to his original plastic mold. He inscribed his autograph on the bird's flank, to circumvent two other lawnware companies that had copied the design: "We're trying," he's explained to me, "to protect its image as the original." Shoppers could now check to be sure that they were purchasing the legitimate, authentic symbol of illegitimacy and inauthenticity.

And so the fifties children entered the multicultural nineties—this peculiarly boundary-conscious era. While some celebrants of cultural diversity insist on the impermeability of boundaries between cultures (and classes and genders), others insist on crossing them, and the boundary crossers tend to come from mainstream groups—notably the white middle class, the keepers of the pink flamingo. In this postmodern era, the crossers cobble together pieces of cultural identity, mixing and matching styles of music, art, clothes, language. They create themselves, and watch themselves while they do. The pink flamingo was tailor-made for this self-conscious brand of boundary hopping. Its notoriety as a symbol of bad taste had made it a perfect symbol of crossing boundaries—and *that* made it a perfect signpost for both cultural borrowing and self-awareness. Now highbrow photographers, for example, use pink flamingos to celebrate pop culture, and to cross into it, but also to comment on the *idea* of crossing. They're letting you know that they're watching themselves.

In 1990, an *American Demographics* poll found that half the residents of Iowa think pink flamingos improve a lawn's appearance. Since 1957, the successive meanings attached to the pink flamingo haven't exactly replaced one another; rather, they have accreted. Sometimes in the same bird. At my East Haven house, I snubbed the birds sixties-style, branding them a violation of wildness, while my landlord found the birds as enjoyably out of place as the green lawn he'd planted twenty-five yards from the ocean. At the entrance to the Anaheim Hyatt-Regency, a set of ten-foot-high flamingos defends the bird's metaphoric claim to glitz and leisure. And I've been told that the chief collector of comics in this country has filled his bathroom with pink flamingos—posting a sign, perhaps, about both the lowbrow character of what he collects and the distinctly self-aware act of collecting. Stories like these have been flying into my files like flocks coming in to roost. An experimental theater company in St. Louis, my parents say, puts pink flamingos out on the lawn on performance nights. And a friend called up one night to let me know that the American man canoeing from London to Scotland on the PBS show *Travels* was carrying a pink flamingo with him. "And he's traveling *really* light," she said—he's crossing political, cultural, and natural boundaries, and watching himself as he crosses.

And my own growing collection of flamingos? Well, I'm an inveterate hiker and camper, a cross-country skier, a longtime birder. I'm a self-identified "nature person," writing about the ways we think about nature. So perhaps I've been marking my engagement (whether consciously or not) with a topic that doesn't seem, on the surface, to be very natural. I'm a baby-boomer myself, a keeper of the object. I'm posting a sign—"Something legitimately subversive going on here"—and watching myself as I do.

Which returns me to the question I started with: "What does a pink flamingo say about how we think about nature? If anything." I have been thinking about flamingos real and fake, and meditating on the connections between real nature and replicated nature. The nature people of America, myself included, have been lecturing to pink flamingos about nature for some time now. I've been trying to imagine what the birds have to say to *us* on the same topic.

First, the pink flamingo's history *has* been an overt dialogue about nature. The lawn-ornament wars have been waged, in at least some small part, over our disparate visions of nature. Arguing about how to beautify the patch of nature that lies closest to the door, we've disputed especially the question of human control—where we should be mucking around, and how much. But the lawn wars have been more obviously about people. They're culture wars, over the definitions of good art, bad art, acceptable art. And they're class wars: we've been using our definitions of the boundaries of both nature and culture to define ourselves. The uses and abuses of the pink flamingo fuel my deepening suspicion that our visions of nature encode a surprising degree of dialogue about human social and cultural norms. Who really thinks of a pink flamingo as an emissary of nature, and not as a class commentary or a statement of taste? Who really thinks about real flamingos? In the case of the flamingo fracas, as we've piled human meanings onto a replica of a bird, we have nearly forgotten about nature itself.

Second, pink flamingos are quite literally made out of nature. Union Products makes the plastics and pink dyes from petroleum by-products, and buys rolled steel (a treated alloy of iron and other ores) for the legs. The bird isn't a flamingo, but *it is real*. It's "natural." It's nature that has been dug up, boxed, shipped, combined, heated, molded, shipped again. It bears a familial resemblance to packaged hamburger at the supermarket, and to electricity from a light switch. While our everyday lives depend upon these pieces of nature from far-flung reaches, most of us can't begin to map the routes that the pieces have traveled. The plastic flamingo's most literal connection to nature may seem trivially obvious, but in the past thirty-five years, perhaps no one has ever asked where the pink flamingo came from.

The pink flamingo replicates nature, and comes from nature. And it says very little about nature. We haven't asked it to say much, just as we haven't asked plastic ducks or stuffed penguins to tell us much about ducks or penguins (or petroleum or cotton). We have asked our totems to tell us very little about the natural world and our connections to it. These creatures inhabit our "placeless," postmodern world, in which we're connected to every part of the globe but fail to keep track of those connections, where television makes the Amazon and the Antarctic no less knowable (or forgettable) than our backyards, where tropical shorebirds populate suburban grass, where the plastic replicas become our closest contact with distant pieces of nature we may never see, and where the mimics have acquired their own realities, their own strange lives. The pink flamingo is a quintessential postmodern object. A replica of a real bird, it was orphaned at the moment of its birth, adopted, coöpted, appropriated for human designs, uprooted into the floating placelessness of modern American society.

But while plastic ducks and stuffed penguins are postmodern creatures, the pink flamingo is unique in the degree to which it tells its own story. What has made this bird so consistently compelling? Originally, postwar suburbanites favored the flamingo for its showiness: the bird stuck out. And just what, exactly, asked the critics in the sixties, was a pink tropical plastic shorebird doing on the green grass of temperate-zone suburbia? An alien by any definition, the flamingo—not Union Products' quietly better-selling ducks—became the archetypal lawn kitsch, and hence a symbol of the inappropriate. And since then, the bird's unassailable out-of-contextness has made it continually perfect for calling attention to new ways of crossing boundaries. In sum, the pink flamingo has worked so beautifully as a cultural statement precisely because it's in the wrong natural habitat. It's *out of place.*

The bird speaks so eloquently about what it's not, and where it's not. The flamingo tells us little about nature, but everything about how we think about nature. And to me, this is the real beauty of the pink flamingo. It's a commentary on the hidden architecture of its own meanings. In the parlance of critical theory, the flamingo deconstructs itself. No matter what statement you use the plastic bird to make, about esthetics or class boundaries or propriety, every pink flamingo also remarks on Americans' disconnectedness from nature. Signposts everywhere, in the venues of nature and culture. Flamingos on the ski slopes, in the wilderness outback, in art galleries, and in the hands of kidnappers. We read the signs, uproot them, and reinvent them, yet the pink flamingos seem to me much like the Jell-O at the bring-your-own-Jell-O lawn parties. The more variations we come up with, the more the plastic birds insist on their essential nature.

CALIFORNIA CONDORS

SUSAN MIDDLETON AND DAVID LIITTSCHWAGER

The California Condor is a rare bird, and an acquaintance with it at firsthand is a coveted privilege. It is so rare a bird that it is doubtful if there are in existence one hundred representatives of the species at the present time (September 1921), and it would not be surprising if there should prove to be not above forty.

—*William Leon Dawson*,
Birds of California,
vol. 4, 1923

The California condor has been a rare bird for a long time. One of the first recognized endangered species, condors were observed becoming scarce in the 1890s. They came perilously close to extinction in the early 1980s, when their numbers declined to about nineteen birds. After much heated debate, the threat of extinction was deemed to be greater in the wild than in captivity, and the remaining condors were captured to create a breeding colony at the Los Angeles Zoo and San Diego Wild Animal Park. By the summer of 1993, there were seventy-six condors, and eight that had been released, with five surviving in the wild. With human will, hard work, and devotion, it now seems possible to revive this species.

Photograph by Susan Middleton and David Liittschwager.

Human intervention was responsible for their demise—through habitat destruction, hunting, and poisoning—and now it is only through human intervention that condors can be saved. Instead of being emblematic of extinction, perhaps the California condor can be a symbol of hope and our human desire to care for life on earth.

Photograph by Susan Middleton and David Liittschwager.

GUJARAT AND RAJASTHAN

PETER MATTHIESSEN

The airplane headed southwest from Delhi to Ahmedabad was a TU-154, leased from Uzbekistan, pilots and all, because of strikes in northern India. (One such plane would crash at Delhi the day following.) In Ahmedabad, there was violent strife caused by Hindu destruction in the weeks before of the Muslim mosque at Ayodhya, and at the bridge over the Sabarmati River a crowd pointed excitedly at a high plume of smoke from that part of town where rioting was taking place. With the old town and many other streets cordoned off by soldiery, the bus made a tortuous passage out of the city. The official death toll at Ahmedabad that day would be seventeen, but other reports claimed it was much higher. Because of the air strikes and the widespread rioting, we would travel the rest of the way by road.

With Victor Emanuel, head of a nature-tour company out of Austin, Texas, I was leading a band of enterprising travelers to observe the exotic birds and wildlife of northwestern India, beginning with the Little Rann of Kutch, a vast pale saline desert a few miles to the west of Zainabad which shelters one of the last three species of wild horses on earth. We also hoped to see four species of cranes—my own special interest. Victor and I had observed cranes together since 1976, when I joined him as a coleader of his new tour company and we led the group to see the wintering whooping cranes at Aransas, on the Texas coast. During that

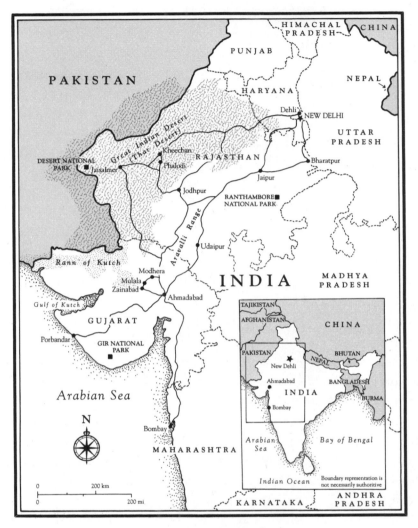

Map by Tracey Wood.

trip, we also observed the other North American crane, the sandhill—one of the few of the world's fifteen crane species not yet to some degree endangered. Now the Indian cranes were the main object of our journey—not only the native sarus of the subcontinent and southeast Asia but three winter visitors: the Eurasian or "common" crane and the elegant small demoiselle from central Asia and the rare white Siberian crane, from the subarctic tundra, which no longer appears anywhere in India except at Bharatpur, in eastern Rajasthan, where we hoped to see it near the end of this Indian journey.

From Ahmedabad, a narrow road led west across flat delta country of the state of Gujarat ("Place of Herders") toward Zainabad, one of the five-hundred-odd principalities of which India was once comprised. Zainabad itself is one of eleven villages in the former principality, which is still led unofficially by a Muslim *nawab* (the Hindi equivalent would be *rajah,* in which case the town would be "Zainpur," as in "Jaipur"). "Here is not like it is in Bombay or Ahmedabad, where the British separated Hindu and Muslim as they did in Pakistan," said Dr. Shabeer Malek, still shaking his head over the senselessness of the rioting, which was taking the lives of hundreds in Bombay. "Here in the villages, we need one another, and so we live nicely together." Dr. Malek's wife was a Hindu, and his daughter had married one, and all were living as nicely as could be expected. Dr. Malek's big house, in a walled grove of figs and neem trees of the mahogany family (Meliaceae), overlooked the bare-dirt village and the thick brown pond, to which animals and humans came for water, the women in bright saris pounding their wash in shallows well stirred by water buffalo and bullocks, sheep and cattle.

In an acacia grove on the west side of the pond, Dr. Malek maintained a desert camp of tents and thatched rondavels protected from the livestock by a thornbush fence, a peaceful shelter in the very midst of abounding village life—a little too peaceful, one felt uneasily, in the light of the human suffering we had left behind us in the cities. At dusk on that first night at Zainabad, I listened to jackals and a dusky eagle owl, and was awakened toward dawn by a coucal, and just as I emerged from my rondavel there came the rolling rattle-cry of cranes out of the east. I reached the thorn fence just in time to see two immense silver-white birds flapping low over the acacia bushes behind camp, flaring wide scarcely fifty yards away, the *tika* red of the crown and upper nape inflamed by the desert sunrise, which turned the soft pearl of the birds to a rare blue.

Unlike the Eurasian and the demoiselle, the sarus crane (*Grus anti-*

gone) lives all year round, in scattered pairs, near the farm villages of the Indian subcontinent and southeast Asia. (In the 1960s, ornithologists discovered a sarus population in northern Australia, but since the aborigines have given it a different name from the native brolga crane, it has probably been there for centuries, perhaps millennia). The sarus gains much of its livelihood at the farmers' expense, yet it is protected as a sacred bird. In Gujarat Hindi, *sarus* means "nice," since this species, like all cranes, is popularly thought to mate for life and is therefore a symbol of probity and fidelity. If one is killed, the people say, its mate will shortly die or do away with itself (how the suicide is performed is not related), and a person who kills one is fated to lose his own mate shortly thereafter.

That morning a second pair of sarus came to the edge of a broad shallow pan, where the last of the monsoon waters had collected. Unlike the hundreds of Eurasian cranes (*Grus grus*) that arrived before them, calling and circling in long wary strings before drifting down finally on the far side of the pan, the sarus flew in low and direct, alighting calmly near some villagers and foraging on the field edges in the same slow and stately rhythms as the human beings amid the bright colors of the women threading slow old paths, copper water vessels balanced on their heads, the herders rising up out of the land, trailed by the slow file of their stock, the slow amble of camels, all along the flat horizon.

The pan lay near the Little Rann of Kutch, which extends eighty miles from east to west and from ten to forty miles north and south, none of it more than a few feet above the sea. According to our knowledgeable and charming guide, Raj Singh, who took time off from his own travel company in London to escort our group through backcountry India, *rann* signifies a "desolate place," as in a wasteland in the wake of war. Kutch ("marshland") is the largest district in the state of Gujarat (in fact, in all of India) and also includes the Great Rann, off to the north on the borders of Rajasthan and Pakistan. The Great Rann is watered by one seasonal river and is dry most of the year; the Little Rann may be flooded by four rivers and the ocean during the strong southwest winds of the monsoon, when solar tides are forced onto the desert from the Gulf of Kutch and the Arabian Sea. In certain seasons of certain years, much of southern

Gujarat may disappear beneath six inches to six feet of water. Even Zainabad, one hundred miles north of the coast, is only three feet above sea level, and most of its roads are built on embankments to keep its settlements from being cut off during the monsoon.

In the afternoon, Dr. Malek, an ironical small man in foulard and frontier hat that did not quite suit him, drove us in his lorry out onto the *rann* in search of the rare *ghor khar,* or Indian wild ass (*Equus hemonius khur,* from the Sanskrit *gaura khara,* or "white ass"). This Indian ass has all but vanished from the Great Rann and from Pakistan and was disappearing from its last redoubt in the Little Rann by 1952, when India's Board for Wildlife intervened on its behalf. Despite raucous cries that the wild ass "belonged, after all, to the ass clan" and that there was "no shortage of asses in this country," a wild-ass sanctuary was established. In 1976, the estimated population of the sanctuary was 720 animals, together with 96 large nilgai antelope, or "blue bulls"; 191 Indian gazelles; and some 62 wolves, which prey on the whole lot. Once there were lions here, but now the last lions in India are confined to the Gir Forest region in south Gujarat.

Our host soon located a small herd of wild asses, which drifted away across the cracked pale alkali of the dry *rann.* In their precautions against men and wolves, the sharp-eyed animals feel more secure out on the pan. From afar, the ass appears white, all the more so since its hindquarters and hind legs are white and it is observed most commonly going away. Seen closer, the animals have pale fawn saddles and rumps, and the black dorsal line of their short stiff mane continues all the way to the base of the tail.

A second herd, ten stallions, at the edge of higher ground—low, bushy islands known as *bets*—paused to peer back at us over their shoulders, as if reluctant to forsake the open desert. Five sarus came from the horizon to alight near the wild horses. "Very unusual," commented Dr. Malek of this group, observing that three birds—two adults with one young—are the most that are normally seen together, except when large flocks of sarus gather at certain localities in the dry season, before the monsoon, after which they return to breeding areas. The lone immature bird resembled the adults except in its smaller size and a shining white nape instead of a pearl-gray one; all of them had pale pink legs, though the tibia, or lower leg, was caked over with dried mud. Oddly, these five cranes on the *rann* maintained dead silence, as if listening for something very far away. And soon long skeins of Eurasians appeared on the horizon, hundreds upon hundreds, until at least a thousand of these lovely gray-brown cranes were drifting in over the desert.

Not far from Muslim Zainabad—an hour's walk across flat fields—was the old whitewashed Hindu village of Mulala, where black-faced white sheep consorted amicably with white-faced black goats, where wild pea-fowl perched boldly on the thatch of the village roofs and picked their way like glorious green turkeys through the earthen streets. Sacred birds, they are fed by the reverent on special platforms elevated for this purpose. Cattle are also sacred, but not buffalo or bullock, which are mere draught animals, yoked forever to ponderous wood-wheeled carts. The camels, too, are draught animals, though occasionally ridden astride, and an in-solent flea-bitten lot whose hauteur and curled lip on big yellow teeth give fair warning to the traveler to keep his distance.

Though Mulala is a Hindu village, a young woman from another village who had married here came down the stone street with her face veiled by her sari—a reflection, said Raj, of the strong Muslim influence in this desert region since the twelfth century. Scattered across the coun-tryside are stone warriors' monuments from ancient days when the Mus-lims, in a series of invasions, were seeking control of all this western country.

Mulala's fields were planted in cotton, wheat, and millet—the ancient strain of cotton has a small, tight boll—and from a slough between two fields two sarus rose trumpeting and sailed away over the yellow-blossomed acacias and cassia, euphorbia and salvadora, figs and neem, and the odd lavender milkweed, Calatropis.

Next morning, along the acacia scrub at the east edge of the *rann,* we searched for the uncommon houbara, or lesser bustard. Not until nearly midday did we flush a rooster-size gray-and-brown bird, which ran a little way distracted, in plain view, before scuttling into the bush. A second houbara, farther on, flashed the broad white bases of the main flight feathers at the tip of its wing as it rose heavily and flapped and sailed toward a *bet* half a mile away.

In this region of the Little Rann, the groundwater beneath the pan is a brine several times more salty than the Arabian Sea, and 40 percent of India's salt is mined here. Shining piles of salt, as white as bone, are scattered across the brown horizon, and here and there are lone thatched huts of the Koli. These people tend the crude bore holes and ancient pumps that sluice the brine toward the center of the pan, where the salt is crystallized by evaporation and piled up to be trucked away. The salt tenders commonly work half a leg deep in brine, and their leg bones become so impregnated with salt that, not being flammable, these bones must be buried after ritual cremation, in contravention of the Hindu religion.

The Koli salt miners are very poor, but they are not "untouchables"—or "sons of God," as Mohandas Gandhi called them. Gandhi himself was a Gujarati, born at Porbandar, on the Arabian Sea. His first social action upon his return to India from South Africa was the famous Salt March south to Dandi from his first ashram, or "shelter," at Ahmedabad, to protest the British tax on salt. These Koli still earn less than a dollar a day for working out here in the white light of hell.

Drifting across these infernal distances, the wild asses were pale and shimmering as a mirage. A lone stallion tended a herd of mares, five of them trailed by foals. Farther on, another stallion left his mares to go sniffing into the scrub after an unattached mare with a yearling and foal. The mare paid his itch no heed. Soon tired of his own ambition, he turned and headed back ruefully toward his own herd.

As the hot sun rose and the cool of the night desert disappeared, strange mirages shimmered all along the merciless horizon, which sinks gradually over the hundred miles south to the sea. Flights of Eurasian cranes appeared and eventually alighted near the wild asses, just as the sarus cranes had done the day before, as if in such emptiness, endangered living things shared an instinct to stick together. A mile away, in the silver shimmer, a solitary camel passed, then a woman's wavering silhouette, far away behind, the large dark vessel on her head like a barbaric crown. Then two cranes, in their vague remote relation, appeared from nowhere in the desert, rising infinitesimally out of the land and blowing across the mirror of white sun, down to the horizon. There was only light beneath them; they walked on water.

North toward the Rajasthan frontier, the roads were no longer built above the land, and stretches here and there were paved (after a fashion); yet the single lane was very narrow, and the drovers and bicyclers and operators of small motorcycle carts and gaudy trading lorries (every one marked GOODS CARRIAGE in front and HORN O.K. PLEASE behind) paid no more attention to our horn than did the livestock, which were quite unaware that the bus was full of people convinced that time was money or at least had value. In north Gujarat, the land softened and the hard cotton crops gave way to fresh green wheat and yellow anise, yellow mustard—the aniseed used as a cooking spice as well as eaten. Three sarus stalked a yellow-flowered field. The light-misted morning sun gleamed on the women's bracelets and on the lacquered red of the camel saddles, from which harnesses were rigged to carts that groaned with their loads of rusty barrels, burlapped millet.

We made a stop at the beautiful old temple at Modhera, built in A. D. 1026 by a Rajput warrior dynasty and mostly destroyed before the end of the century by Mahmud of Ghazni, a notable Muslim invader who made his mark almost everywhere in this western country. Apart from the famous Konarak, on the east coast, the delicate pink sandstone Modhera in its flowered park is the only "sun temple" in India, dedicated to those sun gods of Rajasthan who founded the cities of Udai, Jodh, and Jai.

In the afternoon, crossing the Rajasthan frontier, the north road rose gradually in rocky hills of big-leafed teak woods. We arrived toward evening at Udaipur, where our caravan put up at the wonderful palace that covers an entire small island in Lake Pichola. From here, two days later, the road proceeded northwest into bare brown foothills of the Aravalli Mountains, with mahua trees and guava groves and small terraced fields of sugarcane and wheat and mustard irrigated by wells from which water was drawn up by the slow-circling bullocks. It descended again to Jodhpur (whose maharajah's mislaid polo trousers, replaced in England by British tailors and subsequently affected by the riding gentry, introduced a word containing the letters "dhp" to the crossword puzzle). The next day, we headed west into the Thar, or Great Indian Desert—a land of ravens, white Egyptian vultures, and gazelles.

Near an encampment of nomad Raika people, twelve demoiselle cranes descended among the scattered camels. This is dry savannah patched with thorn scrub, and the dominant acacia is the *khejri*, a lovely dark tree with a taproot that is said to descend ninety feet down in search of water. In dry country, the *khejri* is never cut, not only because it is evidence of water but because its beans are a precious food and its leaves favored by animals for fodder. Perhaps two hundred and fifty years ago, when the Maharajah of Jodhpur ordered that a grove of *khejris* be cut down to make way for a royal road, the edict was rejected by peasants of the Vishnoi sect. The sect was founded in 1451 by one Jambaji, whose vision it was to transform this scrub desert into fertile and prosperous land, and whose twenty-nine commandments forbade the felling of trees as well as the killing of animals. The Vishnois asserted that the black buck antelope, which depended on the tree, was Lord Shiva's favorite, and since the black buck was revered by the Vishnoi together with the *khejri* itself, perhaps sixty Vishnois were killed by the soldiery in defense of "the trees of life," in a very early act of conservation.

Farther west, desert dunes arose, hiding the beehive huts of semi-nomads, who pause during the monsoon to grow a millet crop before moving on. Farther on were brown round-cornered clumps of adobe huts, in a land eaten bare by goats and camels, yet apparently all that could be wished for by the lean-faced Muslim inhabitants, who welcomed our party with curiosity and merriment.

Our road led hundreds of miles west to Jaisalmer, a very strange old fortified town on a desert butte at the edge of Thar. In this barren waste, Jaisalmer would seem to have small reason for existence, but in fact it is located at a crossing of the ancient desert trade routes, north and south as well as east and west. Its former prosperity is evident in the ornate wood façades of its four-story houses, which even today are coveted throughout the Muslim world for their workmanship and beauty. The façades were dismantled and carted away at a great rate to the oil sheikh-doms before the Indian government finally put a stop to it.

West of Jaisalmer, on the Pakistan border, is India's Desert National Park—three thousand square kilometers of semidesert of sparse acacia and dry grasses, fenced off from the livestock-ridden wasteland all around. Inside the park, we saw Indian gazelles—plain delicate brown creatures, astonishingly fleet, much like their relatives in East Africa—flocks of sand grouse, a desert fox, large luggar falcons. But the creature we were hunting was the *godavan,* or great Indian bustard, a bird up to ten times the size of the houbara and even larger than the great Eurasian bustard I had seen the previous summer on the Daurian Steppe in far eastern Mongolia and the kori bustard of the plains of eastern and southern Africa.

Like the wild ass, the great Indian bustard has been recognized as a rare creature since 1952, yet until recent years it was still hunted throughout Rajasthan by trained falcons of the Arab sheikhs, who, on the pretext of pursuing the houbara, constructed three palaces on the Pakistan side of the border to be used as hunting camps. As late as 1978, this park region was hunted by the crown princes of Abu Dhabi and Saudi Arabia and also by the president and vice-president of the United Arab Emirates, despite a ban established the previous year.

A male *godavan* may stand more than three feet high, and it walks, as noted in R. and R. Bedi's book *Indian Wildlife,* with a gait "at once relaxed and majestic," as befits the heaviest flying bird on earth (over forty pounds). Bustards are close relatives of cranes, whose walk might be similarly described. Indeed, in stance as well as lordly manner, the larger bustards look rather like short-necked and stumpy-legged cranes—at least until they struggle to take off, not dancing along and lifting off the ground in the light way of cranes but thundering away with a heavy churning of thick wings. Once aloft and in full flight, bustards again demonstrate their kinship with the cranes, in the up-flick of the wings so pronounced in their more graceful relatives. We saw but one of these rare and wary birds: a massive gray thing throttling aloft not far away, only to glide and plane down quickly, still at speed—not reaching down to touch the earth in the manner of the crane but running and braking to slow its own momentum.

From Jodhpur, on the return journey, we took a lightly traveled road northeast to Phalodi, from where an even more diminished road arrived eventually at Kheechan village, farther north. Here an association of Jain and Hindu merchants had undertaken the feeding of a large flock of wintering demoiselle cranes (*Anthropoides virgo*). The benefactors of the cranes mostly lived and worked in Delhi, Madras, and Bombay, and yet they maintained large silent family houses in this dark red town, where even the fences were constructed of tall upright slabs of blood-red rock, like leaning gravestones. Labor is a lot cheaper than wood in such dry country.

The cranes gathered at two ponds at the edge of town, where a worn-out waste of barren, hard-packed earth stretched away toward a few bent sentinel *khejri* in the distance. The cranes rattled, honked, and creaked in response to inquiring calls from others sailing around and down out of the dusty skies, until several acres of alert blue-gray birds spread back from the brown water. So acclimated to Kheechan had these demoiselles become that camel and bullock carts and women in flame-red, orange, and saffron saris passed within stoning distance, causing no more than a vague shifting of the flocks.

The crane feeding was supervised by Mr. Prakash Jain, formerly a devotee of the controversial guru Bhagwan Shri Rajneesh, lately of Oregon, where his fleet of Rolls Royces awed the populace; the smiling visage of the guru illuminated Mr. Prakash Jain's modest dwelling, where he was kind enough to serve us tea. Eight years ago, Mr. Prakash Jain, whose smile rivals that of his guru in pure beneficence, renounced the world to see to the protection of the cranes, which have been coming to Kheechan for at least a century, and were fed irregularly, like the peacocks and sacred cattle. The feeding was random and the number of cranes rarely exceeded several hundred. It was only when grain was offered twice daily, at appointed hours, that the news spread among *A. virgo,* which soon appeared from all over north India. It also got out among *Homo sapiens,* and the first tourists in the history of Kheechan turned up in small numbers in 1990. By 1991 the flock had grown to some twenty-seven hundred birds, and in 1992 it was estimated at fifty-five hundred. This convocation of large birds consumes four hundred and forty kilos of grain every day from the end of the monsoon rains in December, when the last gleanings in the fields have been exhausted, to early March, when the birds depart on their trans-Himalayan flight for northern Asia.

In midafternoon, from the house of Prakash Jain, cranes could be heard rising from the pond edge and passing noisily over the dark red village, and we walked through empty streets of big old hollow family houses to the western edge of town. The cranes cross the village in both morning and afternoon, performing slow-descending circles before alighting on dunes of fine brown sand outside a two-hundred-by-two-hundred-foot enclosure designed to exclude hogs, dogs, and children. On the sand outside the fence, on the side farthest from the houses, the cranes dropped in slowly, long legs dangling, long toes straining to touch the ground. However, they did not crowd and jostle, and not one presumed to enter the pen until Mr. Prakash Jain's assistants stepped forth to scatter fine white millet seed from enormous metal bowls. Even then, the courtly birds appeared to wait a little, for they are not like gulls or geese, rushing at their food. Then the first danced up into the air and circled the pen about fifty feet above the group before dropping into the corner farthest from the onlookers.

The ranks of birds grew restless then, rising and settling in place, and soon they ran a few light steps and rose into the wind and circled unhurriedly over the low buildings, over the oblivious bicyclists on their way home—including one miraculous small boy who operated a man's bike from below by hanging on with one scrawny arm around the bar and reaching up to manage the handlebars with the other, while the rest of him, not on the seat but just above the ground, labored the pedals. (I wanted to cheer as he arrived home from school, stepped neatly down, took his books, and went inside, for this amazing feat, quite clearly, was his daily habit.) A single bird, then twos and threes, then squadrons of demoiselles entered the pen, dropping in slow against the wind, line after line, as more long Vs of calling birds came over the village from the ponds. Black-fingered wings outstretched, they took unhurried places in the spirals that descended slowly from the sky, or flared off unaccountably and circled around, drifted down, and settled in the thickening flocks of blue-gray mantles, hundreds upon hundreds, several thousand now.

Having fed, the birds returned to the nearby dunes to rest and preen before recrossing the village to the pond edge, and toward twilight, when most of them were gone, we departed Kheechan. At the edge of the village stood a large lone nilgai antelope—also befriended by the people, judging from the fact that it did not run but merely climbed the dune a little way before turning to look back.

After the whooping crane of North America (or even including it, according to the crane authority Dr. George Archibald), the Siberian crane (*Grus leucogeranus*) may be the most endangered of the world's fifteen species, since the red-crowned crane of eastern Asia and Japan, though fewer in numbers, seem considerably more stable in their populations. Like the other two, the Siberian is large and white and specialized in habitat—in contrast to the more prosperous smaller species of cryptic coloration and generalized habit, such as the sandhill and Eurasian cranes. So reduced has the Siberian crane become by human presence in its northern wilderness and hunting in the south that its western population, which breeds in subarctic western Siberia just east of the Urals and migrates by way of Afghanistan to Iran and India, comprises just fifteen known individuals—five at Bharatpur and ten in Iran, on the shores of the Caspian Sea. (It is not known where the Iran flock breeds, and possibly a few more individuals winter elsewhere, but this is by far the most endangered of all of the world's crane populations. The eastern population, which breeds east and west of the arctic delta of the Lena River, is suffering the same attrition. Though more widespread and numerous, its numbers are not thought to exceed three thousand birds.)

In former times, the Siberian crane was described as a common migrant to the Ganges Plain, but it was hunted all along its route, especially in Iran and Afghanistan, and in 1964 a mere two hundred were counted at Bharatpur, and less than half that number (seventy-six birds) in 1976. That year, Dr. George Archibald, of the International Crane Foundation, in Baraboo, Wisconsin, approached the noted Russian ornithologist Dr. Vladimir Flint, who had done extensive fieldwork with the species, requesting eggs from the wild population for artificial rearing. In 1978, at considerable cost, five eggs were located and transferred to America in Archibald's lap. (One of the chicks actually hatched en route in the lap of Archibald's colleague, the late Ron Sauey, thereby relinquishing its status as an egg and causing the ornithologists' detainment by United States Customs for the illegal importation of wild birds.) These eggs were the foundation of a Baraboo flock that currently numbers about thirty birds, in addition to a group of fifteen established in Germany and another of about twenty-five at the Oka Nature Reserve in European Russia.

Victor and I became increasingly concerned about the small band of Siberian cranes that—according to the latest information from Raj Singh's contact, a local ornithologist named Mr. Bholu Khan—had failed to appear at Bharatpur, although it was now nearly mid-January. Our one hope was that they would turn up in the next few days, while we were visiting Jaipur and Ranthambore. The latest date that the Siberians had ever appeared at Bharatpur was January 14.

Already, as we traveled east to Jaipur, the Rajasthan desert gave way to neem-*khejri* savannah—a Vishnoi region, where wild things go unbothered, where small herds of nilgai, some of them attended by demoiselle cranes, have now become quite common. Though these big antelope look clumsy, with their humps and their small heads, they can outrun the tiger and the lion that used to be quite common in the region. Today the lion is entirely gone, and the tiger confined to a few enclaves, such as the Maharajah of Jaipur's former hunting tract at Ranthambore, where we were to spend three days hoping to glimpse one. Along the road traveled a white-robed party of Jain monks and nuns, and a man riding an elephant, and young girls with gold rings in their left nostrils, and a peasant bride-to-be escorted on foot under a canopy of saris in every color of the sun. At the hotel in Jaipur that evening was another sort of Hindu wedding, this one an immense ceremony on a stage that took up most of the huge formal gardens. Even here, wildlife felt welcome, for a tiny spotted owlet flew in out of the dark to perch on a lamppost and cock an eye at the festivities.

At Ranthambore, we failed to see a tiger, but our disappointment (or, at least, Victor's and mine) was offset by the good news that Siberian cranes had at last turned up at Bharatpur, which lies to the east of Ranthambore. We traveled there on the Frontier Mail, that slow old train that has journeyed since colonial days on a roundabout route from Bombay to Delhi and on to Punjab on the northwest frontier. In the railway station, a sadly bent boy dragged his body like a stepped-on insect down the platform, using felt pads to protect his hands. Despite the gray teeth and lifeless skin of bad diet and worse health, he had perfected an angelic smile that worked wonders with the travelers; indeed, he was the prince of the young beggars, dragging himself into the vestibule of the train when it departed, the better to hustle a fresh crop of patrons at the next station. He was very good at what he did, and knew it, for when one shook one's head in admiration and acknowledgment of his heroic con and indomitable spirit, that wonderful smile turned gleeful, even saucy.

In 1981, the Keoladeo Bird Sanctuary at Bharatpur was upgraded as a national park, and the following year grazing livestock within the park (some seventy-one hundred acres, twelve hundred of which become a shallow lake in monsoon and winter) was prohibited, to prevent any disturbance of the birds. Far from helping, the well-intended ban caused many marshes to choke with sedges and close over. In 1986, thirty-eight birds showed up, and three years later, just seventeen appeared, of which nine vanished or departed soon thereafter and did not return. In 1992, only six arrived, among them an immature bird. Perhaps one of those six was the bird reported taken by a golden eagle the following autumn in

Afghanistan, since but five Siberians turned up subsequently in Pakistan—very likely the same five that were there on our arrival.

At Bharatpur, we were informed by Mr. Bholu Khan that five Siberian cranes had arrived the day before, on January 13. By the time we arrived, in the late afternoon, it was too close to dusk to go out looking for the cranes, so we walked instead out the old bricked dike, one of many that fan out across this former wildfowl shooting marsh. Here, at the turn of the century, the viceroy of India, Lord Curzon, with his friend Lord Kitchener and fifteen others, killed five hundred and forty ducks in a single day. On November 11, 1938, a later viceroy, Lord Linlithgow, with his shooting party of thirty-eight guns, killed 4,273 ducks, or well over a hundred birds per man. Even today, Bharatpur is considered the greatest wildfowl marsh in India, with over three hundred species of birds. These include fifteen species of ducks; two species of geese; a great concentration of painted storks and other water birds, including the Siberian crane (which no longer occurs anywhere else in India); and the very beautiful bar-headed goose, which nests at high altitudes on the Tibetan Plateau with the black-necked crane and migrates over the high Himalayas.

That first evening, and next morning from a punt, we saw these handsome geese up close, but I was on crane business here, and anxious to find those five Siberians, which might yet take it into their heads to travel on, like the nine birds that vanished a few years ago. With Bholu and Victor, our group was in expert hands, and with Victor's blessing I set out toward the farthest part of the reserve, where the cranes were said to be lingering since their arrival.

Motor travel on the dikes is wisely forbidden at Bharatpur, and one travels the longer distances by bike-rickshaw. My guide, Mangal Singh, was well acquainted with most of the reserve's more exotic species, and as we creaked along on the main dike his sharp eye picked out four young spotted owlets bunched close in a tree fork, two collared scops owls, some white spoonbills, the gaudy purple moorhen, and nilgai antelopes and sambar deer and mongeese. He even led me off into the scrub to view an Indian rock python, wrapped around the base of a small bush. Finally I entreated him to take me as quickly as possible to the place where the cranes had last been seen, lest they fly off while we dawdled on the path.

And so we did not pause to see the birds that frequented the grounds of a Hindu temple on a point of higher land, but instead turned east on the embankment road and kept on going a few miles more into the early sun. The chilly morning on the marsh was warming quickly, raising fine smells of thorn and mud and reeds, and also the ubiquitous gobble of thousands upon thousands of geese—mostly the common greylags of Eurasia but also a flock of the rare bar-headed geese from alpine lakes of the Tibetan Plateau.

Near the bar-headed geese on the south side of the embankment, not a hundred yards away in open marshland, were two white cranes with extraordinary bald red faces, a red as fresh as roses in the morning sun. These were the first Siberian cranes I had ever seen, and so anxious was I not to scare them, or drive them farther from the bank, that I actually knelt behind a bush in reverence and relief, a move that turned out to improve my line of vision. Pink-legged and red-billed, they probed through the bronze duckweed, immersing red bill and red face right to the eyes to pull sedge tubers out of the mud.

On a separate feeding ground on the north side of the embankment—far enough away to maintain territory but not so far that they could not hear an alarm call from the others—a second pair was even closer, feeding in a grassy pool near the shade of a large water-tolerant acacia. This second pair, too, seemed to have sought out the company of fellow travelers from northern tundras, being all but surrounded by a torpid flock of greylags. Nearby in this parliament of fowls stood other white wading birds ordinarily considered large—openbill and painted storks, white egrets of three species and sizes, the white spoonbills—but compared with the Siberians (which are not nearly as large as the sarus) they looked like mere attendants.

I was now on the lookout for the fifth crane, which I located a mile across the marsh, to the northeast. Apparently unrelated to the others, it stayed off by itself throughout the day.

Bringing up tubers, the Siberians rinse the mud off quickly with a sideways flourish of the bill, which, because of their deeper-water feeding, is longer than in most crane species and slightly decurved. (Like all cranes, they are general feeders, and will also eat small animal life, even young ducklings.) The probing and swishing of these longer bills in comparatively deep water remind one more of spoonbills and flamingos than of the fastidious pick-and-peck of other cranes, and these differences— among many others, including voice, courtship displays, and unison calls—have persuaded Dr. Archibald that *Grus leucogeranus* should not be assigned to the *Grus* genus at all but to its own genus, like the two crowned cranes of Africa (*Balearica*), and the demoiselle and the blue crane (*Anthropoides*).

Exhilarated by the Siberians, I parted with Mangal Singh, since I planned to spend the day on the marsh. Farther east down the dike road, a sarus family fed not twenty feet from the embankment—two adults and two large fledged young, perhaps five months old, their heads and necks still a rich golden brown. The great calm birds are so trusting that one can walk up close to study the black "down" on the long throat (more pronounced in the male) and the small gray auricular tuft protecting the ear in the red wattled skin behind the golden eye.

Moving off without haste, the family split into two pairs, an immature bird trailing each adult. This rearing habit has been noted in other species, such as the red-crowned crane, when both young survive to reach adolescence. Later that day, I saw two more sarus in the distance. A few years ago, the species was threatened at Bharatpur, due to dissemination of poisoned grain by local farmers, but today they have recovered somewhat, and the reserve presently shelters about twenty pairs.

Four boys on bikes came down the path from their village school on the far side of the sanctuary. Excited, they wished to show to strangers three large pythons they had discovered sunning at the mouth of holes and tunnels, off on a side path. Sure enough, there were three pythons in a shining pile of bronze and golden coils, all three larger than the one I had seen earlier and all anxious to disappear, uncoiling and sliding and whispering along the ground in an unhurried yet accelerating process, so swift that it was difficult to tell which snake was which. At least two of the animals were twelve feet long or better and of a thickness greater than my upper arm.

On the far side of the main dike, another path led to open scrub, where later Mr. Bholu Khan showed us a dusky horned owl with two big chicks rearing and straining in the nest. Nearby, on a bush, was an imperial eagle, largest of the *Aquila* genus, which includes the mighty golden eagle of western North America and Eurasia. From the west came the loud two-note horn of flying sarus, in counterpoint with the more distant calls of Eurasian cranes. As the light failed, the Eurasians appeared, crossing the sky in broken strings and ones and twos and threes.

Toward evening, the fifth Siberian drew closer to the others, to a distance of perhaps two hundred yards, and Mr. Bholu Khan confirmed that the outrider was allowed in a little closer when night falls, doubtless for cumulative wariness and protection. He also told me that the Siberians, which are known to be feisty—at least in captivity—in their dealings with human beings, occasionally skirmish with the sarus over feeding pools, and though much smaller, usually drive the big birds off.

On the return, two black-necked storks (one of many disappearing Asian wading birds, with only about 139 individuals remaining in this country) flew across the dike and out over the marsh. In the morning, I pedaled out again and located the two pairs of Siberians near the previous day's feeding grounds, but the fifth bird was nowhere to be found on the broad marsh. Though apparently it had arrived in the small flock, it would not associate closely with its former companions until late March, when the last five Indian migrants of the western population, if they have made it through the winter, will presumably reconvene, calling out to one another, rising from the marsh, circling higher and higher, finally joining together to drift north and west across Rajasthan and Pakistan to resting marshes in Afghanistan and the Central Asian republics. By April, they would be headed north over central Asia and Siberia to the tundra forests and arctic tundra near the delta of the great River Ob, where these last birds of the western race of *Grus leucogeranus* breed and nest.

The next summer in Siberia, Dr. Archibald told me that "these birds have knowledge that no other cranes have. Cranes learn from their parents, and no other bird can teach them their migratory pattern. If we lose these last six, we have lost the knowledge of fifteen million years." Now there are five, the sole survivors of the longest and most arduous migration of any crane on earth—three thousand miles across tundra and desert and high mountains to Turkmenistan and Afghanistan, where they are shot at, with only a few coming as far as India, where they are not.

The following winter (1994) no Siberian cranes appeared at Bharatpur. What became of that small band of five, or whether they will ever be seen again, remains unknown.

TAPIR'S GOURDS AND SMELLY TOADS

LIFE IN A LITTLE-KNOWN RAIN FOREST

DAVID RAINS WALLACE

I hesitated when Pedro Jose Mejia and his family invited me to mount a small, reluctant-looking white gelding at their house in the town of Quebrada Grande. I'd never ridden a horse, so the idea of riding one eleven miles up the slopes of a volcano in the Costa Rican rain forest seemed fantastic. Señor Mejia had recently sold his dairy farm on the volcano to the Costa Rican National Park Service as part of Guanacaste National Park, a new park in the northwest part of Guanacaste Province. The Park Service had then hired him to build and manage a biological station on the site of his former farm. He built it, as he built his farm, with trees from the pastures he cleared, sawing them into boards with a chain saw.

I wanted to visit the biological station, and the Mejias evidently considered horseback the appropriate way to get there. They were unimpressed with my hesitation and avowals of inability, and Pedro's son Walter got on his horse and started to ride away, with my backpack slung over his saddle horn. I imitated the thousands of Westerns I've seen, and got on the little white horse. It seemed as uneasy about the situation as I did, but after some stumbling at my tentative urging, it followed Walter up the dirt road.

The American biologist Daniel Janzen had arranged my visit to the Volcan Cacao Biological Station as part of a tour of the park, which stretches from the Pacific to Costa Rica's central cordillera and contains a transect of ecosystems: mangroves on the coast; dry deciduous forest on the volcanic plateau; rain forest and cloud forest on the peaks. Including deforested areas as well as some of the last significant forest remnants on Central America's heavily populated Pacific coast, the park is an innovative attempt not only to protect enough forest to maintain healthy wildlife populations but to restore damaged land and develop management techniques that will reduce conflict between local people and conservation goals. Hiring the Mejias to run the biological station was an example of enlisting neighboring ranchers in the project.

Janzen had been studying the dry deciduous forest (a much more endangered kind of forest than rain forest) below the volcano since the 1960s and had been living in the area for six months out of every year since the 1970s, but it wasn't until 1986 that he visited Volcan Cacao itself. The volcano was almost unknown, although it stands in sight of the Pan American Highway. Clouds continually cover its summit, so that parts have never been photographed by geological-survey planes, leaving topographical maps with sizable blank spots. Although rain seldom falls from November to May on the Pacific lowlands, the Caribbean trade winds carry almost daily rain to Volcan Cacao. Janzen had discovered that many of the insects he was studying in the lowland dry forest migrated to the volcano's rain forest for parts of their lives. He knew little about the volcano's ecosystem, however, because it had never been studied.

Janzen did know that Volcan Cacao was unusual. It is covered with evergreen rain forest and cloud forest (a forest typical of cool highlands) at elevations of between two thousand and forty-five hundred feet, whereas most Central American cloud forest grows at higher elevation—in Costa Rica, above five thousand feet. Towns, pastures, and coffee plantations have replaced most of the Central American forest growing at elevations between fifteen hundred and three thousand feet. Such forests were extensively cleared even before Columbus, because of their fertile volcanic soils. At Volcan Cacao, Janzen had come upon a kind of forest that wasn't simply disappearing, as most tropical forests are, but that had virtually disappeared. The grizzled biologist seemed slightly bemused by this discovery, as though he had found a living specimen of the elephantlike gomphotheres that inhabited Central America ten thousand years ago. (One of the theories that Janzen has developed about Central American forest is that many of its trees depended on large mammals like gomphotheres to spread their seeds.)

As I urged the little horse uphill, I at first saw no sign that the Volcan Cacao forest still existed. Windblown grassy hills stretched to a horizon fitfully obscured by racing clouds. A few tattered trees stood here and there, but it was hard to believe that rain forest had once covered the hills. Although they were startlingly green after the brown pastures of the dry-season lowland, only a certain brilliance to the rising sun's light and a small flock of emerald-colored parrots indicated that this wasn't, say, eastern Kansas. The air was downright chilly. Volcan Cacao is less of a barrier to the trade winds than are the higher peaks to the north and south, and it has been called one of the coldest parts of Central America.

Riding through these foothills wasn't too hard, because the ground was firm and fairly level. The horse jogged along steadily, with some encouragement from my heels. The wind was the main obstacle: at times, it blew my feet out of the stirrups.

Then the slope steepened, and we came to a gully. Walter said that there had been a sulfur mine there. The gully contained some forest, but my mind was on my horse, who couldn't seem to get a foothold on the gully's brim. It stopped, as though incredulous at being asked to follow the steep, slick track that led down one side of the gully and up the other. I was inclined to agree with it. I dismounted, and we picked our way carefully into the gully after Walter and his bigger, braver horse had thundered across. When we reached the other side, I thought I'd keep walking, but horseback really is much faster, and Walter soon dwindled to a speck below the now dimly visible forested volcanic slopes. I remounted, got back off again to chase my hat, then mounted again. Eventually I caught up with Walter, who was waiting for me by a barbed-wire fence at the mountain's foot.

We crossed a fast, cold stream, and the rain forest began with peculiar abruptness. Almost no intermediate zone of shrubs or saplings stood between the pasture's low bunchgrass and the primary forest's huge trees. The pasture had not been grazed recently, and in a similar North American setting it would have been full of seedling trees. Daniel Janzen later told me that the volcano's rain forest is extremely slow about moving back onto land that has been cleared. He thought that most of the forest's trees needed forest animals, like pacas or tapirs, to spread their seeds, and that since these animals avoid pastures the seeds would stay in the forest. Nobody was sure about this theory, however, because nobody knew much about the volcano forest's trees and animals. Costa Rica has had more success in restoring the dry deciduous forest that grows in the Guanacaste lowlands west of Volcan Cacao, because many trees have seeds that can be carried into pastures by wind or by cows or horses who eat the fruits and deposit the seeds in their dung.

The Cacao forest looked different from other rain forests I'd seen, but it was hard to say how. There were fewer orchids or tufts of epiphytic bromeliads on branches, perhaps because of the windiness or the dry season. The underbrush was taller and denser than is usual under full canopy forest, and the shrubs bore a bewildering diversity of flowers and fruits. Some had flowers like tomato plants and glossy pepperlike fruits, evidently wild forebears of common vegetables. A large shrub with big leaves and blue berries was common—but so were countless other plants.

I dismounted again as we started up the forest path, which seemed too muddy and rocky for my poor stumbling horse. The animal became surprisingly more nimble without me on its back, and vanished uphill. I had to walk only another fifteen minutes until I came to the biological station, a sloping pasture with a bunkhouse at the top. Suddenly I could see westward as far as the Pacific—forested canyons, grassy foothills, brown coastal plain, all part of the national park.

"What a place!" I exclaimed to Walter, who was unsaddling my horse.

"Pura vida," he replied nonchalantly (a Costa Rican expression that translates roughly as "real nice.") He was used to it.

A trail led into the forest above the station, and I walked up it after leaving my pack in a rustic bunkhouse made of tropical hardwood. The forest here was different from the streamside forest below. The trees were smaller and seemed to be of different species, and the undergrowth was sparser. This was only an impression: it's hard to see clearly in a place where most things are unfamiliar, and where one sees more unfamiliarity the more one looks.

The Mejias were ranching people, like most of the people of Guanacaste Province, and weren't intimate with the forest. Lupe, Walter's mother, was afraid of the *terciepelos* (also called fer-de-lance, a very poisonous and aggressive but seldom-seen tropical snake) that lived in the forest, and she wouldn't let Walter's younger brother, Elmer, go into it because of them. Once Walter chased Lupe, Elmer, and a hired girl halfway across the pasture by waving a small nonpoisonous snake at them, the only snake I saw there.

So I was on my own when it came to identifying things. Instead of writing the names of plants in my notebook, I had to draw them, in the hope that I would someday learn what they were. I did see many kinds of plants I'd seen in other neotropical rain forests—*Clusia* trees with succulent, club-shaped leaves; *Cephaelis* bushes with flower bracts uncannily resembling the wax "hotlips" sold by novelty companies; tree ferns; begonias, hibiscuses, philodendrons, heliconians, and climbing aroids. They were probably not members of the species I'd seen before, however; the "hotlips" plants, for example, had purple flower bracts instead of the scarlet ones I remembered. Tropical genera tend to have dozens or even hundreds of species.

Smaller plants were confusing enough: trees were impossible, because their leaves and flowers were a hundred feet in the air. Central American mountain forests usually contain a lot of oaks and laurels, but I didn't recognize any oaks at Cacao. I found some decayed nuts on the ground that might have been acorns, but looking up with binoculars revealed nothing noticeably oaklike about the treetops. Many fruits on the ground probably came from laurels, because they resembled little avocados, which is a Central American member of the laurel family. I knew the trees weren't wild avocados, though, because the fruit of the wild avocado is spherical, unlike the pear-shaped commercial variety, which these Cacao fruits resembled. The only trees whose identities I could be sure of were the figs, whose small green fruits, usually marked with small teeth, littered the ground under their silvery-barked parents. (Figs are the commonest rain forest trees.)

A few days later, Daniel Janzen arrived, with a party of aquatic biologists and potential donors, and I tagged along as he showed them around. He led us into the pasture (in which Señor Mejia had left some trees growing) and showed us a small tree I'd noticed earlier but hadn't recognized. I'd noticed it because it was odd: the bell-shaped white flowers grew from the knobby, whitish trunk instead of from the branches. The trunk had also produced a glossy chestnut-colored pod-shaped fruit, about six inches long.

Janzen said that the tree was *Parmentiera valerii,* a member of the catalpa family. There had been only three herbarium specimens of the species in the world when he came to Volcan Cacao in 1986, but the species has proved to be fairly common in the volcano's forest—convincing evidence that Cacao is a refugium for an almost vanished ecosystem. The tree is also called *jicaro de danta,* or "tapir's gourd," Janzen said, because tapirs are thought to eat the fruit. He speculated that *Parmentiera* might have become rare elsewhere because of a scarcity of large animals to eat the fruit and spread the seeds.

I hadn't seen any *Parmentiera* along the forest trail. As I walked it during the next week, however, I kept finding *Parmentiera* right beside it, as though they'd stealthily planted themselves there when I wasn't looking. They weren't inconspicuous trees: unlike the pasture specimen, with its six-inch fruit (which, however, doubled in size overnight), the forest trees bore two-foot-long objects that resembled a giant cross between a cucumber and a potato. I found one tree when I stumbled over its fallen fruits. I found another when a hummingbird I was watching started to feed on its flowers.

Cacao's animals were easier to recognize than its plants. There were plenty of them—Janzen had seen fresh jaguar scats on the trail—but they faded into the background. Walter told me that he'd never seen a jaguar there and didn't believe that they lived on the volcano; he had seen only a smaller cat, which he described to me in Spanish beyond my grasp. I didn't see any kind of cat, and the animals I did see I saw largely in glimpses. Agoutis—deerlike rodents—slipped across the trail. Small red squirrels eyed me from the canopy. Often I saw only parts—legs or tails of coatis, opossums, spiny rats.

The only conspicuous mammals were three species of monkeys, who seemed surprisingly comfortable in weather that made me very glad I'd brought a down sleeping bag. When I met troops of white-faced capuchins along the trail, the males walked out on overhanging limbs to glare at me, grunting and stamping threateningly. Howler and spider monkeys frequenting a gorge north of the station were less aggressive, but also made their presence felt. They usually saw me before I saw them. Then a male howler with a reddish cast to the long black hair on his back would make deep coughing sounds and pivot back and forth on his forefeet in a way that reminded me of an old black bear. The rest of his troop would just gaze at me, in the profoundly tranquil way that howler monkeys have. Although their howls rival a lion's roar, they're the most peaceful of monkeys.

The spider monkeys, which were a rusty café-au-lait color, with black faces and hands, made squeaking sounds, which I first mistook for tree limbs rubbing together. Adult spider monkeys evidently didn't mind my presence once I came into the open where they could watch me. They would bark a little, then sit quietly on a branch. Once, a half-grown one got excited, squealing and slamming branches around, hanging upside down, then diving headlong into a leafy patch. This apparently annoyed the adults: one of them got up stiffly and departed, while the remaining two grabbed the youngster and tried to quiet it. But it broke away and went into its *enfant-terrible* act again, so they also left. The youngster looked around a moment, then hurried after them.

The forest rang with birdsong, some of it startlingly loud, but I seldom caught more than a glimpse of the singers. Once, I strained my eyes to see a bird that I thought was calling in the treetops, not realizing that it was perched on a branch a few feet away. It was a long-tailed manakin, a chickadee-size blue-and-red bird that looks conspicuous in field guides but is hard to see among the forest's intricate vegetation, even though it spends most of its time calling and performing intricate dance rituals to attract a mate.

The gaudy exotic birds that figure on the jackets of Latin American novels—toucans, trogons, motmots—were common on Cacao, but their colors didn't make them much more visible than the brown or black tree creepers, wood quail, and guans. A trogon with a tomato-orange breast might be a few feet away, but I wouldn't see it unless it moved. There were too many other tomato-colored objects in my field of vision— bromeliad or heliconian flowers. The same was true of collared araçaris and emerald toucanets, although the latter at least made a lot of noise. But I kept forgetting that their harsh croaks and squeals came from birds and not frogs.

Frogs were surprisingly scarce for such a damp place. This might have been because it was the coldest time of year—as Walter and Lupe told me. (They kept remarking on the cold, although they seemed to mind it less than I did. Lying in the bunkhouse at night, I sometimes thought that the entire biological station would become airborne, as the wind strained at the tin roofs.) I thought I heard some frogs calling at dusk— some of these turned out to be cricket calls—and I found some tiny brown frogs in leaf litter. But it was very different from the din I've heard in other rain forests.

Walking the trail early one morning, I first noticed a foul odor, and then encountered a small purple-gray toad. It resembled no other toad I'd seen. Its skin wasn't warty but ridged, like worn leather. Black dots around its eyes gave it the appearance of wearing false eyelashes. When I touched it with a stick (tropical toads can have poisonous skins), the fetid smell increased markedly. It didn't struggle, even when I turned it over with the stick—just sprawled there, belly up. I certainly had no desire to capture it, and when I let go it unhurriedly righted itself and ambled off.

The nasty smell departed too, and so I inferred that the toad had produced it somehow, perhaps as a defense. I'd never heard of a toad doing that, but then little is known about the hundreds of amphibian or reptile species in Central America, many of which have been named only in the past few decades. The toad was probably a known species, but I couldn't be sure even of that, since no field guides for nonspecialists were available.

The rudimentary state of Central American herpetology was the cause of my visit to Volcan Cacao, as it happened. David Wake, a herpetologist who headed the Museum of Vertebrate Zoology at Berkeley, had told me about it; he'd been at Cacao the year before, looking for salamanders, his speciality. Daniel Janzen had found what he thought might be a new salamander species, which wasn't unlikely, because Wake and his associates had found dozens of new species in the past twenty years.

Central and South America are the only parts of the tropics known to have salamanders—amphibians that live mainly in temperate forests. A single North American family—the lungless salamanders, or plethodontids—migrated south, evolving into more than one hundred and forty tropical species in the process. These species live throughout forests from Mexico to Brazil. All use their tongues to snag insects and other prey, as frogs do. Some have become so thin and elongated that they can live in the soil like worms; some have prehensile tails and live in the treetops. (David Wake showed me some of the latter in the museum, placing them along a string like a row of elfin acrobats.) As many as thirty individual salamanders have been found among the leaves of a single epiphytic bromeliad of cloud-forest canopy.

Wake and his students had spent weeks at Cacao, examining moss and epiphytes and digging in the forest floor. They found only one species besides Janzen's, however, and both species appeared to be known, common ones. This seemed an unusual lack of diversity for a country in which twenty-one salamander species have been found within a forty mile transect of lowland, foothills, and mountains.

Janzen evidently still had hopes for new salamander species, because he told me to "hang on" to any I encountered on Cacao. Then he returned to the lowland with the aquatic biologists, who also seemed puzzled by Cacao, although it was insect abundance rather than salamander scarcity that puzzled them. They couldn't understand why there were so many caddis-fly larvae in the streams, because these larvae eat algae and the streams were too shady for algae to grow well. But the larvae's abundance was undeniable. The local species lived in a case that it constructed out of circular pieces of leaf; the shrubs overhanging the streams looked like Swiss cheese.

David Wake had found new salamander species in the California desert, a more unlikely place than even the chilliest of Central American volcanos, so I didn't expect to find any new salamander species if he couldn't. I had already turned over dozens of logs trying and had found only a small brown crab.

Cacao was capricious with its secrets, however. The day after Janzen's visit, I climbed farther up the volcano than before, following a recently cut trail through the dwarf cloud forest. Because the trees beside the steep trail branched only a few feet above the ground, it began to seem as if I were climbing in the forest canopy. Bromeliads grew at eye level or on the ground, which was often hidden by sprays of flowers and low bamboo thickets so rain-soaked that I sometimes felt as if I were doing more swimming than climbing.

First, there were stubby light-green bromeliads, with white flowers. Then I passed through a zone of slimmer, dark-green ones, with a reddish tinge; then through another zone of the stubby light-green variety, striped with pink. I looked inside all these and found grubs, bugs, worms, cockroaches, a large colorful weevil, and an iridescent green jumping spider, but no salamanders. The volcano was constructed of a series of steep ridges, and they began to seem endless. I'd reach the top of one only to see the next looming through the mist. I saw little else in the distance, although open patches that drifted by gave me glimpses of the forest canopy below. It was brilliant with flowers I'd never seen from the trail.

Fallen trunks increasingly entangled me, and I found myself more and more *in* the trees, climbing several feet above the ground and sometimes falling through slippery branches. I sat down to rest in a temporarily sunny ridgetop glade full of pink-striped bromeliads. I'd examined dozens by this time, but I summoned the energy to glance into one perched beside me on a branch. A chocolate-brown silver-speckled salamander was curled up in one of the leaves and remained motionless until I touched it. Then it exploded in such energetic wriggles that I barely managed to get it into a plastic bag. I stuffed moss and leaves after it to keep it moist, and climbed back down to the station.

I hung the bag in the dormitory for the remaining days I spent at the station. I could hear the salamander moving around in it. I didn't dare open the bag, for fear it would get away. I knew Janzen would be unimpressed with hearsay evidence.

When it came time to return to Janzen's headquarters in the lowlands, I feared the salamander wouldn't survive the horseback ride down the mountain. The Mejias provided a bigger, bolder horse than the little white one I came up on, perhaps hoping to hone my equestrian skills. When I'd kicked my heels into the white one, it went into an equable walk, but when I tried this with the new horse it broke into a bone-jarring trot that threatened to crush bag and salamander between my thigh and the saddle.

In Janzen's cinder-block cottage at park headquarters, I described the medium-size chocolate-brown, speckled creature, and Janzen said that it had to be a new species for the volcano, because it wasn't like the two he and Wake had found. His salamander had been big, with a pale band around the tail; Wake's had been small, with a prehensile tail. Then we opened the bag.

"I don't see anything," Janzen said.

Anxiously, I pulled out the wad of leaves and moss, and the salamander emerged onto the table. It appeared as glossy and bright-eyed as when I'd found it, although the lowland's ninety-degree heat must have been a new experience for it.

"Yes," said Janzen, "that's different." He whisked the salamander away into his inner sanctum, where a computer sat in a nylon tent under a ceiling festooned with plant and insect specimens in plastic bags. He eventually sent the salamander to David Wake in Berkeley, and that was the last I heard of it for a while.

It was intriguing to think that I might have discovered a vertebrate species new to science simply by climbing partway up a small mountain. It also seemed unlikely. The next time I talked to David Wake, I asked him what it was. He said that it probably was a species called *Bolitoglossa subpalmata,* which is among the commoner Costa Rican salamanders between three thousand and eleven thousand feet, and is known to live in bromeliads at lower elevations. He wasn't sure, however. My salamander was unusually small for that species, and no other specimens of it had been found at Cacao. Since there are over thirty species in the genus *Bolitoglossa,* identifying one from a single specimen is dubious. Wake added that the small salamander he had found at Cacao, which he'd thought belonged to a common species, had turned out to be a new one.

Hearing how scarce salamanders continued to be at Cacao made me a little regretful about having collected one. Although I knew that my salamander was extremely unlikely to be the last of its kind, extinction is such a pervasive threat in the tropics (particularly the extinction of amphibians, which are rapidly dwindling worldwide for unknown reasons) that I felt an almost superstitious apprehension.

When David Wake began studying tropical salamanders in southern Mexico and Guatemala in the late 1960s, in some places he and his colleagues found salamanders in half the bromeliads they examined. They identified fifteen species in a transect running from the continental divide to the Pacific slope. But in 1980, after political violence had put an end to his biological work in Guatemala, Wake wrote:

> The forest had been removed and pasture occupied nearly the entire area between 1500 meters and 2300 meters (4500–6900 feet). Below 1500 meters traditional coffee plantations, which feature large shade trees and extensive plantings of bananas, had given way to a near monoculture of coffee grown in hedgerows without any suitable cover for arboreal salamanders.

Since my days at Volcan Cacao, I've found another obscure salamander in Central America. It was a big brick-red-and-cream-colored salamander in a rotten log at the base of Pico Bonito, on Honduras's north coast. This is one of the most beautiful landscapes in the world, with cloud-forested, waterfall-hung peaks looming startingly above the golden-green gallery forest and the crimson boulders of the Bonito River, so the salamander's resplendence seemed appropriate. David Wake thought it might be *Bolitoglossa dofleini*, a species that he'd seen in Honduras, but he couldn't be sure—partly because on this occasion I had let the salamander go. Pico Bonito is one of Honduras's national parks, so perhaps there will be time to learn more about its resplendent salamander, as there will be time to learn about Volcan Cacao's small brown one.

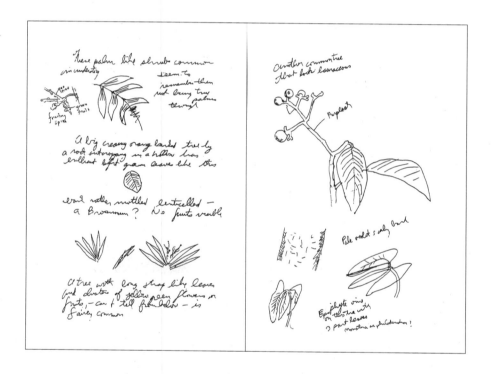

THE SWEET SMELL
OF SUCCESS

THOMAS EISNER

The observation that set me off working on *Utetheisa ornatrix* was a casual one. I had always been fascinated by this moth. It was relatively abundant in the area of central Florida where I do my research, and it was beautiful. With its speckled white forewings and pink hindwings, it was impossible to miss on the wing. It flew as readily in daytime as at night, unlike most moths, which are strictly nocturnal. *Utetheisa,* I had come to think, had to be a gastronomic "no-no," gaudily colored not for show but as a warning to its enemies. I had done some tests with local birds, which I found to ignore the moth, but I had never witnessed an actual encounter between *Utetheisa* and one of its predators.

Then one day, at a site I often visited to study insects, I saw an *Utetheisa* fly into a spiderweb. Instead of trying to flutter loose, as moths typically do when entangled in webs, the *Utetheisa* became instantly motionless. The spider, alerted by the impact, scurried over to the moth and inspected it, but instead of following through with a bite, cut the moth loose. Systematically, by use of its fangs and with the help of its legs, it snipped one after the other the strands that were restraining the moth, until the moth fell free. Before even striking the ground, the *Utetheisa* unfolded its wings and flew off.

Utetheisa, at rest on a pod of its *Crotalaria* foodplant.
Photograph by Thomas Eisner, Cornell University.

To ensure that it was not for lack of appetite that the spider had rejected the moth, I collected a dozen or so *Utetheisa* and flipped these live, one after the other, into individual spiderwebs. Without exception, whether male or female, the moths were freed. *Utetheisa* was evidently unacceptable to spiders, and the reason was probably its taste.

But what could make this moth distasteful? I put the question to our laboratory group at Cornell, with the result that we began thinking about *Utetheisa* in earnest. We have now worked for over twenty years on this moth, delving deeper and deeper into the secrets of its success—secrets

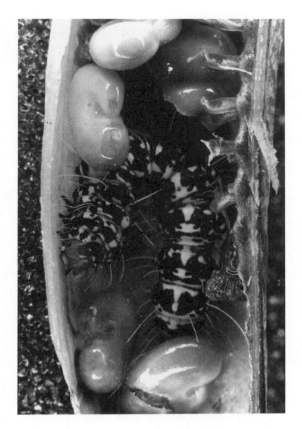

Utetheisa larva, inside pod of *Crotalaria*, feeding on seeds.
Photograph by Thomas Eisner, Cornell University.

which we came to learn were essentially chemical. The story is still unfolding.

Figuring out what made *Utetheisa* noxious to spiders was relatively easy. *Utetheisa* was known to feed on poisonous plants as a larva. The plants, of the genus *Crotalaria,* had been intensively studied, because they were occasionally eaten by cattle, to whom the experience could be fatal. The toxic substances in *Crotalaria* belong to a category of compounds called pyrrolizidine alkaloids—comprising substances such as monocrotaline—of well-known chemical structure. The alkaloids serve *Crotalaria* for defense. They are intensely bitter and potentially deterrent to any

The pyrrolizidine alkaloid monocrotaline, present in the *Crotalaria* foodplant of *Utetheisa*.

number of plant eaters. *Utetheisa* is exceptional, in that it has somehow, in the course of evolution, become tolerant of the alkaloids and able to feed on the plants. What occurred to us is that the moth might have taken its evolutionary advantage a step further. Could it be that it incorporated the alkaloids into its body and by so doing used them for its own defense? We analyzed *Utetheisa* caterpillars and found that they were laden with alkaloid. But more important, we found that the alkaloid was present in the adults as well, indicating that the chemical did not disappear during metamorphosis. And then we found that we could rear *Utetheisa* in the laboratory on two alternative artificial diets, one made up with *Crotalaria* seeds and containing pyrrolizidine alkaloid (known as the CS diet), the other based on pinto beans and devoid of alkaloid (the PB diet). We were now in a position to put our hypothesis to the test. We took moths from both cultures into the field and offered them to spiders. The results were dramatic. Those raised on the CS diet were consistently cut from the webs, while those reared on the PB diet, which we proved chemically to be alkaloid-free, were killed and eaten by the spiders. We also tested for the deterrency of the alkaloids themselves by adding these in crystalline form to the surface of insects that spiders ordinarily consumed, and we found that the crystalline addition made such insects unacceptable. There could be no doubt that the alkaloids were the basis of the moth's defense.

Utetheisa mating. The male, at lower right, projects partway from beneath the wings of the female. *Photograph by Thomas Eisner, Cornell University.*

Being able to rear *Utetheisa* meant that we could also study some other aspects of the moth's life. We chose to look into the courtship. *Utetheisa* court at dusk, and it is the female that takes the lead. Perched on a branch of *Crotalaria,* she "calls" the male by means of a volatile chemical attractant. The attractant is a mixture of compounds, each a long unbranched chain of carbon atoms. We were able to identify the chemicals because we located the two glands in the female's abdomen that produce them. It took dozens of glands, dissected from laboratory-reared *Utetheisa,* to obtain sufficient secretion for analysis.

To emit attractant, the female undertakes rhythmic compressions of

Scent brushes of the male. *Photograph by Thomas Eisner, Cornell University.*

her abdomen, which cause the glands to be squeezed and the attractant to be forced out in "puffs." These puffs are invisible but can be demonstrated indirectly. Male *Utetheisa* detect the female's attractant with olfactory sense cells located on the antennae. Olfactory signals conveyed by the antennal nerve of the male can be picked up with special electronic instruments. When a male antenna appropriately "wired" for signal detection was placed downwind from a female *Utetheisa* during "broadcast time," we obtained a pulsed signal output from the nerve, indicating that the attractant was impinging upon the antenna in discontinuous bursts.

We thought initially that the female, by pulsing, might be adding a diagnostic, species-specific feature to her chemical message, but this turns out not to be the case. Other moths are now known to pulse their attractant, and they all seem to emit puffs at the same rate—between one and three per second—as *Utetheisa*. The current view is that pulsation increases the efficiency of the signal output. By pulsing, females need less attractant to lure males than they would if they were to emit their scent in a continuous stream.

Courtship in *Utetheisa* involves more than mere attraction of males by females. Once a male locates a female, which he does by flying along the aerial plume of attractant that drifts downwind from her, he does not at once proceed to mate. He first flutters around the female at close range, circling her erratically, and periodically flexing his abdomen forward while thrusting himself against her. We monitored this behavior, which ordinarily takes place in near darkness, with special television cameras sensitive to infrared light. Such light is visible neither to insects nor to us. We positioned females outdoors, where we knew they would "call," illuminated them with infrared light, aimed our cameras at them, and watched. We discovered that when the males were performing their abdominal thrusts, they extruded from their abdominal tip a pair of conspicuous brushes, which we later found to be glandular and which the males ordinarily keep withdrawn in pouches.

We extracted the brushes chemically, and found a new compound, which we called "hydroxydanaidal," or HD for short. There were several remarkable things about this molecule. Most interesting was its obvious structural similarity to pyrrolizidine alkaloids, which suggested that it might be derived chemically from these toxins. This in itself called for an explanation. Why should a male insect use a derivative from defensive substances to communicate chemically with its intended mate? We assumed, of course, that by displaying its brushes the male was conveying some kind of message to the female. But what might that message be? Why should a male moth have anything to "say" to a prospective sexual partner when the two are already within mating range? Why should there be foreplay in an insect?

To prove that the brushes were important to the male's ability to mate, we took a group of males from which we had surgically removed the brushes, released these outdoors where we had set out females that were ready to court, and watched with our television cameras. We had cut little notches into the wings of the altered males so that we could tell them apart from any normal males in the area that might also make an appearance. The treated males flew to the females, performed their aerial acrobatics and abdominal thrusts, but were less often accepted by the

Utetheisa male, everting its scent brushes during courtship. *Photograph by Thomas Eisner, Cornell University.*

Hydroxydanaidal, the chemical in the scent brushes of male *Utetheisa*.

females. The females tended simply to remain quiescent, keeping their abdomens tucked away beneath their wings.

We were also able to show, in chemical tests, that the males produce HD from their alkaloid. Males that we had reared on the alkaloid-free PB diet proved to have no trace of HD in their brushes. We released such males outdoors and tested them with females, and found that they too were less likely to be accepted. With the surgically treated males there was always the possibility that their lack of success had been due to some effect of the surgery, other than the lack of HD, but the PB-diet-raised males had fully functional brushes. Physical possession of brushes was therefore not in itself sufficient for male success. The brushes also had to have the right "smell." We showed further that if you stroked a female with a set of excised brushes, it was possible to cause her to part her wings and present her abdomen, but only if the brushes contained HD.

But there remained the question of the nature of the brushes' message. Was HD simply the male's way of announcing his arrival—of saying to the female, "I'm here, I've heeded your call, raise your abdomen, and let's mate"? Or might he be telling her something more subtle about himself? I had an idea that I dismissed at first but which continued to nag me. (I remember having it—I was watching sea otters off the California coast, near Carmel.) We knew from earlier chemical work that *Utetheisa* differ in their body alkaloid content. Adults that we caught in the field could contain either high levels of alkaloid or graded lower dosages. We didn't know the reason for this, but speculated that *Utetheisa* might differ in their larval ability to obtain the chemicals. In *Crotalaria,* alkaloid is present at highest concentration in the seeds. This makes sense, given that the alkaloid is a deterrent to most insects; by putting alkaloid into its seeds the plant is essentially protecting its offspring. The seeds are also the parts of *Crotalaria* preferred by the *Utetheisa* larva. Yet if there are too many *Utetheisa* larvae at the same site (or larvae of competing moths, such as *Etiella zinckenella,* which also feed on *Crotalaria* seeds), the seeds can be in short supply.

Utetheisa larvae might thus have to compete for the parts of their

Cluster of *Utetheisa* eggs on a leaf of *Crotalaria*. *Photograph by Thomas Eisner, Cornell University.*

foodplant most richly endowed with the defensive chemical they need. Larvae might differ in their ability to locate the seeds, or to gain access to them (they could be variously "pushy" vis-à-vis other larvae), or they might differ in their ability to absorb alkaloid from the food. These abilities could be under genetic control. If so, might not HD be an indicator of the male's competitive ability? Might this molecule, which we knew to be derived from alkaloid, be used by the male to tell the female how much alkaloid he possessed and therefore, indirectly, how good he was at competing for the chemical? And did it not make sense that the female should show preference for males able to offer proof of a potentially heritable, beneficial capacity? Should she not favor males that "smelled sweetly of success"?

We did experiments that offered some support for these speculations. We found that the HD content of the brushes was indeed a measure of the male's alkaloid content. The greater the amount of alkaloid in the male's body, the higher the HD level in the brushes. But the story got more complicated, and it became clear that I was not being nearly imaginative enough. The female *Utetheisa,* it turns out, transmits alkaloid to the eggs. The amount is substantial, and suffices to protect the eggs against some of their enemies. Eggs are a vulnerable stage in the life cycle of an insect, and many females conceal them from view or protect them by addition of chemicals. *Utetheisa* eggs are exposed to a multitude of predators, including ants, ladybird beetles, and green lacewing larvae. The alkaloid protects the eggs against all of these. But what is remarkable is that the alkaloid in the eggs does not stem from the mother moth alone. Some of it stems from the father. *Utetheisa* males transmit their sperm to females in a so-called spermatophore, a package so large that it can amount to over 10 percent of the male's weight. Mating takes hours in *Utetheisa* (the pair typically remains coupled through the night), in part because the males are slow in depositing the spermatophore in the female. Packed with the sperm in the spermatophore is a substantial quantity of nutrient (which the female puts to use in the manufacture of eggs) and a sizable fraction of the male's alkaloid. In bestowing alkaloid upon the eggs, the female uses both the amount she obtains from the male and a share of her own supply. Egg protection is therefore a biparental endeavor in *Utetheisa.*

We had to expand our thinking. It seemed that HD could be an indicator also of a male's alkaloidal offering. Indeed, when we did the appropriate chemical analyses, we found the brushes to contain HD in amounts proportional to the quantity of alkaloid the male transmits to the female at mating. HD could thus serve both as proclamation of a genetic capacity and as promissory announcement of a nuptial gift. For the female, the compound could provide the basis for assessment of male "worth."

Our latest findings tell us that the *Utetheisa* female is selective not only about which male she mates with but about whose sperm she uses after mating. Male and female *Utetheisa* mate with a number of partners over their life span. Spermatophore remnants provide a telltale record of a female's mating history. By checking for such remnants it was learned that females in natural populations mate on average with from four to

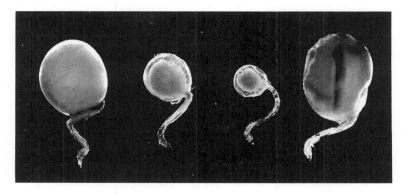

Sperm packages (spermatophores) of *Utetheisa. Photograph by Thomas Eisner, Cornell University.*

five males. Occasional females mate with as many as ten or more. In the course of her life, a female can therefore receive multiple nuptial gifts. The nutrient she receives in this fashion has a major impact on her fecundity. Each spermatophore provides her with enough nutrient to produce an extra thirty eggs or so, an increase of 15 percent over her basic output. The repeated matings provide her also with multiple alkaloidal gifts, all of which she bestows upon the eggs. What we discovered is that the female does not necessarily utilize the sperm of all her partners. *Utetheisa* offspring can be checked for paternity. Females can be mated with males of known genetic constitution, and the offspring can then be examined for presence of the various males' genes, or traits associated with these genes. We checked the offspring of females that we had mated with two males, and found that it was almost always the sperm of the larger male that won out. Mating sequence did not seem to matter. The larger male tended to father the offspring whether he was the first or second of the partners. The reproductive system of *Utetheisa* is a complex labyrinth of ducts and chambers. While we do not know precisely how the various components of the system operate, we have hypotheses about how the female might manage anatomically to favor one set of sperm to the exclusion of another. And we have evidence that the female herself controls this process. If she is anesthetized in such fashion that she cannot operate her musculature, including the many pumping muscles of her reproductive organs, the sperm-sorting mechanism breaks down.

The female strategy is an interesting one. By accepting multiple partners she can accrue multiple gifts, which is of obvious benefit to her, since she can thereby promote both her fecundity and the survival of her offspring. But why is she selective about which sperm she uses, and why specifically does she favor sperm of larger males? We cannot provide definitive answers to these questions, although we have some ideas. Larger males are also the ones that contain the most alkaloid and bestow the largest alkaloidal gifts. There may be a simple reason for this. Males rich in alkaloid are likely to be the ones that as larvae fed predominantly on the seeds of the foodplant, the parts not only richest in alkaloid but also richest in nutrient. By favoring sperm of large males, the female is therefore reinforcing, after copulation, the choice mechanism that she already exercised in the precopulatory context. Postcopulatory assessment provides the female with the option of taking corrective action. If on a given evening she accepted a male of moderate size and alkaloid content, she can still discriminate genetically against that male by utilizing the sperm of a larger, more alkaloid-laden (and therefore genetically superior) individual that she is able to lure on a subsequent night. But the earlier mating is canceled in the genetic sense only. Nutrient and alkaloid that she receives from the losing male is utilized, together with all such gifts she obtains from other mates.

We have some idea of how the female assesses the size of her mating partners. She appears to do so indirectly, by gauging the size of their spermatophore (which is proportional to male body size), for which purpose she may use special stretch receptors that female moths are known to have in the "bursa," the chamber in which the spermatophore is deposited. Male *Utetheisa* can be caused to produce inordinately small spermatophores, if they are induced to mate repeatedly beforehand. If such males are put into competition with physically smaller males, whose full-size spermatophore is larger than their own submaximal one, they lose their reproductive advantage. We predict from this that males, under natural conditions, do not sexually overdo it. It is obviously to their reproductive advantage not to mate again until they are able to produce spermatophores of full size. That restorative period, in *Utetheisa,* is about a week.

We also think we may have a tentative answer to the question, Why don't smaller males of low alkaloid content "lie" to females during court-ship? Why don't they masquerade as desirable males by producing ex-aggerated levels of HD in their brushes? These males would be "found out" after mating, unless they also provided large spermatophores. Smaller males, even if able to convert extra alkaloid into HD for inflation of their chemical message, might simply lack the extra nutrient for com-parable inflation of their spermatophores. Perhaps it is in part to check on liars that the female evolved her mechanism for reassessing males after mating.

We have fallen in love with *Utetheisa.* The moth has introduced us to levels of complexity of insect life that we never imagined could

Utetheisa larva emerging from the egg. *Photograph by Thomas Eisner, Cornell University.*

exist. It taught us to ask questions, and it was generous with its answers. *Utetheisa* is a widely distributed species, successful in many habitats. We draw comfort from the knowledge that it is not endangered, and that it might perhaps, through its extraordinary revelations, increase our appreciation of the many species not so lucky.

Postscript. Many friends and associates contributed to our research on *Utetheisa*. Chief among these is Jerrold Meinwald, my collaborator for many years, in whose laboratory the chemical work was carried out. Others include William E. Conner (courtship study), David E. Dussourd (nuptial alkaloid transfer), Craig W. LaMunyon (sperm selection), Angel Guerrero and Robert K. Vander Meer (characterization of alkaloid, hydroxydanaidal, and female sex attractant), Maria Eisner (microscopy, predation studies), and Ken Amerman (countless favors). It was William Gass who exclaimed "Sweet smell of success!" when told about *Utetheisa* in conversation. I hope he doesn't mind my appropriating the analogy.

MILLIPEDE SUMMERS, SILURIAN NIGHTS

SUE HUBBELL

At last summer's end, I was talking one morning on the telephone with Dr. Rowland Shelley, of the North Carolina Museum of Natural History, in Raleigh. Dr. Shelley is one of only three millipede specialists in the Western Hemisphere, and he had generously taken the time to identify two millipedes for me and had gone on to tell me something of their biology and behavior.

How had he come to specialize in a field with so few researchers? I asked him, at the end of our conversation. Had he studied them in college?

"How could I?" he replied, in his soft drawl, countering my question with one of his own. "None of the professors knew much about millipedes, and what little they taught was usually wrong. No, I came to work here at the museum about twenty years ago, and the curator of invertebrates wanted to know what group I'd like as a specialty. I gave it some thought and remembered the first time I'd ever seen a millipede—a thing creeping along that looked like a cigar with legs. I'd asked my father, 'Daddy, what *is* that?' and he said, 'Son, that's a millipede.' Well, I remembered wondering about it, so I said I guessed I'd like to specialize in millipedes. There were only two researchers, both of them in Virginia, and they were kind enough to let me come and work with them every year for a couple of months. I would just sit with them and ask questions, until eventually I learned enough to go on with work of my own."

I come from a family of writers, and we specialize, too, after a fashion, although much more broadly. For instance, my brother, Bil Gilbert, writes about vertebrates quite a lot and kindly leaves invertebrates, all millions and millions of them, to me.

One afternoon earlier that summer, I was sitting out on the patio of the house in southern Pennsylvania that Bil shares with his wife, Ann. We were looking out at the stream that meanders through their front yard and talking about millipedes. More summers than not, Ann and Bil's house is invaded by millipedes, who make quite a nuisance of themselves there. It isn't that individual millipedes do anything bad. They don't bite or eat clothes or nibble on the ceiling beams. About the worst thing they do is emit an unpleasant odor. But thousands upon thousands of them creep under the kitchen door, find their ways through cracks and crevices, crawl up the walls, and because of their sheer numbers become a cleanup problem. Each morning, Ann has to sweep up the nighttime travelers by the bushel-basketful. All the neighbors along the creek have a similar housekeeping task during the millipede summers.

Millipedes, those hard "worms" with legs that Bil and I used to call "thousand-leggers" when we were children, come in a variety of sizes. Ann and Bil's summer invaders were small, a couple of inches in length, dark in color, hard to the touch, and coiled up when disturbed. Their tiny, paired legs ran the length of their bodies and looked like a row of bristles. They were invertebrates, to be sure, so Bil started peppering me with questions. He knew that they weren't worms, but what were they, exactly, anyway? Were there different species? What were they up to? What did they eat? Why did they appear in such hordes from time to time? Lemmings, he knew, massed in periodic eruptions, and he said that there seemed to be some sort of "social irritability" factor causing this behavior. Could something like that be at work with millipedes?

I had no idea. All I could tell him was that millipedes belonged to a class of invertebrates all their own, as did their far-distant cousins, the centipedes—the sinuous orange creatures with fewer but longer legs that you mustn't pick up when you turn over a rock and find them, because they can administer a nasty dose of venom. And millipedes weren't insects; those had their own classificatory home—Class Insecta, for animals with six legs and three body segments. Spiders, ticks, and daddy longlegs were members of Class Arachnida, for animals with eight legs. Millipedes had a separate class, but I couldn't remember its name.

A few weeks later, at my request, Ann gathered up a couple of stray millipedes she found on the kitchen floor, popped them into a pimiento jar filled with 70-percent alcohol to kill and preserve them, and gave them to me. I'd begun reading up on millipedes and had made an appointment to see Ron Faycik, in the Invertebrate Section at the Smithsonian Institution, in Washington, D.C., where I have a second home. He was going to give me what help he could.

When I met Ron, he shook his head and grinned. "With invertebrates around here, we more or less divide 'em up as those with six legs and those with more," he said. "I've called the spider guy to come take a look, but while we're waiting, let's pull out some drawers and see what we can find." He started taking out metal drawers of millipede samples—preserved, described, labeled—which researchers use for identification and study. I'd read that the Smithsonian had one of the world's outstanding millipede collections, but still I was startled to see how many sizes, shapes, and colors of millipedes there were—ranging from ones even smaller than mine to big, fat, colorful ones coiled and filling their huge jars. We'd come across nothing that looked like my samples when the spider expert found us. "I don't know *anything* about millipedes," he said, "except to tell you who does. Rowland Shelley comes up to work on our collection now and then, and he can probably help you out." He gave me a telephone number. I called Dr. Shelley, and he agreed to identify my specimens. I sent them off in their pimiento jar and settled down to read the scientific papers that seemed interesting and a 1991 book, *The Biology of Millipedes,* by Stephen P. Hopkin and Helen J. Read (Oxford).

Millipedes are part of a grouping called Myriapoda, which includes not only the millipedes, Class Diplopoda (the double-legged), but centipedes, Class Chilopoda (the foot-jawed, from the Greek *kheilos,* "lip," since the foremost pair of legs are jawlike), and a couple of other classes of many-legged small animals. People who study them are called myriapodologists and meet regularly as the International Congress of Myriapodology, in Paris, France. They like to remind the world that there are more things creeping around than just insects and spiders, which (if my reading of their papers is correct) myriapodologists believe get all the attention. "Millipedes are fascinating and, dare we say it, endearing creatures," write Hopkin and Read.

Millipedes do not literally have a thousand legs. The record-holding species is one with seven hundred and fifty, and most have fewer than a hundred. Millipedes are called Diplopoda, the double-legged, because all of them—no matter the order, family, genus, or species—are made of doubled but fused segments, out of each of which grow a pair of legs. Infant millipedes are only a fraction of adult segments long when they hatch from their eggs. They add segments—and, consequently, legs—as they grow with each molt. A typical millipede has a hard, tough, mineralized cuticle, ideal for an animal that burrows through the upper layer of soil or leaf litter, feeding on scraps of decomposing leaf. By the time it has become an adult, it has consumed five times or more its own weight, in the process helping to turn vegetable debris into soil and generally tidying up the world.

Millipedes, as invertebrates go, are fairly long-lived. Although some grow, mate, and die within a single year, many species live for three or four years. Some, with a poor food supply, can live a considerable time—eleven years is the record, in captivity. (Recent studies show that slightly underfed animals live longer; rich food supplies simply hasten developmental stages.)

Millipedes have separate sexes, and there is considerable variation among species as to how they comport themselves to assure new generations. Their sexual parts, typically, are aft and underside, only a few segments behind their heads. Female millipedes have specialized reproductive openings in which they receive the males' sperm, to be stored in spermathecae, where they keep it until they use it to fertilize their eggs. Females of some species take up the sperm, which males have secreted in droplets upon a spun web of threads on the substrate. Among other species, the male takes a more active role, clambering up his partner's body and wrapping himself in a coil around her until their reproductive segments meet. Joined to her in this fashion, he uses a modified pair of legs, called gonopods, to transfer his sperm to her. Mating may last from a few minutes to several hours. After they have separated and she has fertilized her eggs, she lays them; the eggs are protected in a variety of ways (depending on the species), ranging from a simple protective coating secreted from the mother's body to an elaborate nest. Young millipedes hatch out of these eggs and begin to molt and grow and add segments immediately, relying on stored food energy from the yolky maternal egg to take them through several molts before they are able to feed and live an independent life.

Among some millipedes, males exhibit a curious bit of biology called periodomorphosis, a five-dollar word that describes a midlife crisis of sorts in which, for reasons unknown, a sexually mature male reverts, by molting, into an immature stage with sexual parts that are no longer developed, and then molts back again into a fully mature sexual stage. The function of this step backward is a puzzle to myriapodologists, who suggest a number of theories to explain it: it may be an adaptation to extend reproductive life in times of stress or scarcity, a way to conserve metabolic resources for additional sperm production, or a response to a gender imbalance in the population. All agree that additional investigation may turn up some entirely different explanation.

Millipedes are slow-moving animals, despite their many legs, and seem, at first, to be vulnerable to predators. But in fact they do not become dinner very often. Their tough mineralized exterior is remarkably strong. One experimenter has shown that an individual millipede can support twenty-five thousand times its own weight (one hundred grams) without being crushed. Some defecate when they are touched; some are bristly; some produce chemicals that are not only antifungal, antibacterial, and stain blue but are "repugnatory" (in biological parlance), defending the animal from being eaten. Of these, some are bright-colored, or even luminescent, to advertise their inedibility and scare off predators. In addition, when disturbed, touched, or endangered, most millipedes coil, tucking in their vulnerable heads, antennae, and feet. This serves not only to protect them within their hard, armored surface but also to position optimally the openings to their repugnatory glands, which secrete those smelly, itchy, blue-staining chemicals. The secretions of these mild-mannered, plant-eating millipedes vary according to species; they are not poisonous, and they range from offensive in odor to pleasant (at least to humans). Dr. Shelley's own particular specialty, he told me, was a family of millipedes that produce a sweet odor (the family belongs to the Order Polydesmida). Millipede secretions are chemically complex but include some compounds that sound familiar: cyanides, with their almondlike odor; terpenoids, which smell of camphor; and benzaldehyde, familiar to any beekeeper who has used that commercially produced substance to drive bees from the honey in the hives at harvest time.

Whatever antibacterial, antifungal qualities millipedes contain in their bodies, and whatever defensive effect their secretions and hard cuticles may have, a few predators have managed to circumvent them.* There are a number of diseases that attack millipedes, including a bacterial one introduced by nematodes, which opens the possibility of biological control of millipedes when they become pesty. Occasionally birds, turtles, armadillos, and a variety of amphibians, as well as some insects and spiders, manage to ignore or overcome all millipede defenses and dine on them. Easily the most entertaining example of this comes from Thomas Eisner, of Cornell, who discovered that one kind of African mongoose had learned how to unwrap the protective coil of a large millipede. The banded mongoose (*Mungos mungo*), Eisner writes, picks up millipedes of the genus *Sphaeotherium* in its front paws and, standing, hurls them backward be-

---

* A 1981 paper by J. Tinliang et al. indicates that extract of millipede halted the growth of tumor cells for six hours ("Observation of the Effect of *Spirobolus Bungii* Extract on Cancer Cells," *Journal of Traditional Chinese Medicine,* vol. 1). Some millipedes also produce natural sedatives.

tween its legs at rocks, where the hard, shell-like cuticle shatters and uncurls, allowing the mongoose access to the morsel of food within.

At a time in our intellectual history when we seem to have gone mad for numbers, millipedes—which today are found in perhaps a mere ten thousand known species, compared with the more than a million species of the Class Insecta—may not seem to be one of life's notable experimental successes. Yet if we consider all the various failed experiments that millipedes, had they powers of observation, could have witnessed during the more than four hundred million years they have been creeping around on this planet, maybe we should think otherwise. There were no vertebrates back in Silurian times, except the fishes swimming in the ancient seas. Myriapods probably got their start in the water, too. The oldest known myriapod fossil is a centipedelike animal found in Upper Silurian sediments, and the earliest known definite millipede, named by paleomyriapodologists *Kampecaris tuberculata,* was found in Silurian Old Red Sandstone. Somewhere back in those times even before there is a record of insects, the millipede emerged from the seas and began adapting modestly to life on land: stepping along on those paired legs; developing defenses against whatever strategies other life-forms came up with in attempting to turn them into dinner; outlasting many flashier experiments; enduring—with only modest changes down to the present—cataclysm, mass extinctions, and climate change. If that isn't success, I don't know what is.

Not long after I'd sent them, Dr. Shelley telephoned me about the millipedes in the pimiento jar. Although to Ann and me the two had looked pretty much alike, he told me that they were females of two different species. Identification is chiefly made by noting differences in male sexual parts, so one of them, belonging to the genus *Abacion,* could be either of two species; both had the roughened, crested cuticle of the sample. The other, the smoother one, was so familiar to Dr. Shelley that he could identify even a female. Its name was *Ptyolis impressus* (Thomas Say), and it was a member of a widespread family—the Parajulidae, Order Julida. It was less frequently found, he said, but not really rare—something of a wanderer. It was unusual in its feeding habits, for unlike other millipedes it was omnivorous, occasionally adding animal scraps to its usual vegetable diet. From his knowledge of their habits, he didn't think that either of these millipedes would gather in the great hordes of Ann and Bil's millipede summers.

I'd asked Bil to describe the odor of the mass invaders. He'd said, "Something like crushed elderberry leaves: musty, ancient, dank." I repeated that to Dr. Shelley, who said, "Well, then, they are probably *Oxidus gracilis,* family Paradoxosomatidae, of the Order Polydesmida. They are often the ones that erupt and invade houses, and they smell like that. They've been little studied, because they probably came here from southeast Asia." He went on to explain that there were still so many interesting things to be learned about our native species (some one thousand, in forty families, in North America) that researchers would rather spend time working on them than on a species that may have made its way to our shores in the soil of imported plant materials or by similar means. He sighed and said, "People always wonder why this or some other question relating to millipedes is so little studied. There are ten orders of millipedes found worldwide, and they are very diverse in their biology and behavior; their behaviors are interesting to a myriapodologist, but maybe they don't seem dramatic to others. After all, millipedes are not harmful and have little economic importance that we know of. If they did something bad, the government would spend a lot of time and money figuring out how to kill them, and in the process we might learn something about them."

There have been many printed reports about periodic eruptions of millipedes, several of them referring to *O. gracilis,* some to other species. Some of the eruptions seem to be annual, others cyclical, still others unique. All reports are anecdotal, and no real science has come out of them. But in reading the reports I noticed similarities to Ann and Bil's invasions. In nearly every case, the millipedes came in the summertime, in places near streams; they traveled more often at night, attracted to artificial light. One report stated that millipedes were present in such numbers that it was impossible to walk without stepping on them; another spoke of wells having been filled and contaminated by them as they drowned. In yet another, farmworkers were overcome with nausea and dizziness when the fields they were working were invaded. Some said the millipedes moved purposefully in the same direction; others said they milled about, occasionally wadding up together in big balls. Stories of millipedes massing on railroad tracks range from eastern Europe to the American West. In some cases, sand had to be strewn on the tracks lest trains be derailed by their numbers. Possible explanations of their eruptions include population migrations of an animal with only modest mobility, dispersal to adjust the gender imbalance of a population, dispersal to favorably damp surroundings to avoid dessication in a period of drought. One writer suggested that each millipede eruption had a different cause. When I talked to Dr. Shelley, I asked him what the current thinking was about eruptions. Could they possibly be the result of "social irritability," Bil's term to describe the eruptions of lemmings? Dr. Shelley didn't think so. "Lemmings have a lot more mobility than do millipedes, and they are behaviorally more complex," he explained. " 'Social irritability' would imply a more organized consciousness than a primitive invertebrate probably has, but some invertebrate equivalent of it might be described as a density-dependent population factor, in which crowding, depletion of resources, and lack of mates might all be contributors."

In 1742, Charles Owen published *An Essay Towards a Natural History of Serpents,* a compendium of information known to the literate Western world about such "serpents" as snakes, griffins, sea monsters, tarantulas, honeybees, and millipedes, which he calls *Scolopendra.* That Greek word originally meant "millipede," but has been transmogrified through Latinate taxonomy to become a contemporary genus of tropical centipedes. But never mind. Owen's description and drawings lump together the two kinds of myriapod anyway, giving a hodgepodge of misinformation about a generic animal. His illustration is an example of pack-rat scholarship, a drawing copied and recopied by literary gents who had never seen either a millipede or centipede. It resembles a millipede in the same way that the final tale resembles the original story after it has been passed around a circle of ten-year-olds playing Rumor. The many paired legs have been transformed into feathers on a beastie listed between "the Sea Serpent" and "the Mistress of Serpents." Here is his entry:

The Scolopendra *is a little venomous Worm, and amphibious. When it wounds any, there follows a Blueness about the affected Part, and an Itch over all the Body, like that caused by Nettles. Its Weapons of Mischief are much the same with those of the Spider, only larger; its Bite is very tormenting, and produces not only pruriginous Pain in the Flesh, but very often Distraction of Mind. These little Creatures make but a mean Figure in the rank of Animals, yet have been terrible in their Exploits, particularly in driving People out of their Country: Thus the Inhabitants of Rhytium, a City of Crete, were constrained to leave their Quarters for them (Aelian, lib. xv, cap. 26).*

So far, Ann and Bil have not been "constrained to leave their Quarters" because of millipedes, although Ann has thought about it, I know. But our understanding of these eruptions seems to have expanded little since the days of Aelian, a second-century Roman writer. Ann and Bil and their neighbors along the creek have millipede invasions more summers than not, and it is as interesting to speculate why there are some seasons when they *don't* have them as to wonder why they do. When we were once again sitting outside their house on the patio, drinking coffee, I relayed to them what I'd learned about millipedes. They had tried to correlate the lack of millipedes in the past two summers and occasional other summers with changing weather patterns, cycles of winter cold, and rain, but could find no correspondence. We sat quietly musing, and then I looked at Ann. She was wearing that private look I have come to know over the years. She got up and went into the kitchen. She returned with a smile on her face, and held out to me, on the palm of her hand, a raffia figure clothed in a scrap of red cloth. "I was in Mexico a couple of winters ago," she said, "and a woman gave this to me. She said it was a spirit who could grant one wish. I'd been getting pretty tired of sweeping up millipedes by the dustpanful every summer morning over the years, so when I brought it home I put it up in the kitchen window and wished we wouldn't have any more millipede summers. Maybe it worked!"

SUMMER

DIANE ACKERMAN

Summer is like a new philosophy in the air, and everyone has heard it. From atop a chestnut tree, where spiked fruits hang like sputniks, comes the sound of a bottle band and the kazoo-istry of birds. On the ground, a blanket of dry leaves gives sound to each motion: falling berries, scuffling voles, a skink rising from its bog. Small fence lizards do rapid push-ups as part of their territorial display. All along the weedy roadways, crickets rub shrill songs from their legs, and grasshoppers thrash and rustle in the brush. The grass has grown tall at last, and the trees offer shade for the first time in a year.

Expectant and rowdy, animals enter the green metropolis of summer through the tunnel of June and July, and they all have noisy errands to run. They bustle about their business of courting, warring, and dining. Only humans fret over meaning and purpose. Animals have appointments to keep. Even the June bugs, though clattering against the window screens—humming and buzzing, bumbling and banging—are on a mission of romance. Related to Egyptian scarabs, which were buried with pharaohs, they sometimes batter their way indoors by mistake, and then run around in beetlemania like wind-up metal toys.

Spring meant scant food, faint light, and hardship. But summer is a realm of pure growth, the living larder of the year, full of sprouting and leafing, breeding and feasting, burgeoning and blooming, hatching and flying. Now the mallards are dancing as they ceremonially mate. Baby garter snakes lie like pencil leads in the grass. Wild strawberries ripen into tiny sirens of flavor that lure chipmunks, rabbits, deer, and humans alike out into the open to graze. A vast armada of insects sails into the rosebeds, and groundhogs dig among the speckle-throated lilies.

Countless birds seem to be auditioning for their jobs. A bad-tempered wren will haze a rabbit across the lawn by dive-bombing straight at it, beak ready to impale. There's no way the rabbit can climb after the chicks, but wrens are pint-size scolds and highly territorial. Large glossy crows sound as if they're gagging on lengths of flannel. Blackbirds quibble nonstop from the telephone wires, where they perch like a run of eighth notes. I sometimes try to sing their melody. Because every animal has its own vocal niche (so that lovesick frogs won't drown out the hoarse threats of a pheasant barking at a dog), summer days unfold like Charles Ives symphonies, full of the sprightly cacophony we cherish, the musical noise reassuring us that nature is going on her green evitable way and all's right with the world.

Drawn by a familiar chirp, I look out my kitchen window to see a cardinal couple feasting together on sunflower seeds. Scarlet red with a black mask, the male eats first, lifting a sunflower seed, rolling it to one side of his beak, where a built-in seed-opener cracks the hull, then rolling it to the seed-opener on the other side to finish the job. Meanwhile, the dusky female stands nearby and shivers. Puffing up her feathers and squeaking, she looks helpless and cold, but actually she's inviting her mate to court her. Though acting like a hungry infant bird, she is perfectly able to feed herself, and will. This dramatic appeal is the time-honored way that female cardinals (and many other birds) play house. When the young are born, the parents must feed them nonstop, so she wants a mate who knows the plaintive signs of infant need and how to respond. The male cardinal observes her display and cocks his head, as if listening, but what he's really doing is looking hard. Because most birds have poor stereo vision, they see better if they look with one eye at a time. Lifting a plump seed, he pogo-hops over to her and places it carefully in her mouth.

Meanwhile, two robins are running relays to feed their squawking brood in a nest they've placed in a yew tree near the door. The chicks are all gaping mouth and yammer, just fluff and appetite. How do the parents keep from feeding the same chick over and over? Birds have a reflex that makes them pause a while between swallowings. If a parent robin puts a worm into the mouth of a just-fed chick, the worm will sit there and not go down. Then he or she simply plucks it out and gives it to a different chick.

Nearby, the lavender garden is a den of thieves, as dozens of plump bees fumble the flowers. Dressed in yellow sweaters, the bees aren't stately and methodical about their work but rather clumsy. Skidding off shuddery petals, they manage to grab a little nectar, but also get smeared with pollen as they career out of the blossoms. Hovering for a moment, they then dive headlong into the next flowers, and spend the day in a feast of recovered falls. One rarely notices the uncertainty of the bee, wallowing and sliding, or how flower petals are delicately balanced so that they will appear firm, but waver and flex suddenly without actually breaking off. The purpose of the design is to unsettle the bee.

When night starts seeping through glossy dark leaves, a whippoorwill cracks the long three-stage whip of its voice, flaying the air alive. It belongs to a family of birds whose Latin name—*Caprimulgidae*—means "goat-sucker," because they were often seen traveling with herds of goats and were thought to milk them dry during the night. Now we know that it was the goat-sucking insects the birds hunted. But the name stuck, replacing the more common "night jar," which was a better-fitting alias for a bird whose boomerang voice can jar the night right off its hinges.

Midsummer's Eve, on June 23, falls two days after the summer solstice. Once it was said to be the witches' sabbath, when an evil spell could dishearten the coming harvest. On that night, if a maiden put yarrow sprigs beneath her pillow, she would dream of her future husband. On that night, bathing in fern seed could make a man invisible, and walking backward with a hazel twig between his knees would lead him to treasure. Summer solstice is just a little sabbath with the sun. Indeed, summer officially begins with the solstice, from the Latin *solstitium,* "sun standing still." For a few days, the sun rises and sets in almost the same spot on the horizon, a prelude to the longest day of the year, and then the sun begins to crawl south through imperceptibly shorter days, toward a still-unimaginable winter. But for the moment it is early, spine-tingling summer. Jasmine and pine leaden the scents of evening. Spores like manna drill the sky. Pheasant eggs sneak life out of damp sod. Summer disavows any passion stronger than earth's in the sound of rain, in open field, when drizzle breaks into downpour.

Invitation to
a Rainy Day

JANET LEMBKE

It's raining.

Raining? No, "rain" is far too neutral, too paltry a word for what is drenching the North Carolina coast at Great Neck Point. The sky fitted the earth like a snug, gray, felted cap this morning when I waded out in the wide and salty river to fish the gill net. Before I'd hauled the catch ashore, the sprinkles had started, pocking the dark water like scattershot. While I cleaned croaker and spot, the drops grew heavier, the far shore disappeared in fog. Now that packaged fish are in the freezer, and I've exchanged scale-covered fishing clothes for dry and ordinary garb, sozzle and showers and pure inundation have taken possession of the day. Mostly, the drops rat-a-tat on the trailer's roof like seeds pouring out of a hopper, but sometimes the quick, distinct sounds merge into one when rain intensifies and the water falls in steady sheets. Rain rolls down the window letting us see light but little else.

While Dog naps on the sofa, my husband, a retired petty officer whom I call the Chief, inspects our old, weatherbeaten trailer for leaks. But no water drip-drips this time through the window frame above the bookcase on the east wall, nor does it seep through the west wall onto the shag rug by the spare bedroom's door. The Chief has fought that floor-level leak with caulk and monumental cussing for years. Satisfied that he's finally waged a successful holding action, he comes to rest at the kitchen table with coffee and plans for building a boat ramp off our seawall. We might be better off if he were making plans to build an ark.

Watching him, I think of all the things I could be doing on this confining, gully-washing, cataractal day. I could read, write letters, knit, or make a fancy dinner, the kind that takes hours and many herbs to prepare. I could fold laundry—the basket of clean clothes holds three loads' worth—or I could undertake a wrestling session with the house python, as the Chief has chosen to call our vacuum cleaner with the long hose that can coil around legs in an instant. Lord knows, we've tracked a Sahara of sand onto the shag rug and the kitchen linoleum. I choose instead to contemplate this streaming, soaking phenomenon for which the English language has a hundred words and none at all.

I do know some plain facts about rain. Today's rain is made of primeval water—water that has existed constantly and in the same quantity since molecules of oxygen and hydrogen collided and joined not long after the planet was formed. Earth's oldest oceans and its earliest rains are still with us, though their water has since appeared in myriad guises, from ice cap to bog, from snow to steam or invisible vapor. And water rolls on a great wheel called the hydrological cycle: evaporation, condensation, precipitation. This morning's downpour began in the clouds. Up there, dust specks and other infinitesimal bits of floating matter provided the nuclei needed for vapor to condense into minuscule droplets. And the droplets merged, plumping out until they were heavy enough to fall without evaporating down to the earth, to the parched soil of Great Neck Point.

I also know things about rain that have nothing to do with the facts:

It's raining, it's pouring,
The old man is snoring,
Bumped his head and wet his bed
And couldn't get up this morning.

That's an American version of the childhood classic—the one learned at recess out of adult earshot. The more polite old man endorsed by our parents simply went to bed. The verse that English children sing to the same "A-Tisket A-Tasket" tune ignores the old man and his doings altogether and compares the rain to pepper falling from a box "and all the little ladies are holding up their frocks."

The deluge slacks off. Chanting playground singsong, I open the back door to sniff the air and listen. What I get is a faceful of cool raindrops, the scent of wet earth, and—not an old man's snoring but the whistles of bobwhite announcing their name and the briskly bugled chow-call song of the orchard orioles.

Some rains are not so benign—from the ancient skyburst that sent Noah drifting across new-formed seas for forty days to here-and-now downpours that do not cease for days on end but flood the Mississippi, break its levees, and drown a thousand thousand hopes and dreams, along with the new-planted seeds in the fields. But today's rain is water from heaven. And, oh, we have needed it.

For the last three weeks the world has been sweltering, the air holding its moisture-swollen breath. My grandmother, a mistress of the art of delicate speech, told me that horses sweat, men perspire, ladies glow—or "dreen," if they're old-fashioned South Carolina ladies, sitting on the porch swing with lemonade and a gently fluttered fan. In my grandmother's book, I'm a horse. Weeding the garden, walking, cooking, cleaning fish, working at any activity, I flat-out sweat. Not only do I soak the underarms of my shirt but the back and front as well. As for the Chief, his brow and upper lip become beaded as soon as he opens his mouth to talk. But we can endure the humid heat, can compensate by moving sluggishly, drinking gallons of iced tea, and showering away the sweated salt when darkness brings temperatures down from the high nineties to the comparatively arctic high seventies. And day or night, we can always plop our wilting bodies in the river.

The trees, however, have been coated with dust from the dirt lane. The garden has panted with thirst, and even prolonged watering with the sprinkler has not put the pep back into drooping bell peppers. Nor have the birds escaped punishment. The heat has made them silent and re-clusive, hoarding their energy. Nor have they had ready sources of water for drinking and baths. Even the nearly everlasting puddle on the dirt lane has dried up. The birds were looking elsewhere for water—in buckets and barrels containing the algae-green remnants of past rains, in the river itself. Several mornings ago, a pair of cardinals chose the river for their ablutions. I saw the cock glide down to perch on the moving rim of a wave; the hen flew with him but caught herself in time and rose intact. Scarlet leaf bobbing on gray-brown water: the handle of our dip net was half a foot too short for me to reach him. I do not know if he was able to come ashore. Only the river's children seem to have fared well through these sultry weeks. Though superheated winds have desiccated the land, frequent southwesterly gusts have churned the water into oxygen-trapping whitecaps. There's been no fish kill, with air-starved bodies floating on the surface. Instead, the finny creatures have been swimming all along into our nets, and the blue crabs scuttling into our pots.

We deserve today's fat, juicy drops. For three weeks, we've been tantalized, grasping at storms that disappeared before they reached our shore. Late afternoons and evenings, thunderheads have regularly built themselves over the river's far bank in tall, gray columns crowned with dazzling bursts of sunlight. Brilliant chains of lightning have connected heaven and earth. Thunder has followed, like an old man's timber-shivering snores, like rumbling growls from some great Olympian gut. Or perhaps Zeus was laughing. Watching the storms roll out of reach, we sighed and sweated.

Today, no lightning slashes down, no thunder booms. I hear rain and the revitalized birds, not just bobwhite and orioles but bluebirds, car-dinals, three kinds of warblers, and the cheerily loudmouthed wrens. Their wet feathers are plastered to their bodies, but they've waked from torpor, they're singing up a shivaree. "Whee!" I holler back. My shirtfront is soaked this time with deliciously cool, clean water, not salty sweat. It's as if we walking, flying, wriggling, hopping creatures of the land have needed water-laden air as much as sea creatures need oxygen-laden water.

Now we all celebrate the quenching of heart's thirst. Drops pelt on the world like grains of rice flung at a bride and groom.

We're also celebrating something else, something primordial. To-morrow, though I'll encumber myself with rubber boots to slog through puddles and the mud of the dirt lane, though the mosquitos will be resurrected and thirsty, my shirt will stay dry. I'll smell newly cleansed air and see the bell peppers standing erect. Toads and frogs will croak in full, a capella chorus. There may be a hatch of dragonflies. The birds will definitely put themselves on tuneful display. We've all been guests at a wedding—*hieros gamos,* the sacred marriage.

Twenty-five hundred years ago, the playwright Aeschylus saw mois-ture leached by hot winds from Greek soil. He saw rivers vanishing beneath their beds, plants withering, sheep and goats nibbling at parched vegetation, and human laborers sweating as profusely over dusty fields as warhorses in the dusty thick of battle. And when the rain came sweet-ening the land, filling streams, plumping out the flocks and their keepers, he listened to the primeval language of storms and translated it into his own tongue and his own understanding. In the final play of a prize-winning trilogy, the fifty daughters of Danaos plot at their father's behest to murder their fifty bridegrooms, brutal men, before the marriages can be consum-mated. One daughter, only one, looks on her new husband's face and chooses to think not of past violence but of future promise. She drops her knife. He lives. And she is tried for filial disobedience but exonerated because she has bowed to something more powerful than her father's wishes: she has honored a timeless and divine command. Aphrodite her-self, the incarnation of realized sexuality, appears and blesses the couple's mortal marriage in terms of the eternal marriage from which all living things have sprung. The play is lost now except for the goddess's words and the recurrent miracle they praise:

> Desire   yes   Sky's holy quickfire longs
> to pierce the curvèd world.
> Desire desire   grips Earth and reels her
> toward the coupling.

And Sky's rain   showered in their blissful bed
impregnates Earth
and She gives birth   the herds' grass and the grain
for man's joy and continuing.
By that torrential wedding   life learns its seasons—
the sprout, the flower, the completed fruit.
And I within   am accomplice.

Today it's raining cats and dogs. It's pouring orioles and bluebirds, snapping turtles, lizards, pollywogs, and gallinippers. It's pouring butterflies, not to mention fire ants and ticks. It's pouring pines, live oaks, hickories, and holly, trumpet vines, honeysuckle, poison ivy, grass for Dog to roll on and the Chief to mow, weeds to be yanked from the garden, and dozens of sweet California Wonder bell peppers for me to stuff and freeze or put on the supper table. And people are flowering, bursting out of their tight, dry pods. We're waterstruck, all of us, and all of us are not only guests at the wedding but witnesses to its consummation. We're also sopping proof of the primal couple's measureless fertility.

"Whee!" Dog comes to the back door to see what I'm whooping about. She pokes her nose outside just long enough to get it splattered. She looks at me just long enough to tell me I'm crazy and walks primly back to the sofa. Well, she can snooze away this lusty, pelting weather. Her people won't. We owe this day our reverent jubilation.

THE NATURE OF NATURE

DAVID E. FISHER

To my mind the most important mystery of nature is the mystery of the nature of nature. Is it red in tooth and claw, as Tennyson would have it, or is it a benign Garden of Eden, as the most extreme environmentalists insist? The question is not one of philosophical interest only; its answer will form the basis of our response to the most important danger facing us today: How do we respond to the changes in our environment which we ourselves have wrought?

The red-in-tooth-and-claw crowd sees nature in the purest Darwinian terms: the fittest survive, the rest are eaten. As Bertolt Brecht put it: "What keeps a man alive? He feeds on others." And, conversely, the world is full of creatures who want to eat *us*. We can forget the wolves and tigers now, for though they are stronger than we are, and their teeth and claws are sharper than ours, they are no longer a threat; our intelligence has put us far beyond their powers. But mosquitos still bite us, and when they fly away they sometimes leave their legacy behind, in the form of plasmodia, which burrow deep into our bodies and breed their offspring there in hordes of millions upon millions. These creatures want only to live and die in peace within our bloodstreams but they incidentally cause a malfunction in our mechanisms which goes by the name of malaria and affects literally hundreds of millions of people and kills several million a year, mostly children.

Insect-borne diseases are not generally a cause of concern in this country. I frequently ask groups to whom I lecture what the most disastrous viral or bacterial diseases in the world are, and the overwhelmingly popular answer is AIDS, or tuberculosis, or pneumonia, or—it doesn't matter what. The diseases people worry about here are not the insect-borne tribe, because those are endemic generally in tropical, undeveloped countries. But in those countries malaria, elephantiasis, sleeping sickness, and a horde of other microbial horrors strike many hundreds of millions of people, and are seen by the Tennysonians as violent proof of the antagonistic nature of nature: each species lives by feeding on another.

Nor are the nonliving aspects of nature any more mild, goes the argument. The beneficent sun warms us all, but it warms also the tropical oceans, which transfer their heat energy to the winds, which then begin to whirl around and flow in and gather up more and more of the oceans' latent heat, until they are whirling in giant hurricanes at speeds of more than a hundred miles an hour. And though we have learned to spot them with our satellites and so to steer our ships away from harm, though we have learned to watch them as they swirl playfully across the oceans, we can only stand transfixed helplessly and with horror when they swarm ashore and knock down our buildings and fling people with deadly force through the air. Add to the hurricanes a longer list—volcanic eruptions, earthquakes, floods, tornados, tsunamis—and then bring in the litany of viruses and bacteria, and end finally with the cacophony of such man-made terrors as global warming and ozone depletion and heavy-metal poisoning and radioactivity, and it's clear that we don't have to worry about wolves and tigers and hobgoblins and cacaedemons and things that go bump in the night: nature itself rises against us on every side, and will devour us in a moment once we let our guard down.

But these are merely anomalies, blemishes in a larger landscape of benign beauty, argue the Edeners. For every example of a virus killing its host or a jackal chasing down a deer, they quote examples of symbiosis in nature. Sharks, which are the example *non pareil* of monsters who live by devouring others, also exhibit the most gentle symbiotic relationship with their remora. These are fish that attach themselves to the shark with suckers and hang on for a free ride. When the shark slows down to feed after a kill, the remora slip off and dine on the scraps. To pay for all this, they clean the shark's skin of parasites and dead cells.

There are numerous examples of similar relationships in nature. Fungi live with plants, using the plant's ability to synthesize organic carbon from CO_2 and giving the plant in return a network of burrowing tubes that provide pathways for the plant's roots. And, of course, there are the host of beneficial bacteria living within our guts and producing (for example) vitamins K and B for our use.

Viewed from this perspective, the entire earth is a largely well-managed system of interactive creatures in a natural society, all of which evolved together into today's "balance of nature," in Rachel Carson's powerful phrase, and are therefore suited to one another if only—and this is a big *if*—humanity would stop interfering. Not that we should go away or become extinct—not at all! We are part of this balanced garden and are entitled to live here freely and happily. But we are not its masters; we are not entitled to kill those species we don't like, to tame those winds we feel uncomfortable with, to remake this garden into a concrete-paved condominium or a high-rise housing project.

From this perspective, the miseries of our world, including but not limited to AIDS and malaria and hurricanes and global warming, are due to our shortsightedness, our lack of insight and compassion when dealing with nature. Not that we create hurricanes, for example; we are not responsible for them. But we are responsible for overbuilding our cities on the subtropical coastlines without regard to the natural order of things—and among the elements of that natural order are hurricanes. So when they come—as come they must, in order to bring the necessary quantities of water to the vegetation natural to those areas—they ravage our jerry-built cities and kill us. It's not their fault, it's ours for butting in where we don't belong.

The Edeners present the same sort of argument for diseases: Africans have lived with malaria as an endemic but low-grade infection for millennia; they have built up a resistance to its worse ravages, and it is only when new settlers come into the area that the disease strikes and kills.

AIDS can easily be seen as a preventable disease; all we have to do is alter some aspects of our lifestyle, goes the argument. Sleeping sickness is carried by the tsetse fly, and we simply have to accept the fact that certain regions of the world belong to the fly and not to us and that we had better stay out of them.

Edeners have eagerly supported the Gaia hypothesis, which states that the earth itself is virtually a living organism, that all life and all processes are interrelated, and all operate for the good of the organism Earth. Only man, who has lost his oneness with nature, violates the Gaiac pact. It is we, not the tsetse and the anopheles and the hurricane, who are out of step. And if we attempt to confront nature as an adversary, we are bound to fail, for with all our powers we are still just one species among billions of others. Instead we must search for our rightful niche, stay within our ecological boundary, and all will be well again.

This basic mystery of the nature of nature is one that we have put off understanding for far too long and is now about to destroy us if we do not learn to come to terms with it, for the difference between these two views constitutes the difference between two long-term strategies of survival. We emerged out of the duskiness of prehumanity to find ourselves in a jungle full of carnivores, and we banded together and fought them. We countered the wolf's teeth with spears and arrows, we domesticated (enslaved) animals to act as beasts of our burdens, we learned to draw sustenance from the earth and comfort from superstitions and religions. We warmed our environment when we were cold and cooled it when we were hot; we cleared it of insects and paved it and pushed it out of our consciousness. We grew from wee beasties cowering in the dark to masters of all creation.

Or so we thought. We learned about the Second Law of Thermodynamics and its corollary, that all forms of energy production must include a waste component, but we didn't worry: we threw our wastes into rivers and lakes and into the oceans and the air; and we forgot about them, as currents of water and air drew them away from us. But as we became fruitful and multiplied, as we filled the earth, we found that it is a finite earth and that "the breakfast garbage that you throw into the Bay, they drink at lunch in San Jose," as Tom Lehrer put it. We found that the wastes do not disappear as the winds swirl and the oceans circulate; they simply go round and round and come right back at us.

And we found that though we could eliminate anopheles mosquitos and malaria from developed countries above the tropics, we were helpless in hotter, wetter, more undeveloped areas. Forty years ago, we bathed India in DDT in a massive effort to eliminate the disease, but today there are more cases of malaria there than ever before. Twenty-five years ago, we mounted an extensive campaign to combat hurricanes, to predict their paths with certainty and even to steer them away from our coasts and weaken them so they wouldn't hurt us when they hit. The campaign was a total failure, and today we aren't even trying to affect their course or strength; we have admitted defeat.

Of course, say the Edeners. For all our vaunted technology, we are weaklings when it comes to confronting nature; and not only are we doomed to failure if we try but the effort itself is evil. It would, if it succeeded, destroy the "balance of nature." Nonsense, say the Tennysonians; the common fate of all species in this world of nature is to die, to become extinct, and if we alone are to survive, it must be by confounding nature, by raising ourselves above her level.

I would like to suggest that the truth lies somewhere between the two. The Edeners are right when they say that we are simply too weak to challenge nature head-on: dropping a nuclear bomb into Hurricane Andrew wouldn't even have made him burp, and bathing India in DDT only backfired and led to vaster populations of resistant anopheles. The Edeners are middling right and middling wrong when they hold that primitive people live easily with endemic diseases such as malaria; after all, most of the millions of children who die every year from that disease are native-born. And they are outright wrong, I believe, when they argue that the attempt to rise above nature is evil in itself. We have wiped the smallpox microbe off the face of the earth (except for samples maintained in safe labs), and who would debate the relative benefits of biodiversity versus human health in this case?

The Tennysonians are right to note that if we are to survive we must somehow raise ourselves above the natural order of things, for in that order all things must eventually perish; but they are wrong to suggest that nature operates only by tooth and claw, and that survival depends on strength alone; there are many examples of coöperation between and among species and individuals. And in some manner, I think, we must find a way to coöperate with nature, or at least to bedevil her with subtleties—to learn to live with her power but to evade her worst onslaughts.

That is, after all, how we rose above the wolves and tigers, which were so much stronger and faster than we were; it is how we built our civilization—an achievement distinctly different from anything produced by any other living or natural organism on our world, ants and corals be damned. And we now have within our sights the possibility of bypassing evolution and achieving immortality as a species. (That is, at least until the galaxy dies, many billions of years from now.)

To achieve that immortality we must solve the mystery of nature's nature, we must find our place in the scheme of things. We must recognize, first of all, that nature is more powerful by far than we are, from her smallest weapons to her most powerful. From viruses to insects to the awesome fury of a hurricane, we have nothing to match her armaments. We have won a few battles against our microbial adversaries, as in smallpox and polio, but the ravages of malaria, elephantiasis, and AIDS are with us still, with little relief in sight, and with more and deadlier emergent viruses still to come. We have wiped anopheles out of North America, but it still reigns supreme in Africa and India. As the biologist Thomas Eisner has put it, "It's time to recognize that we don't share the world with insects. They own it." And Hurricane Andrew reminded us that we are helpless when the winds rise up out of the oceans and roil in upon us. From the smallest to the largest, from viruses to insects to hurricanes, nature is not only too much with us but too much for us.

But we must also recognize that though we are part of and one with nature, we are also different from the other refuse of evolution. We are not merely one more species among billions of others; we have developed a complex consciousness capable of understanding the universe, and with even the beginnings of this understanding come the ability to manipulate. Unfortunately, another concomitant of understanding seems to be hubris, which leads us to think that we can not only manipulate but actually conquer the universe. And this—at least for the moment, and perhaps for all time—is beyond us. We must learn to live at the fullest extension of our powers but within our limitations. We cannot nuke the hurricanes, as was suggested in the 1960s; we cannot bomb them into submission, for the energy of our largest hydrogen bombs pales in comparison with the energy of these monsters. We cannot wipe anopheles off the face of the earth, both because we haven't yet developed a poison specific to the species and because it develops a resistance to those poisons we do throw at it. We cannot command the sun to cool down or the ozone layer to increase at our will, we cannot direct the oceans' circulation or the tsunami's path; we cannot enforce our will on nature—nor can we even collectively decide what our will should be.

But before any of this, we must strive to understand the world we live in; we must demystify the nature of nature. I think that when we do we will find she is neither evil nor beneficent but simply uncaring; that we as a species are immaterial to her; that she could not care less if we thrive or shrivel, if we exist or join the dinosaurs in oblivion. There is an old joke about how a surgeon screws in a lightbulb: he holds it up to the socket and waits for the universe to revolve around him. But Copernicus and his successors showed us that we are not the center of the universe, and now we understand that the galaxy swirls on its way oblivious of us, and the universe expands without regard to our own particular location within it. It's time to face up to the fact that even our own earth doesn't care whether we live or die. For if we douse the world in radioactivity or warm it beyond the temperatures of all past climates with greenhouse gases, nature will yet endure. As conditions change, nature will change with them and go on as serenely as before. If some species disappear, well, that's all in the scheme of things, isn't it? It matters not one whit to nature.

Ay, there's the rub. For if we change nature sufficiently, we may find that we are no longer welcome on this planet. And so we had better tread softly, until we understand better how nature works and how we fit into the nature of things.

HUMAN NATURE

PETER J. FERRATO

Photographs by Peter J. Ferrato.

Of all the known types of nature in this world, human nature is the most important. We must always strive to understand it; and try to correct the human psycho-social aberrations which threaten not only the other creatures of this world, but also the very survival of all members of *Homo Sapiens,* and the world itself.

OF WHALES AND MEN

VICTOR PERERA

In July 1993, a humpback whale was spotted off the coast of California, struggling to stay abreast of its pod while dragging a salmon gill net wrapped around its body and part of its head. The valiant whale faced the prospect of slow starvation as it fell farther and farther behind its companions, who were headed for the Farallon Islands feeding grounds.

After two centuries of hunting whales to the brink of extinction, we have passed laws to protect most of the surviving cetaceans in the world's oceans. Our undeclared war against the whales may be over, but we continue to kill these creatures in silent, careless, and insidious ways that may ultimately prove crueler than the clean thrust of a harpoon.

Several years ago, the corpse of an eighty-foot female blue washed ashore on Northern California's Año Nuevo beach, near Santa Cruz. With hundreds of my fellow Lilliputians, I marveled at the dainty pink patches under her massive flukes, the grooves under her throat that opened and closed accordionlike to the rhythm of the waves. The whale's tongue, half-hidden behind the huge plates of baleen attached to the upper jaw, was the size of a hot-air balloon, and nearly a ton heavier. Her spine stuck out the back of her head like the mast of a ship. Although she had been dead for days, and the rotting baleen gave off a barely tolerable stench, her sulphurous blue color, the roseate sheen under her flukes, and her movement in the water made her seem alive. Impossible to imagine a single soul inhabiting that delicate, expansive hulk. A week after the University of California hauled the carcass off to Santa Cruz, their marine lab disclosed that the whale, years away from her full growth, had been pregnant. The cause of her death remains a mystery, although scientists suspect that pollutants may have poisoned or suffocated her.

The drama played out in the Arctic Ocean in 1988, when Inuit Eskimos and American and Soviet technicians worked together to save—at enormous expense—two gray whales trapped in an ice floe, aroused the sympathy of millions of TV viewers. But for all the excitement created by the worldwide media coverage, the rescue of those two young whales, who may have been strays doomed to perish in any case, did not translate into a larger concern for the preservation of their kind.

Shortly after the rescue, a story in the *New York Times* about the growing pollution of the lagoons and bays in Baja California, where fifteen hundred gray whales mate and calve every winter, went virtually unnoticed. The following winter, the grays reached the breeding lagoons months later than usual and in reduced numbers. Although no direct link was established between the pollution of the bays by chemical waste products and the whales' tardy arrival—other disruptive factors may have included temperature fluctuations caused by the El Niño current and oil spills off Huntington Beach and the coast of Alaska—the press hardly troubled to sound the alarm, and the story never made the six-o'clock news.

Gray whales belong to the ancient suborder of Mysticeti, or baleen whales, and their yearly migration between the Bering Sea north of Alaska and Baja California is probably the oldest continuously transited nomadic route in existence. (Another group of migrating grays, in the North Atlantic, was exterminated by Basque whalers in the eighteenth century.) Unlike the larger blue and sperm whales, which are pelagic, grays rarely stray more than a few miles from shore. For that reason, they are especially vulnerable to oil spills, heavy traffic in shipping lanes, and the toxic discharges of coastal factories and cities. Every year, the Pacific gray whales' migration approximates more closely a seven-thousand-mile obstacle course, with no winners, only casualties and survivors.

More alarming than the predicament of the gray whales—whose numbers have stabilized at around twenty thousand, thanks to a 1930 international ban that kept them from being hunted to extinction—is the threat to the largest of the baleen whales, the rorquals, whose members include the blue and fin whales. Exact figures are not available, but the surviving blue whales probably number less than three thousand, out of an estimated population of a quarter million before the start of commercial whaling; fin whales, the next largest rorqual, have been cut down to less than a quarter of their prewhaling stock. Of the remaining large Mysticeti, the humpback, right, and Greenland whales total approximately twelve to fifteen thousand—a fraction of their original numbers. Of the Odontoceti, or toothed cetaceans, male sperm whales were hunted nearly to extinction for their coveted ambergris, a waxy substance produced in the whales' intestines that is used as a fixative for perfume. Of the remaining baleen whales, only the smaller sei and minke, targeted by Japanese and Norwegian whalers, are still relatively abundant.

There is a demon in human nature that blinds us to the intrinsic value of another life-form—and its relevance to our own survival—until we are on the verge of snuffing it out. The global alarm over disappearing rain forests has come too late to save hundreds of thousands of irreplaceable animal and plant species—most of them unknown to us—that will have vanished from the face of the earth by the end of the millennium.

If we are to "see" the importance of the remaining whales before they are lost to us, we might begin by realizing that they are not just another relatively bright creature, like chimpanzees or dogs, from whose behavior we gather evidence to reaffirm our perch on the top rung of the evolutionary ladder. The dolphins and great whales—members of the order Cetacea, which also includes porpoises and the spiral-horned narwhal—have brains that are as large or larger than ours, and we are only beginning to understand how they work. The mind of the whale is designed to function in a wholly different medium than ours, a medium in which our conventional yardsticks for measuring intelligence are simply irrelevant. Our typical IQ test—the Stanford-Binet, for instance—assesses memorization, quickness and range of association, and accuracy and speed of computation. None of these problem-solving skills are of any use to a large mammal in the ocean, where the competition for survival assumes altogether different forms. The whale's and the dolphin's mastery of echolocation takes care of most of their food-finding and navigational needs and frees the remainder of their brains for communication, recreation, "thinking," and other functions that remain a mystery to us.

We are learning that dolphins and some whales are able to draw astonishingly accurate "sound pictures" of distant objects; that they are sensitive to the pull of the magnetic poles, which serve them as navigational aids along the equator; that their brains process as large a volume of acoustical information as ours do visual input; that they may be able to scan and appropriately respond to one another's physical and emotional states. We are discovering that they have highly individualized personalities, that they engage in social relationships and lead communal lives of astounding richness and complexity. Their use of echolocation has become the subject of intense study by scientists—including Navy technicians, who employ the dolphin's skills to carry out undersea military and intelligence operations. The use of marine mammals for these purposes raises fundamental ethical issues. Animal-rights activists have denounced the Navy's secret training of bottlenose dolphins to kill or maim enemy frogmen by ramming them with .45-caliber nose guns, as reported in the *New Yorker* and elsewhere.

Whales and dolphins are not our "lesser kin," separated from us—as are the apes, our evolutionary cousins—by a turn on the road an eyeblink ago in geological terms. If anything, the cetaceans are our oceanic counterparts, our peers, who have made adaptations to their environment which in many important respects have proved far more successful than our own.

The Koryak Eskimos of Siberia's Chukchi Peninsula, who still hunt the Greenland (or bowhead) whale with nets and spears, may be among the last to honor the whale's place in human culture. When the hunters set out, their wives dress in ceremonial finery, and wear crystal charms to soothe the whale's spirit, inviting it to offer up its life to the hunters' spears so that their families may live through the winter. After the elders slaughter and cut up a captured whale, the careful apportionment of the meat, bones, and baleen helps define the community's cohesiveness. During their annual whale festival, the Koryak perform dance rituals to accompany the whales that they have captured and eaten back to their spirit home, as if they were departed relatives. The Koryaks recognize their dependence on the whale as a sacred trust, and their elders believe that when the last whale dies, the Koryak culture will die as well.

The growing popularity of commercial and professional facilities offering humans the opportunity to swim with dolphins has led to some surprising discoveries about dolphin behavior. Trainers in oceanariums have long known of the dolphins' love of mischief; even in captivity, healthy dolphins love to tease, and they resort to various ruses to keep their trainers on their toes (and themselves, quite likely, from dying of tedium.) A dolphin trainer at Marine World, near San Francisco, confessed to me that he could no longer keep up with his wards, who hoodwinked him repeatedly in order to obtain more food or weasel out of performing their tricks. As we spoke, one of his dolphins began playing with a balled-up tinfoil wrapper. Alarmed, the trainer offered to swap the hazardous toy for two whole mackerel, a deal the dolphin readily accepted. After swallowing the mackerel, the dolphin dove and retrieved another ball of tinfoil to play with, which he had squirreled away at the bottom of the pool. That trainer had come to the conclusion, as have other trainers I have interviewed over the years, that dolphins should not be kept captive and that their interactions with humans should be entirely voluntary.

There is a world of knowledge to be acquired from free-swimming cetaceans who seek out human companionship. John Lilly, one of the first modern investigators to swim with free dolphins, released the captive dolphins he worked with after they became despondent.

The propinquity between dolphins and *Homo sapiens* was remarked on in the ancient world by Plutarch, who noted that dolphins are the only creatures who like human beings for their own sake. Visitors to Crete and to Athens museums have been struck by the murals and sculptures that depict humans disporting with dolphins. The murals in the palace of Knossos, the dolphin mosaics on the island of Delos, hint at the seminal role of these creatures in the ancient Minoan and Greek chthonian Mysteries. Best known of all the ancient stories, perhaps, is Pliny the Elder's account of the dolphin who, frolicking with a youth he had befriended, drew crowds to Hippo, on the North African coast, to celebrate a joyous act of interspecies communion.

What has taken us so long to renew a bond that goes back at least twenty-five hundred years? Is it not our apprehension that these creatures may challenge our implicit claims to species superiority? Perhaps only an individual or a society secure in its identity can trust enough to avail itself of all that a dolphin or a whale has to teach us.

The songs of the humpback whale continue to attract scientific study, in part because of their variety and range and the fuguelike repetition of complex sounds and phrases. The cosmologist Carl Sagan has suggested that these symphonic medleys are a whale approximation of epic poems, in which are encoded collective experiences passed down from generation to generation. Their large brains may function as extensive memory banks—equivalent to our libraries and archives—for storing their Odysseys and Iliads. In a study conducted in the Caribbean and off Maui, in the Hawaiian islands, marine scientists Linda Guinee and Katharine Payne found distinct rhyming patterns in the humpbacks' elaborate and stylized songs. Guinee and Payne also discovered that although these compositions alter dramatically from year to year, they are sung almost exactly alike—and repeatedly—by courting males thousands of miles apart. (The publication of this report coincided with the discovery that African elephants produce infrasonic sounds in order to communicate with one another across miles of veld or scrub forest.)

One of many odd things about whale song—apart from the mystery of how the sounds are produced—is the eerie sense of familiarity, or "déjà entendu," that they evoke, not unlike the weird thrill one experiences on first hearing the thrumming songs of Australian aborigines. A fascinating possibility opened up by these findings is that humpbacks may use songs as musical maps to identify and conserve ancient, invisible boundaries. This suggests another parallel with the aborigines, who composed songs about geographical features of Australia's outback and the magical creatures attached to them. Whale songs may be the oceanic correlative of the aborigines' songlines, mapping undersea canyons, rift valleys, and mountain ranges reverberating with a cetacean testimony millions of years in the making. Perhaps humpbacks sing their watery realm into renewed existence, season after season, just as the aborigines reclaim *their* ancient world when they go on walkabout, by singing the stories of the outback's earliest inhabitants.

Is it coincidence that the great whales are disappearing just as we are ridding the planet of the last aboriginal cultures that cling tenaciously to their founding myths and legends? In the past forty years, four great whaling nations—the United States, Japan, Norway, and the former Soviet Union—have killed two million blue, fin, sei, right, humpback, and sperm whales, or nearly as many whales as were slaughtered by all nations during the entire nineteenth century.

As with most wars, economics may have been the precipitating factor, but we continued and accelerated the slaughter long after we found synthetic or natural substitutes for every important whale product. In the closing phase of this war, our weapons became increasingly sophisticated. In the mid-1940s, whalers introduced sonar and harpoon bombs that exploded inside the whale's head, lungs, or heart, giving the creature no chance whatever to struggle or escape. The carcasses were processed in giant factory ships, which reduced them to drums of oil, sushi steaks, or barrels of cat food in less than an hour.

The International Whaling Commission was created in 1944 to set quotas among its members, which include the world's great whaling nations; as whale populations have plummeted, the Commission has assumed the role of custodian. In 1986, the United States, which had declared a unilateral moratorium on commercial whaling seven years earlier, successfully pressed the Commission to declare a worldwide moratorium. Under intense American pressure, Japan, the Soviet Union,

Norway, and other holdouts finally agreed to the ban, but Japan and Norway have continued selective whaling through a loophole that permits the killing, taking, and treating of whales "for purposes of scientific research." In each of the past eight years, Japan and Norway have sent out their fleets to capture a minimum of four hundred minke whales between them, purportedly to determine the minke's reproductive rates and feeding and migratory habits. Japan sells the whale meat—amounting to twenty-five hundred tons a year—to restaurants for its gourmet diners.

At a meeting of the IWC in Kyoto, in May 1993, Japan pressed hard for a resolution permitting resumption of limited whaling near its shores, in the interest of conserving its "whaling culture." Japan bought the votes of new members of the Commission—the nonwhaling island nations of St. Vincent, St. Lucia, Dominica, and Grenada—with the offer of economic assistance. The power play by Japan and its allies was defeated by the antiwhaling nations, who voted as a bloc to keep the existing ban in place. However, the loophole in the Commission's bylaws continues to permit Japan and Norway to hunt several hundred minke whales a year for "scientific research." Japan also showed its muscle by mustering the votes to defeat a French-sponsored initiative to create a whaling sanctuary in the South Seas, south of forty degrees latitude, where most of the world's whales live.

Japan's whaling czars continue to denigrate the Western nations' concern for whales as "sentimental." Kazuo Shima, Japan's whaling commissioner, claimed that France's proposed whale sanctuary was politically rather than scientifically motivated, and Norway's self-styled environmentalist Prime Minister, Gro Harlem Brundtland, scoffed at bleeding hearts who would turn the whale into the ocean's "sacred cow."

At a meeting of the whaling nations on Norfolk Island in February 1994, Japan produced "scientific data" to support the resumption of commercial hunting of the minke whale, whose total population they estimate at between five hundred thousand and one million. At the same meeting, Russia's whaling commissioner Konstantin Shevliagin—who supports France's call for an Antarctic ban—discussed the findings of a recent investigation led by President Boris Yeltsin's ecology adviser, the biologist Alexei Yablokov, into classified records of the Soviet Ministry of Fisheries. The result was the shocking revelation that the Soviet whalers' slaughter of humpback and blue whales from the 1960s to the 1980s—and perhaps for decades earlier—had been more than twice what they had reported to the Commission. One factory ship, the *Sovietskaya Rossiya,* also took twelve hundred right whales, which had been protected since the 1930s.

In June 1993, Norway had made good on its threat to resume whaling near its shores. Conservation groups immediately launched a worldwide boycott of Norwegian export goods.

At the meeting of the IWC in Puerto Vallarta, Mexico, in May 1994, a majority of 23 of the 40-member body ratified a ban on whaling in the Antarctic. Japan cast the lone dissenting vote, and six others abstained, among them Norway and Japan's Caribbean allies. The ban prohibits commercial whaling in all waters south of Australia, Africa, and South America, a total of eight million square miles. Roughly 90 percent of the world's whales spend all or part of their lives in these waters. Passage of the ban was hailed as the biggest victory for opponents of whaling since the 1986 global moratorium, but the Japanese were unfazed by their setback. "The sanctuary is an emotional, not scientific decision," reiterated Kerno Iino, Director of the fishery division of Japan's Economic Affairs Bureau. The IWC turned down Iino's appeal for an exemption to the ban that would permit Japan to kill two thousand minke whales a year inside the Antarctic sanctuary.

Japanese and Norwegian whaling supporters made clear they intend to press next year for a lifting of the ban on whale species that are not in danger of extinction. In the meantime, the loophole that allowed Japan to kill three hundred minkes for scientific investigation last year, remains in place; that and the continuing slaughter by pirate whalers who sell their catch in the black market, should reassure the thousands of Japanese diners with an unquenchable yen for whale meat.

How to account for this persisting atavism from one of the world's wealthiest and most advanced nations? Two decades ago, before the tide started running against uncontrolled whaling, Japan's chief lobbyist for the whaling industry—who also happened to be a leading conservationist, responsible for the protection of a hundred and fifty migratory bird species that fly between the United States and Japan—was asked how he could reconcile his two advocacies. "It's very simple," he replied. "With my left hand I stroke the birds and with my right shaft the whales."

Not that whales are strangers to contradiction. As Herman Melville understood so well, paradox is their natural element, a trait that they share with *Homo sapiens* and that is part of our peculiar bond. The blue whale, thought to be the largest creature ever to inhabit our planet, is the least aggressive cetacean, and subsists by consuming swarms of the tiniest and most abundant crustaceans, called krill. Only a partial ban declared in 1965 by the erratic IWC prevented the Japanese and the Soviets from hunting the blue whale to extinction.

Killer whales, or orcas, one of the fiercest of ocean predators and the only cetaceans to kill and eat their own kind, are the friendliest toward humans. For the most part, orcas become quite docile and pliable in captivity. (A stunning exception was a female orca who rammed and killed her smaller rival during a performance in San Diego's Sea World, in 1991. The sale of Sea World a few weeks earlier and the consequent decline in staff morale may have been a contributing factor to this unusual event. Like those dogs and cats that mirror their owners' idiosyncrasies, whales and dolphins are keenly sensitive to their trainers' moods and mental dispositions.) One wonders why killer whales, the pariahs of the whale nation (Inuit Eskimos identify them with the wolf) regard us with such peculiar affection. Do they see us as their earthly counterparts? Would they describe us—to borrow John Lilly's phrase—as killer apes?

Cetaceans have achieved an ease, an at-oneness with their environment, that we might well envy. Since baleen whales, which employ their roof combs as giant strainers to harvest their food, are distantly related to cows, camels, and other ungulates, we might conveniently regard their passivity as typical bovine behavior: meek cattle being led to slaughter. And yet, would we have been less ruthless if they had forcefully resisted our hunting? Chances are, had there been more aggressive mother whales and Moby Dicks among them, we would have muttered "Exterminate the brutes!" and finished them off a long time ago.

Even if a total ban on whaling could be enforced tomorrow, the survival of the great whales would by no means be assured. So few blue whales are left in the Antarctic that individuals have to roam thousands of miles to find a mate, thus heightening the risk that they will collide with a tanker plying the busy trade lanes, or chance upon a massive oil spill.

Blue whales couple for life and are the most single-mindedly devoted of all the whales. Before the advent of engine-driven ships, blue whales could communicate with their kin by sending low-frequency signals across a web of deep sound channels that extended for thousands of miles. The noise produced by ship turbines, undersea drilling, industrial explosives, oil-rig construction, submarine sonar, and other man-made devices has critically interfered with these whale communication channels, creating an enforced isolation. Not only are contacts between potential mates disrupted but vital information on the location of feeding grounds or a menacing oil spill—to name two possibilities—cannot be reliably exchanged. These disruptions would be aggravated incalculably by an experiment of the Scripps Institute of Oceanography, whose investigators plan to transmit low-frequency sound pulses from seabottom loudspeakers off Monterey Bay's Point Sur and the Hawaiian island of Kauai. The objective of the Acoustic Thermometry of Ocean Climate, as the project is officially known, is to determine the rate of global warming—if any— by measuring fluctuations in ocean temperatures worldwide over a period of years. The experiment is opposed by many marine scientists and mammalian specialists, who fear that the loudspeakers—which are to be placed in marine sanctuaries frequented by migrating blue, gray, and humpback whales—would drastically compound the damage already done to their undersea communications.

In any event, the blue whales' numbers may already have been depleted to the point where an adult male's search for a suitable mate is so hazardous that the remaining blues will simply allow themselves to die out. The sighting last year of pods of blue whales off Provincetown, on Cape Cod, and the blues' continued presence in sizable numbers off Big Sur allow a small margin for hope (a margin that could be wiped out by high-decibel accoustic transmissions from neighboring Monterey Bay.)

If the approved Antarctic whale sanctuary fails to materialize, the most serious long-term threat to the whales' survival is the gold-rush fever that will overtake the world's oceans in the coming years. As land resources are exhausted, the United States, Russia, Japan, and the lesser maritime nations will stake out their claims on the oceans' mineral and food resources. As the oceans are carved up into private mining and oil-drilling reserves, not only the whales but most other marine mammals are likely to find their grazing pastures of krill and plankton increasingly under siege. The large oil spill by an Argentine ship in the Antarctic in 1989, followed by the grounding of the *Exxon Valdez* in Prince William Sound, took a calamitous toll on krill populations at opposite poles of the globe; the *Exxon Valdez* disaster—the largest of its kind in United States history—directly endangered migrating whales and wiped out thousands of northern sea otters. Since the disaster, Exxon has made cosmetic changes, such as purchasing larger oil-containment booms, but it has steadfastly refused the expense of replacing its outmoded fleet of single-hulled tankers with double-hulled tankers, which are the only credible safeguard against another calamity of comparable or greater magnitude. It remains to be seen if Exxon and other oil carriers will comply with the Oil Pollution Act passed in 1990, which will require double hulls on all new large cargo carriers built in the United States over a twenty-year period, starting next year.

Jacques Cousteau has conjectured that humans and killer whales may one day form a partnership to help clean up and rehabilitate the polluted oceans. That day would arrive not a moment too soon, as increasing quantities of petroleum, hypodermic needles, and industrial and nuclear wastes wash ashore on our beaches. For hard evidence of the effects of our pollutants on the cetaceans, suffice it to mention a pod of beluga whales in the St. Lawrence River, whose skins are peeling off as they die agonizing deaths of pneumonia and other diseases caused by the chemical by-products of the river's large paper mills. The continuing mass beachings of whales along the Chilean and Argentine coasts may be another early warning that we are irreversibly poisoning our oceans, and thereby ourselves as well. And the widening hole in the ozone layer above the Antarctic threatens migratory whales with a new catastrophe, as scientists warn that rising levels of ultraviolet radiation could wipe out or cause mutations in the vast populations of krill and plankton the whales feed on.

It is not difficult to foresee a time when the surviving whales, elephant seals, dolphins, and walruses will be confined to reservations and stud farms—the oceanic counterparts of wildlife-breeding zoos. In herding and domesticating whales, we would render them as powerless as their distant land cousins, cows and sheep. And they would soon fade from our consciousness as the mysterious and potent "others" they represent. In like manner we have rendered invisible the large felines, the apes, and the pachyderms by confining them to the zoological parks that the art historian and philosopher John Berger calls "the epitaph to a relationship which was as old as man."

There is a tendency among natural scientists to demysticize the whales by dismissing any speculation about them that is not supported by hard evidence. In the view of these debunkers, whales have evolved hardly at all in millions of years; they have at best a primitive cognitive capacity; and their intelligence is far inferior to that of chimps and gorillas, who can learn a rudimentary language and even pass it on to their progeny. The humpbacks' songs are explainable as territorial or courtship displays, little different from birdsong. The dolphins' sonar and communication skills are said to be about on a par with those of bats, and their play patterns are said to show little improvisation. As for their legendary friendliness to humans, these skeptics point out, dolphins may have drowned as many sailors as they have saved, by shoving them out to sea rather than landward.

The answer to these charges is that even if one considers only the most obvious and verifiable features of cetaceans, they remain among the most

VICTOR PERERA

remarkable creatures on earth. We are still confronted with the unexplained complexity and disproportionate size of their brains; their close family and communal bonds; their intricate webs of intraspecies communication; and the harmony they have achieved with their environment. The ancient Greeks and the Hebrew scribes knew next to nothing about dolphin sonar or the humpback's song, yet they held the whale in reverential awe, and the Hebrews named him Leviathan. We moderns, for all our technological advances, have acquired far less knowledge about the living whales than we have inherited concerning Egypt's pharaohs, or—for that matter—than we have deduced about the dinosaurs, which became extinct sixty-five million years ago.

On the beaches of northern California and off the Pacific coast of Mexico, I have observed gray whales pause in their migration to ride a high surf, or dance in troika formation to an unheard mazurka. I have watched a humpback clear the water repeatedly in a calligraphy of heart-stopping leaps motivated—as near as anyone can tell—by the sheer exhilaration of self-expression. Whoever has witnessed a school of dolphins riding a ship's bow wave is unlikely to mistake their acrobatic display for goal-directed activity.

What are the whales doing with those marvelous large and complex brains of theirs, as they turn and turn in the water, rising and falling to the primordial rhythm of their breathing? (Appropriately, the word "whale" derives from the Norse *whal,* or "wheel.") Who is to say that they are not absorbed in a profound meditation for the strengthening and purification of their spirit, or that they are not offering up prayers, after their own fashion? More than one observer has noted the eerie parallel between the wheeling motion of a migrating whale and the whirling of Tibetan prayer wheels.

The whale kingdom is one of the last refuges of the shell-shocked imagination. By hunting or domesticating the whales out of existence, we eliminate not only the refuge but the fugitive imagination whose frayed threads bind us to the whales. Aristotle, who wrote one of the earliest and best studies of whales and dolphins in his *History of Animals,* and who gave us the foundations of modern logic, was a stranger to the modern sin of anthropomorphic fallacy. Our high-school teachers' warning never to attribute to animals our own emotions and desires originates in the Cartesian premise that *Homo sapiens* is the only creature with a soul.

Yet meditating on a whale's soul compels reflection on the nature of soul, or consciousness. The whale's "cogito" is so radically different from ours that we can only approach it by observing his behavior, the outward manifestation of his "sum." And this leads us from one mystery to another, *cogito* to *sum, sum* to *cogito,* and back again.

Aristotle believed that the differences between a human's and an animal's virtues and defects are quantitative, not qualitative. And, in common with the Koryak Eskimos, he saw no contradiction in the "existential dualism" (to borrow another phrase from John Berger) that allowed people to revere whales as potent "others" endowed with souls and at the same time to hunt them for their subsistence.

Greek philosophers and Eastern mystics understood that ocean mind and earth mind are two halves of a single consciousness, which has been called Gaia in honor of the earth goddess. In the mind of the whale, whose seniority over ours extends to twenty-three million years or more, Ocean has apparently found stability. Earth mind has proved more contentious. The nonrational, or "reptilian," part of our brain continually usurps our reason and drives us on to destroy not only our own environment but that of the whales as well. From the viewpoint of a "cetacean ethos," a God-fearing Christian, Jew, or Muslim who kills, eats, or otherwise exploits a whale is morally inferior to a Koryak hunter, whose very existence is entwined with that of the whale. The "primitive" Koryak's outlook is rooted in an ancient shamanistic tradition of cyclical world deaths and rebirths—a tradition that evolved eleven centuries ago into the sophisticated cosmology of the Mayas.

The whale's message to us is so simple that it is easily ignored; it is imparted by most land creatures as well, including reptiles and birds (not to mention our direct ancestors the Greek philosophers). Even the aggressive dinosaurs achieved a balance in their far simpler world, enabling them to survive for hundreds of millions of years. Whales are the largest and most intelligent of living creatures to have mastered the trick of harmonious coexistence, and that should earn them recognition not only as models and peers but as our potential teachers.

We could do far worse than to approach the whales and dolphins as allies, to invite them into our psyches and allow them to imbue us with their gentle, peaceable natures, their conjugal loyalty, their joyousness and ageless propensity for play. An enhanced awareness of whales is tonic for our spirits, and it liberates ancient linkages to our mammal ancestors encoded in our cells that can help us become deeper, worthier beings.

And yet these days we are preoccupied with the "monsters" of the animal kingdom—with dinosaurs and sharks. It is as if we were reenacting, in our cultural imagination, a premammalian stage of our evolution when we were finned or clawed and sharp-toothed predators, roaming our planet's vast plains and oceans—streamlined machines designed for killing and devouring, governed by blind instinct.

As popular culture appropriates the whales and converts them into marketable dolls, jewelry, cartoons, and TV serials, many pioneer investigators in cetacean intelligence have gone underground, or they have fallen silent. I know people who feel so deeply about whales that they cannot talk about them with outsiders. Sometimes, when I watch these remarkable creatures wheeling and breaching far out at sea, I imagine whales who feel the same way about us, nursing a sense of betrayal that lies too deep for words.

What is it we kill in ourselves by exterminating the whales? In Aristotelian terms, our moral accountability differs not a jot whether we harpoon a whale for its flesh or its ambergris, slaughter a rhinoceros for the magic properties of its horn, or massacre elephants for their ivory tusks. And we are equally culpable when we patronize chimpanzees and gorillas as our lesser cousins, carry out exhaustive studies of their motor skills and cognitive abilities, and confine them to zoos and laboratories, even as we go on destroying their forest habitat. How do you distinguish between humiliating an adult dolphin by turning him into a performing clown, and planting an out-of-focus TV screen in front of a caged gorilla, as primatologists do in the Washington Zoo?

As we hurtle with a deepening foreboding toward the threshold of the twenty-first century, we stand to lose our sanity, and something else besides, if no whales remain to accompany us on our journey. Even a TV-jaded child's dawning realization that Leviathan is not a Great Fish but a warm-blooded, intelligent, and sentient being very like ourselves—and yet different—can strike him with the force of revelation. In destroying the whale, we snuff out that precious spark of recognition in a child's first encounter with a cetacean. If we know this about the whale, and still go on killing and eating it, then what sort of creatures are we? In exterminating the remaining whales, along with other intelligent beings on our planet, we forfeit all hope of salvaging any shred of meaning or coherence from the universe, and we embrace with both eyes wide open a cold, dark, and irredemptive isolation.

By admitting whales into our consciousness, we take a giant step toward a new Copernican worldview, in which man ceases to be the measure of wisdom for all living creatures. Cetaceans could help rid us of the demeaning stereotypes that prevent us from approaching as sovereign beings each whale, gorilla, dolphin, chimpanzee. Whales can help us understand that human intelligence is only one part of a cosmic Logos that seeks harmony and balance in all its component elements. By exterminating other intelligent creatures, we upset that balance and magnify the destructive contradictions in our own intelligence, which may well be the youngest and least stable on our planet.

Unlike most fishes, whales are not scaled creatures; but we are. We wear our scales over our eyes. The whales could help us remove the scales, save for our determination to keep them on for fear of what we might see.

SAVING THE WHALES

——⌒——

ROBERT FINCH

On Monday morning, September 30, 1991, Kathy Shorr, a friend who works at the Center for Coastal Studies in Provincetown, called to tell me that sixteen pilot whales had just beached themselves on the shore of Cape Cod Bay east of Sesuit Harbor, about a mile from my house. These were the same whales that had tried to beach themselves in Truro the day before, but members of the Cape Cod Stranding Network had managed to push them off before they got in. I do not belong to the Stranding Network, whose members are trained to aid stranded marine animals, so I wasn't expected—actually, might not be allowed—to help; but Kathy asked me if I would watch what was going on and report back to her.

I drove down to the harbor in my pickup truck and found the whales, most of which were clumped on a single stretch of beach, about two hundred yards east of a long rock jetty. Several dozen cetologists and volunteers were already tending to them, while several hundred onlookers crowded behind yellow-tape police barriers staked in the sand. Four of the whales had died, but the rest had been covered with sheets and blankets and were being kept wet with buckets of salt water. The crews had dug shallow pits around them, so that water would seep in. This would help keep them wet and also partially buoyant, so that they would not be suffocated by their own weight.

The whales had first been spotted about 6:00 A.M. by a fisherman on the jetty. It was now about 10:00 A.M., dead low tide, and there would be no chance of refloating them for several hours. I asked a man who seemed to be in charge if anyone from the Center for Coastal Studies was there. He said, "Not yet, but you can help us turn this next whale." He led me over to two whales off by themselves next to the harbor jetty: a young eight-foot whale and a fourteen-foot female, who was thought to be pregnant. She was obviously uncomfortable and very active, thrashing and wedging herself deeper into a puddle. She had already vomited a couple of times, and her torso was cut in several places by the rocks below the sand. The smaller one did not seem to be in very good shape either; it had trouble breathing and remained rather quiet.

This was the first time I had been near live stranded whales, though on several occasions I had seen them dead and watched them being autopsied. I have been ambivalent about the practice of "rescuing" pilot whales. The species has a long history of apparently voluntary strandings on these shores. To the early Cape Codders, these strandings were considered a gift of Providence, supplying them with meat and high-grade whale oil from the rounded "melon" in the front of the whale's head. When a whale herd was spotted coming in, the people around here regularly set out in small boats to "help" the animals ashore. I have a photograph from the 1930s showing several men in my town posing proudly with spearlike flensing knives and standing on the bodies of a couple of dozen stranded pilot whales. The stripped carcasses were buried in the dunes. A few years ago, tides and currents exhumed the whitened skeletons, which tumbled out onto the tidal flats like a xylophone junkyard. Beachcombers picked up some of the vertebrae to use as drink coasters.

For reasons that are not yet clear, pilot whales largely disappeared from local waters after the Depression. But in the mid-1970s they began to show up and strand again. Most strandings occur from September through December. No one knows why these whales strand—though a number of theories have been offered, including mass suicide, the traplike configuration of Cape Cod Bay, and viral brain infections that disrupt the animals' navigational and echolocation systems. Most stranded pilot whales appear healthy, yet even when they are successfully gotten off a beach, more often than not they try to strand somewhere else, as these had.

A lot of time, energy, and money is spent in these rescue efforts, even though there is no clear way of determining their value. Some research scientists seriously doubt that it is a wise use of limited resources, but they are reluctant to say so, since attempts to save the whales give their organizations good publicity, resulting in donations. Others justify the exercise as an opportunity to learn more about the whales' physiology and behavior. For the volunteers, it is certainly interesting and exciting to work with these animals close up; and there is, of course, a kind of guaranteed satisfaction in being part of any group effort working toward a clear, altruistic goal for a limited time.

But the rescue attempts have bothered me not only because it remains unclear whether or not we are actually helping the whales but because we seem to go at it with the same kind of unexamined certainty with which we used to drive them ashore only a generation or two ago. I find myself suspecting that some of the people who give generously of their time and assets to help whales, spotted owls, or cats could care less about chronic poverty, drug abuse, inner-city violence, Third World hunger—or, for that matter, a neighbor who is alcoholic, depressed, or unemployed. Were we doing something worthwhile here on the beach, or were we just making ourselves feel good while having an undeniably interesting time?

I have harbored these doubts for a while, but this was the first experience I'd had actually working with stranded whales, and it changed my perspective a bit. For whatever reason the whales had stranded, they were obviously in distress. One female had given birth to a stillborn fetus and then had died; I saw the bloody placenta hanging out of her genital opening. The people who have worked with them know that, if not seriously injured, the whales do respond to care—whether or not they are "grateful"—and that given sufficient opportunity they will regroup and swim off, sometimes only to strand again. In the absence of hard evidence that these efforts are actually harming the whales, one can argue that it makes sense to err on the side of compassion.

I spent the next few hours helping to tend our two whales, carrying buckets of water several hundred feet in over the flats, trying to keep the sheets over them wet, digging out the puddles in which they lay, and shoveling sand under their heads to prop them up. During this time, each of the twelve surviving whales was measured; a blood sample was taken from each, and the animals were marked for future identification by attaching a numbered plastic tag to the trailing edge of the dorsal fin.

I noticed that the whales kept their eyes closed—probably to keep out sand. They breathed through their blowholes in great puffs of air and water vapor at uneven intervals. The blowhole is a black, ribbed, three-inch-wide tube that goes deep into the head cavity. Each blowhole has a tight-fitting operculum, or cap, that closes between breaths. A few times I got a faceful of whale breath, and, surprisingly, it smelled clean and fresh, like the smell of ozone in the air after a storm.

It is hard to think of whales as fellow mammals. They seem so artificial and impervious to the touch—cold, wet, slick, and rubbery. Yet when I was pouring water over the larger whale's tail, I accidentally nicked a fluke lightly with the shovel blade. Bright red blood began to flow from the cut and pool in the cloudy water around her. I felt sick. The tail apparently acts as a heat exchanger, so that the blubber is thin there and the blood close to the surface.

As the tide began to come in, I walked off the beach to go back to the truck for my waders. In the dunes between the beach and the harbor was an amazing sight. Over a thousand iridescent blue-green tree swallows were flocking among the bayberry and goldenrod, buzzing, perching, then taking off in sudden mass bursts of flight, only to turn around and group again in a kind of constant dynamic cohesiveness, their white bellies flashing, morning light glinting off their shiny backs. It is an old cliché in nature—vibrant, fecund vitality going on indifferently side by side with helpless, pathetic mortality. But I was held there, mesmerized. At such times it seems not that natural and human values are at odds but that nature encompasses our values and goes beyond them, to realms of meaning that we may not be fashioned to comprehend. All we have is our humanity and affinities, and the hope that these may be enough in this world.

During the morning, some staff from the Center for Coastal Studies had arrived, led by Dr. Stormy Mayo. Stormy (he was born on a boat during a coastal storm) is a fifth-generation Provincetown native and the chief cetologist at the center. The tide had turned and was beginning to reach the whales. Stormy and Dan Morast, a cetologist with the International Coalition for Wildlife, decided to move as many of the animals as possible off the beach and into the harbor, so as to be able to maintain them in a calm, deep-water situation, which would give the whales the best chance to reorient themselves and recover before being let go. The move was accomplished by slipping a large plastic stretcher, with holes for the flippers, underneath each whale, then slipping long aluminum poles through the stretcher sides and attaching the stretcher by chains to a large front-end loader, which carried the whale off the flats and over to the boat ramp inside Sesuit Harbor, some five hundred feet from the beach.

This was not as simple as it might sound—especially getting the stretcher under a two-ton whale, which was liable to start thrashing around when it was disturbed—but we managed. The two whales I had been working with were among the first to be taken off the beach. We followed them over, and as the larger whale was lowered into the water, six or seven of us held onto the stretcher to contain her. On the other side of a small pier, another half-dozen workers in wet and dry suits held three of the transported whales upright in a small penning area.

As soon as our whale was in the water, she seemed to sense the other whales nearby and began to get excited, vocalizing with whistles and clicks and trying to get out of the stretcher. All of a sudden, we realized that there was no holding her. She surged forward and dove, swimming beneath a yellow oil-slick boom that had been roped around the penning area. We thought we had lost her, but almost immediately she dove back under the boom and joined the whales in the pen. Pilot whales are extremely social animals, and the strong herding instinct is suspected of having something to do with their mass stranding behavior.

Transporting the whales off the beach continued throughout the afternoon. A parade atmosphere developed as increasing numbers of onlookers lined the route and cheered each passage of the front-end loader with its cradled, dripping cargo. No one knew how long the whales might have to be kept penned. Stormy said it might be all night. For the time being, the people in the water were simply trying to hold the weakened and disoriented whales upright to keep them calm and together, and waiting for decisions. Since I had no wet suit (and in any case wasn't trained in in-water care), I drove back to the house to get a camping stove, some water, pots, coffee, and hot chocolate. When I got back, I went over to the center's van, which had just arrived with more wet suits. David De King, the center's director, asked me, "Do you want to put on a Gumby suit?" Not having the faintest idea what that was, I said, "Sure." A Gumby suit is a bright-orange one-piece foam dry suit with oversize feet, attached mittens, and a hood. Wearing it, one looks and moves remarkably like the gum-eraser character made famous by Eddie Murphy on the old *Saturday Night Live* show.

I staggered down into the water and joined the other suited people and the whales. There were now nine whales in the pen, in three to five feet of water. High water had prevented the front-end loader from getting the last three off the beach, so they had been let go, in the hope that they would make it on their own. Three people were assigned to each whale in the pen, one holding on to each flipper and a third holding on to the tail. By chance, I was assigned to the large female I had cared for on the beach, with two young students from the Massachusetts Maritime Academy, in Buzzards Bay.

By now, the whales seemed to have calmed down considerably. We tried to keep them in a rough circle with their heads together, and we could hear them occasionally vocalizing. Gumby suits are buoyant, made for swimming and floating rather than diving. As the tide continued to rise in the harbor, several of the lighter people were having trouble keeping their balance without weights. Some lost their footing and ended up floating helplessly on their backs, like small children in snowsuits. I had no such trouble, since my left suit-leg had a leak in it, soaking and weighing down my lower half. At intervals, people were asked if they wanted to be spelled, and at one point a woman waded among us feeding us pieces of fudge, as we opened our mouths like nestling birds.

It was now dusk, and Stormy and Dan decided that we would make an attempt to let the whales go. Two of them had been fitted with temporary radio transmitters on their dorsal fins, and all had been fitted with Cyalumes—flexible plastic light sticks—so that they could be tracked out of the harbor after dark. On signal, we released them slowly and stepped back. The whales began to act like a bunch of drunks, bumping into one another, turning over on their stomachs, swimming upside down. Novices like myself were distressed, but apparently this was expected behavior for stranded whales. Stranding skews their balancing mechanisms, much as ours would be if we were hung up by the feet and spun around fast. An initial reorientation period is normal. Some of the whales recovered sooner than others, and it was clear that the former were trying to aid the latter to keep above water. Gradually, they all began to swim normally and to circle together in a clockwise direction. A plastic net hanging from the boom kept them from swimming under it out to sea, and the rest of us stood in the shallow water, pushing them off when they tried to come into shore.

I say "pushing," but it is clear that a whale of that size will do what it wants to. ("Where does a two-ton whale swim?" is the cetacean version of the eight-hundred-pound gorilla joke.) "Guiding them off" would be more accurate. It was then that I began to think of them as horses—large animals that we pretend we can actually control. They moved like a herd of horses in slow motion. They even sounded like horses, with their heavy, throaty bursts of breathing. It was quite a sight: nine large black fusiform shapes with carnival lights attached to their fins, swimming inside a circle of bright-colored human erasers. It really did look like a circus act, and there was a festive and anticipatory sense as Stormy gave the order to move the boom away and let them go.

Just above us, a line of boats had formed across the inner harbor to keep the whales from going farther in. The crews gunned their motors, blew horns, and beat their hulls with oars, and the rest of us shouted and splashed the water in front of us to encourage the whales to head out (precisely the same tactics, though with an opposite end, employed by earlier generations of Cape Codders). At first, they continued to circle, without going beyond where the boom had been. Stormy surmised that they had "learned their containment." Gradually, however, two large males began to lead the others out. We all began to cheer, but after a hundred feet or so the whales became disoriented again and started to swim to the sides of the channel. We regrouped and tried to steer them back to the middle, but they seemed to become more confused and a little panicky.

After a while, it became clear that they were not going to go out of the harbor. It was now totally dark, and the tide was beginning to ebb. I also realized that I had been in cold water for several hours and that my bladder was about to burst. I slogged up onto shore, where I found someone to unzip the top of my suit; then I slogged back out of the glare of the spotlights to relieve myself. When I got back, a decision had been made to close the boom again and let the animals regroup inside the pen. I asked David De King what the thinking was now. He began to explain the options, then stopped and sighed, "Oh, hell! We don't know what we're doing. Nobody's ever had whales contained this way before. We're making it up as we go."

A half hour later, Stormy, Dan, and the other scientists agreed that the whales should be kept overnight and a release tried again at first light. Wet, cold, and tired, I decided I had had enough. Reinforcements had arrived from the Massachusetts Maritime Academy and elsewhere, so I climbed out, shed my thoroughly soaked "dry" suit and handed it to an eager volunteer. When I got back to my pickup, I found that the bed had been commandeered as a general canteen for making coffee, soup, and sandwiches, so I left it there and called my wife to come pick me up. It was now 9:30. A warm bath and a can of Dinty Moore later, I felt very pleased with myself and slept well till 6:00 A.M., when Kathy Shorr showed up at the door to ask if I wanted to come down to see them let the whales go. I did.

For a while, it looked once again as though the whales wouldn't get the idea, but then they began to move purposefully out into the channel and headed toward the open water of Cape Cod Bay. This time we withheld our cheers and walked beside them cautiously, apprehensively, all the way out to the end of the rock jetty. A crew from the center followed them out of the harbor entrance in a Zodiac (a powered rubber raft), and soon both the whales and the raft were out of sight. We walked back, nourishing a tentative sense of finality and accomplishment, but the most anyone would say was "Keep your fingers crossed." Later that morning, the Zodiac radioed in that the three whales that had been let go off the beach the afternoon before had rejoined the pod, and that they were all swimming off into deep water.

In the next three days, the pod stranded three more times in Yarmouth and Barnstable, the next towns over. Six more died. The volunteers and the staff were exhausted, but they felt they had to keep trying as long as there was a chance for a viable group to survive. The remaining six were pushed off a marsh at Old Wharf Lane in Yarmouthport a day later. After that they were not seen again.

THE PACIFIC COAST
OF CALIFORNIA

JOHN A. MURRAY

The 5. day of June, being in 43. degrees towards the pole Arctike, we found the ayre so colde, that our men being grievously pinched with the same, complained of the extremitie thereof, and the further we went, the more the colde increased upon us. Whereupon we thought it best for that time to seeke the land, and did so, finding it not mountainous, but low plaine land, till wee came within 38. degrees towards the line. In which height it pleased God to send us into a faire and good Baye, with a good winde to enter the same. In this Baye wee anchored, and the people of the Countrey having their houses close by the waters side, shewed themselves unto us, and sent a present to our Generall.

—*The Voyage of Sir Francis
Drake into the South Sea,
Begun in the Yeere of Our Lord,
1579*

I first saw the Pacific in late August of my twenty-fourth year. There it was, shining bright and blue as a polished stone at the end of Wilshire Boulevard in Santa Monica, California. Seagulls overhead. Tall green palm trees. Sidewalk cafés. Newly arrived millionaires in red Corvettes. Former heroin addicts pushing grocery carts on the way to the methadone clinic. We got off the city bus at the intersection of Wilshire and State Highway 1 and walked west over a sidewalk spray-painted with peace signs. The scent of coconut oil guided us past the wooden pier and down the concrete steps to the beach, which was about as hot as the inside of a Monterey pottery kiln. Mercifully, a breeze rolled inland from the breakers, bringing with it the memory of saltwater fish and the promise of cool water beyond. As they have been every Saturday since before I was born, the sun worshipers were packed as thickly as elephant seals on a haul out. They avoided eye contact—the territorial imperative—as my friend Ken led the way. Another pair of Marines back to the world from their noisy base among the Joshua trees and scorpions of the Mojave Desert.

One glance told me the Santa Monica littoral was an ecological disaster area. The fertile salt marshes and grassy dune fields that Sir Francis Drake would have seen in 1579 were long gone, not to mention the floating rafts of California sea otters (*Enhydra lutris nereis*) that were plentiful until the Russians built Fort Ross on the Mendocino coast in 1812. The gentle Indians, of course, were all buried back in the madrone canyons, with their beautiful seashells. The giant California condor (*Gymnogyps californianus*) might as well have been in the Rancho La Brea tar pits by then (1970s), and the last Los Angeles County grizzly bear (*Ursus arctos horribilis*) died in a hail of gunfire at the head of Tujunga Canyon in the San Gabriel Mountains on May 16, 1894. His crime? Being alive, I guess. Of the wolves (*Canis lupus linnaeus*) not much has come down, except that they have not been reported in California since about the same time the first domestic sheep were driven up from Old Mexico. Numerous other vanished plants and animals are now consigned to the insolence of museum drawers, barely known even to the curators. The whales—alas, the poor whales. And each time it rains for three or four days, the sewers overflow and the waste-water treatment plants break down and all sorts of unspeakable filth pours like something out of Charles Baudelaire's *Les Fleurs du mal* into the Pacific.

After centuries of aimless wandering, we finally dumped our seabags on an unclaimed spot, rented a psychedelic-colored umbrella, and settled back to cold pizza and warm beer. We were ostensibly celebrating my promotion to corporal, but the mood was bittersweet; seven men in our unit had just been killed in a helicopter crash. From the parking lot, above the tidal-wave zone, Janis Joplin belted out "Piece of my Heart" from a fairly good set of car speakers. About a dozen volleyball games were in progress just below the seawall. Everywhere, the radiant sun darkened taut oiled bodies that could have been legitimately displayed in a living gallery at the Louvre. (Oncologists must be kept busy with melanoma cases in L.A.). What few elders were about seemed, outwardly, to be in equally fine shape. I suppose it is axiomatic that when you walk around all day in a bathing suit you tend to look after your physical appearance more carefully than when you are dressed in a down parka. In a crowd numbering in the thousands, the only people working that day were the lifeguards. Sitting on top of sturdy wooden towers with oversize binoculars, they vigilantly scanned the surf for five-ton, twenty-five-foot great white sharks (*Carcharodon carcharias*). Each year, three or four people are attacked and seriously injured in the Pacific, although most incidents occur in the turbid seas of the Land Down Under, where the shark is referred to as "White Death." As Ken and I looked over our shoulders at the Santa Monica Mountains, it was easy to imagine, with the steep dry hills fading from olive to gray in the morning haze, that we were on the French coast near St. Tropez, or somewhere up the road from Naples in southern Italy, just across the Straits of Sicily from Africa. Trace Santa Monica back far enough historically and you arrive on the rat-infested docks of Europe. The vast Mediterranean where Ulysses roamed for ten years is, as a point of information, about one-sixty-fifth the size of the Pacific.

In those days, I carried the Everyman's Library edition of *The Voyage of the Beagle* with me at all times, as a kind of scripture and also as an antidote to the deracination of military life. Through Darwin's narratives—those panoramic Victorian word pictures before landscape photography began to supplant descriptive prose—I voyaged, like Emily Dickinson, far out on the world: to the Galapagos, New Zealand, Tahiti (some of the best writing in the book), Botany Bay. Darwin's Pacific was not unlike the body of water before me: ancient, enormous, silent, long-abused, uncaring. A nature that was both the source and repudiation of civilization. My friend and I spent the day on the front lines, fighting the sand fleas, quietly reading our books, talking to our new neighbors about their unemployed alcoholic boyfriends and the winter mud slides and the autumn forest fires and the inscrutable San Andreas fault, body surfing (the water is colder and the drop-off more sudden and the swells more powerful than in the Atlantic), and finally watching the sun set beyond the offshore oil rigs and incoming freighters and jumbo jets outbound for Seoul and Shanghai and Sydney. After dark, we walked an hour to find a hotel with a vacancy.

Northern California was quite a different experience, many years later. This was the mid-1980s. I was in graduate school then, toiling like a monk at Anglo-Saxon and *Finnegans Wake* in my tiny book-crammed apartment three blocks from the University of Denver. My parents had moved to San Francisco from the nation's capital, after my father was beaten up by a gang in the parking lot of the headquarters of the Environmental Protection Administration, where he worked. Each time I visited San Francisco, Dad and I drove north over the Golden Gate Bridge to explore Marin County. (Long tall bridges always make me uncomfortable, especially the devilish twenty-nine-mile causeway over Lake Pontchartrain, in Louisiana, which I discovered by accident—nearly passing out at the wheel from vertigo—while exploring Cajun country in December 1989.) First stop was the Marin headlands, on the far side of the bridge. Hour after hour, we sat among the sagebrush and wild sunflowers, watching the great tides sweep in and out, the sea fogs build and dissipate, the tremendous flocks of ocean-dwelling birds go about their daily affairs. Once, a huge aircraft carrier steamed in from patrol, bristling with antennae and phalanx guns and surface-to-surface missiles, the broad decks covered with all species of deadly aircraft, a thing of terrible beauty. What would Drake have thought if he had seen that ship looming out of the fog? The sea lions and harbor seals at the bottom of the cliffs were oblivious to the nuclear leviathan, more concerned with roving packs of killer whales.

San Francisco is lovely from that perspective—the gleaming steel-and-glass towers of downtown finance, the solemn eucalyptus groves of the military cemetery at the Presidio, the mossy ramparts of Fort Point, the rhythmic rise and fall of the bridge—but why does that city, or any city, have to keep forever expanding? Over seven million people now inhabit the Bay Area. Studio-apartment rents on the Peninsula are like house payments elsewhere. Parking can be impossible. Quality of life dwindles with each passing year. A eucalyptus tree (native Australian) grows until it reaches maturity, and then maintains a stable size. Theoretically, it could live forever. Gravity, terrain, soil, exposure, the seasons, the root mass, the liquid-nutrient transport system—all act as fixed but gentle limiting factors. Cities, especially those around the Pacific rim, become ever larger, until people are forced to live as they now do in Tokyo, where entire extended families are confined to six-hundred-square-foot cubicles. This is no way for human beings to live. We are not bacteria, not termites, not ground-dwelling rodents. People evolved on the plains and steppes of Africa and Asia, with plenty of space around them, and they require space to fulfill all that is human within them. We have voyaged beyond the atmosphere, walked on the moon, landed our first scouting probes on Mars. We have seen our destiny in the stars, in all the distant worlds of the galaxy. We deserve better here on Earth. Unfortunately, given present trends, an increasingly crowded twenty-first century faces our grandchildren in San Diego, Los Angeles, San Francisco, Seattle, and Vancouver. Wouldn't it be nice (title of a Brian Wilson song) if we modeled our societies on the eucalyptus tree, living in restraint and harmony with its environment, and not the carcinoma cell, greedily and suicidally destroying the body that sustains it?

A few miles up the coast from the Marin headlands is Muir Woods, an isolated five-hundred-acre stand of redwoods at the base of Mount Tamalpais. Before the Golden Gate Bridge was built (or even imagined), people took a ferry across the narrows and then rented a horse-drawn surrey to reach the forest and the coast past Inverness around Point Reyes. In the sheltered valley, the two-hundred-fifty-foot-tall coastal redwoods (*Sequoia sempervirens*) loom like the pillars of heaven over a lush understory of dogwood, big-leaf maple, tanbark oak, rhododendron, laurel, and wild azalea. Black-tailed deer (*Odocoileus hemionus columbianus*) tiptoe through the moss, and gray squirrels scamper up and down trees ten feet in diameter. Ferns abound: wood fern, sword fern, bracken fern, deer fern, licorice fern, Western five-finger fern, and one not found in any guidebook I simply call the Murphy fern. Each winter, when the heavy rains fill Redwood Creek in Muir Woods, mature salmon and steelheads fight their way upstream to spawning beds. (Across the northern Pacific, clear-cutting and hydroelectric-dam projects have all but deprived salmon of access to their breeding locations.) Once, flying reptiles nested in redwood groves, and miniature dinosaurs, the ancestors of the human race, ran through the branches, gaining dexterity and agility. Redwoods, in many ways vitally linked with our evolution, have been on Earth for a hundred and thirty million years. Sadly, of the two million acres of old-growth present in California in 1840, only sixty thousand acres remain in parkland today.

It is a lovely place, Muir Woods—the trails offering a walk back in time to when redwoods were found abundantly across North America. There is a sense of timelessness in the groves, of trees that were seedlings when Caesar took his ill-fated walk to the Forum, of a ground sanctified by age and beauty. It is always twilight under the thick canopy, always April cool, with the morning freshness of the biblical garden. It is also always crowded. The last time I was there, I overheard a man joke that in the forest his shoes left the ground and the crowd carried him up and down the trail to Cathedral Grove twice before his feet finally touched earth again. Anyone who has been to Muir Woods, or a day's ride to the east, among the sequoias of Yosemite, knows that California needs more and bigger parks. Muir Woods is the most—I hesitate to use so sentimental a word—magical place I have ever seen. One almost expects Ansel Adams to step out from a shadowy green wall of ferns with his priceless Hasselblad camera in hand. "Dead? Me? Why, goodness no! I've been here taking pictures in the forest all the while. Wait a moment. I'll be right back. John Muir and Ed Abbey are calling for me."

On our third and final trip to Point Reyes, which is about an hour beyond Muir Woods, my father and I took a long walk on North Beach. This is as wild a beach as you'll find anywhere in the world. Even Alaska has nothing to surpass it. Row after row, the white churning combers charge like Tennyson's cavalry, beating relentlessly against the land, never retreating. One day, according to the geologists, the Pacific will win the assault, and the whole beach—in fact, the entire first fifty miles of California coastline—will be submerged beneath the sea. The continental plate, it seems, is steadily slipping beneath the Pacific plate, which is much larger and stronger. But on the day of our hike the edge of North America was, thankfully, still holding its own.

Here Sir Francis Drake came in June of 1579, after having plundered Spanish forts and ships from Chile to Peru. (Shakespeare was fifteen that summer, still uncorrupted by Anne Hathaway, still discovering the marvels of Plutarch and Ovid.) Drake's cargo bay fairly bulged with captured gold and silver, and he knew that a return to Plymouth, his home port, by way of South America was not feasible. The entire Spanish Pacific fleet was waiting with a vengeance, somewhere between the *Golden Hind* and Cape Horn. The Captain's only hope was to sail west around the backside of the planet, following Magellan's pioneering 1522 route past Indonesia and around the Cape of Good Hope. After an abortive probe up north to Oregon, searching for a northerly wind, the royal pirates wound up in California, at thirty-six degrees north latitude, where they put in for rest and repairs. As a result of that historic visit, we now have Drake's Bay just down the coast; Sir Francis Drake Boulevard, over in Inverness; Drake's Seaside Curio Shop; Drake's Bait and Tackle; and Sir Francis Drake Bed and Breakfast. I'm certain Drake would appreciate the humor, for the Elizabethans—one of the endearing qualities of their age—loved nothing more than to laugh at themselves.

The country around Point Reyes is similar to England—green rolling pastureland, clear running streams, bird-filled oak woodlands nestled in ravines—and, perhaps as a consequence, the crew of the *Golden Hind* felt at home and stayed awhile. Exactly how long we don't know. Perhaps two weeks. Drake was reminded most of Dover in the south of England, with the white-chalk cliffs, and so he named California "Nova Albion," and claimed it for Elizabeth, the petite red-haired monarch who proved that women can lead nations four hundred years before the issue came up for discussion in the former colonies. There were in Nova Albion, according to Drake's scribe, "hordes of Deere by 1000 in a company, being large and fat of body." Black-tailed deer are still abundant today, and seen by the dozens, along with the Tule elk, but most prevalent are the cattle and sheep, which are present in the thousands. Also noted by the British were "a strange kind of Coney" with "the taile of a Rat being of great length" and "a bag" on either side of the chin, in which the animal "gathereth (its) meate." The Indians made "great account" of the fine skins of this animal, and fashioned the coat of their king from them entirely. These were beaver, and they are still industriously building trout and duck ponds in the broad upland valleys. Drake did not mention grizzlies, but they were certainly about. The Spanish explorer Sebastian Vizcaino wrote in 1602 that he had seen a number of grizzlies at Monterey feeding on whale carcasses. Today the bears are found only on the California state flag. Someday they may be returned to the Sierras.

The coastal Californians were friendly and each day brought gifts down to the beach where Drake and his men had pitched their tents. The men wore the skins of deer and beaver, and the women wore cloth skirts fashioned from "a sort of hempe." Eventually, Drake and a squad of marines followed the natives inland and visited several of their villages, noting that the houses were dug into the earth, with wooden roofs overhead. On one of these occasions, they assembled for a sort of party, singing songs and making speeches to one another. Neither side understood a word the other was speaking. I would give the state of Ohio to travel back in time and observe that spectacle: a seasoned band of Elizabethans—educated in Latin, Greek, French, Italian, and English; fully aware of the movements of the planets around the sun and of the moon around the Earth; practiced in the compass and the astrolabe and the sea chart—meeting for hours with a nation of souls whose cosmos was radically different, whose faces were painted (in some cases black, in others white), who could not imagine how the ships were built or where they came from or what the metal cannons and muskets were for. Not one non-European Native was killed, injured, or enslaved on Drake's voyage, which must be some kind of record for the age—a time when Sir John Hawkins was already transporting the first West Africans to the Caribbean, in exchange for rum he then sold in England.

We walked for miles down the beach that winter day, watching the storm (waves oblique and from the northwest, driving from the arctic), looking for beautiful shells, stopping to examine a washed-up redwood tree, and following deer trails around the dunes. In the sheltered hollows behind the foredunes, we found bay-berry and beach plum, sea grape and prickly-pear cactus, and on the larger hills farther back the pygmy forests of bishop pine and dwarf oak and maple. Here the deer lived in plentiful numbers. At one point, I came across the sun-bleached skeleton of a young deer curled up in the wild raspberries, and we marveled at the smooth perfection of the bones and left them there undisturbed, out of reverence. The oldest dunes, a quarter mile back from the sea, had soil mixed in with the sand, and canopied forests, and there were freshwater ponds behind, with many of the birds—tundra swans and loons and white-fronted geese—I have seen in the Alaska Range every summer for half a dozen years.

Back on the beach, the long-legged sandpipers cruised the edge of the waves, stopping to pluck morsels from the seaweed and driftwood. Gulls scavenged the wave troughs, swooping down to pick up small fish and crabs, and then fighting over them in the air, dropping their catch sometimes back into the sea. About every quarter mile, a prominent sign warned hikers not to go near the water. Great white sharks were about, it seemed, and there was a fierce undertow and a sudden drop-off that made for "sleeper waves." Apparently, the sea will appear normal, a steady seven- or eight-foot surf, and then suddenly a massive wave of fifteen or more feet will rise up out of nowhere like Poseidon and overwhelm you. According to the sign, several people had been full-fathom-fived by these rogue waves, and a couple of others had been returned to the food chain by the sharks. So my father and I kept a respectful distance. We would have, anyway, because a storm was coming in fast on the high tide. We had heard about it on the car radio driving up the coast; it was "the storm of the century," as they are always called. Thick clouds the color of a gun muzzle were building to the west, pushing in front of them a pale pearl-colored fog bank. The sea was being driven wild by the winds, and it was something to behold. Though we were walking side by side, my father and I had to shout to be heard over the surf. It was the sort of storm you might see if you could peer into the imagination of Beethoven as he sat at the piano pondering his next creation, about to pound out the clashing, violent major and minor chords of his titanic anguish.

After a while, we retired to a bunker of sand just out of the wind, watching the unruly sea, the otherwordly fog, not saying much. What is there to say, when you have known each other, in all moods foul and fair, for over thirty years? Love is all that is left, and love is best expressed in the things we do, the time we take together. So we sat there buried in our winter coats, staring out at that gray-and-white expanse, me thinking of the empty quarters ranging beyond, of the far-off coast of Japan and all the secret worlds of Asia (that amazing grove of giant redwoods in the Szechuan Province of China, for example, which was not discovered by Westerners until 1944), and Dad no doubt meditating on the long drive down the coast past Stinson Beach and over the bridge we both disliked but pretended not to mind, to my mother's bright, warm kitchen. The waves were not so much crashing now as exploding. In the middle of a thought, Dad abruptly said that he was cold, stood up and turned back, and left me there to be alone with the sea.

Why do we need churches, synagogues, temples, I thought, when we have this? What more proof could a skeptical mind require? What better place to pay our respects? Bring those proud atheists John Stuart Mill and Bertrand Russell to Point Reyes, and let them walk around for a month or two breathing the fresh air and looking at the wildflowers. Let the architects come here, too, and build places of worship that truly do justice to the beauty and grace and originality of creation. Complete instructions on how to live, how to govern, even how to die—everything is around us in nature, in the tides, in the storm, in the way the sea grass, moved back and forth by the wind, etches a curve in the sand. A child can read the book, understands the language, looks at us with pity, because we do not. We spend our lives trying to learn what we knew before we were taught how to read and write.

I started to make a list of all the amazing facts I'd ever heard about the Pacific. I decided the most amazing was that the heart of a blue whale weighs one thousand pounds, and after that the fact that in 1820, off the western coast of South America, an enraged sperm whale repeatedly struck and sank the two-hundred-and-thirty-eight-ton Nantucket whaler *Essex.* But then I thought a bit longer and concluded that the most amazing thing is that we know so little about the Pacific. All the books ever written on the subject could be placed in one large wooden crate and dropped into the waves and have just that much effect on the universe. An insignificant splash. Can we create a storm, even a small one? Can any man ever born or ever to be born follow a sperm whale to the basement of the Pacific, where he feeds at eight thousand feet on bottom-dwelling sharks? Can we translate the language of the porpoise, even a single phrase? How does a golden plover navigate, year after year, from Antarctica to Alaska? Thoreau was right. We need to know that there are forces—like the Krakatoa volcano, or El Niño—greater than history; lovely undersea gardens, with strange seahorses, that we will never see; typhoons and tidal waves that can swallow an aircraft carrier whole and not leave one floating cork; and animals gentle and wise, like the blue whales, that have lived as we see them now for millions of years. Their hearts are large, but think of their brains. Consider a brain that has not a hundred and fifty thousand years of evolution behind it but two million years. What marvels do those frontal lobes contain? What do the humpback whales sing about, in those half-hour symphonies off the coast of Hawaii each winter? I listened to the waves for a long time, hearing many things, reassured that there is so much we will never know, realizing that only in such humility will we as a species, like the long-persisting whales, ever endure.

Sometime after that, the cold rain hit my face, and I turned to look for my father, but he was long gone, lost in the fog, and so I followed his tracks over the wet sand, putting one foot after the other in each of his steps. I would catch up farther on, even after his tracks disappeared in the rain that was coming hard now from the north and west, from a place I would never know.

LOGGING

~

TED KERASOTE

In a valley of quiet, we empty the sky, felling trees with horses, among a circle of sweat and friends. Some would call this logging. I don't know what to call it: life . . . building a cabin . . . being a mindful citizen of my home? I search for a name, using my hands and teeth, my nose.

The tinkle of the bell mare drifts down the slope, the hand-turned winch clicks, the heady, musty smell of working horses mixes with the odors of spruce and sun-warmed resin, huckleberries. Standing on the arch—the mobile winch that hoists one end of logs off the ground—Woody says, "Back," to the two draft horses, their hooves the size of buckets. He wears a torn shirt and filthy jeans, gold-framed spectacles, and a hard hat shaped like the First World War helmets of American soldiers.

At his command, each horse takes a diminutive step backward, moving the arch into place. Woody wraps the horses' reins around a metal tender on the front of the arch, both designed and welded by himself, then jumps lightly from log to log like a marten, prying apart the trees with a pike and circling them with hook and chain. He moves with long-time practice and care.

Across the valley, the hillsides rise to granite outcrops—meadow and aspen; meadow and conifers; meadow and sky, as empty and crystal blue as the sound of the bell. Here, on the north-facing side of Mosquito

Creek, the fir and spruce rub branches, allowing only rough circles of light to pool on the forest floor.

After helping Woody top off the load and watching him drop out of sight down the skid trail with the horses, I walk back along our cut, through an old stand of lodgepole pines we are about to fell. White of bark, straight and tall, the trees have lost their green. However, unlike Yellowstone's lodgepole forest to the north, they've seen no fire. No life-giving holocaust has seared their trunks, providing a blaze to pop their dormant cones and start a new grove, the centuries-old story of this fire-dependent species. In the course of time, they've simply grown old, growing and growing until their trunks have fattened to sixteen, eighteen, twenty inches in diameter. Such trees are no more than sticks in the Pacific Northwest, but here, in the high mountains of Wyoming, they're not only good-size—when it comes to lodgepoles, they're venerable. Woody has declared them the best house logs he's cut in the state.

Touching the trunk of the largest, I sight up to where its crown sways, slowly, gracefully, through the oh-so-blue sky. A slight breeze courses up there, eighty, a hundred feet off the ground. Down here, all is still. Once upon a time, the people who called this place home cut smaller lodgepoles into lengths of ten to twenty feet during the spring, peeled the bark, and set the poles aside. Come fall, the two-inch-thick trunks would have dried to a weight of only seven to ten pounds and would be stiff, strong, and virtually impossible to split. Lashed together and covered with buffalo hides, they formed the framework of a tepee, hence the name lodgepole. The poles were also good for making a travois, which served as the means by which Plains Indians, journeying to the mountains for tepee fixings, dragged the bundled lodgepoles back to the prairies.

When the first settlers came to the Rockies, they used the lodgepole (*Pinus contorta*) for fencing corrals, and also for sheds, stables, and sometimes even for cabins, as I'm about to do. The naturalist Donald Culross Peattie recounts in his great work *A Natural History of Western Trees* that the species was also made into fruit boxes and telegraph and telephone poles. Bridge pilings, mine props, railroad ties . . . these, too, were once fashioned from this two-needled pine. In fact, across the next divide at

Horse Creek, lumberjacks would fell lodgepoles during the winter, saw them into six-foot lengths, trim them square with broadaxes, then stack them near the frozen streams. During the spring spate, these future railroad ties were floated to the Green River, boomed (held by cables stretched across the creek mouths), and floated south when the water reached its best height.

So today, up here in Mosquito Creek, we stand in a long line of loggers. I rub my palms against the tree, put my nose into its bark and inhale. Dry for years, it has lost its scent. Then I wrap my arms around its girth, measuring its bulk. Having counted the rings of trees already down, I know that this tree is a little over a hundred years old, which is notable for the species but not senescent. Four-hundred to six-hundred-year-old individuals have been recorded. Still, compared with me this tree is an elder. It was a seedling before Wyoming became a state and before any white person homesteaded these valleys. It was already a little tree before my grandfather was born. It felt the ashes of the Katmai and Mount St. Helens eruptions fall on its needles and heard the silent mountains fill with the coming of trucks and atomic bombs and jets. It has witnessed the trapped-out beaver return and four generations of humans making deer and elk into meat. It has been present as these valleys were clear-cut and then reseeded, and now it is watching us take out the standing dead, of which it is one.

Even though our logging is selective and horse-drawn, and completed in this circle of sweat and friendship, I'm not totally at ease with what we're doing—especially because the trees are old and ready to serve others besides me. Left alone, they might provide food and homes for sapsuckers, great horned owls, a small bear. If I were a member of the family Ursidae instead of a human, such a fallen tree would be a delightful smorgasbord of ants and grubs, and, excavated a little, also a snug winter den. Eventually some of these trees would be split by lightning, others would be toppled by the wind; they would rot into soil. Our logging will short-circuit an entire community's changing shape, going on as it has done for eons.

Still, I'm neither bird nor bear, and our species hasn't lived like these beings—seamlessly, totally within nature—for hundreds of thousands of years. This old tree will feel no rot, won't mingle its juices with the soil it has known. No sapsucker will tap on its trunk, no black bear fill its bole with soft hibernal breath. It will ride down the valley on Woody's flatbed truck and become the ridgepole of my new house, hear the laughter of children, parents, and friends, listen to banjos and Beethoven, smell baking potatoes, Christmas pudding, and shampoo, watch moose and deer nose to its grovemates on the lower courses of the house, and feel ravens walk upon its back, as they once did here in Mosquito Creek. It will shelter my world—a sheltering that is, by my lights, as necessary as the sheltering of the bear. And I guess that the only way I can remain easy with its transformation from tree to human home is to be present as it happens, midwife as much as logger.

Above me, Tonio, Woody's helper this summer and also a naturalist from Costa Rica's Monteverde Cloud Forest, cajoles Milo, the huge chestnut gelding, backward toward a log. His voice, "Gee, haw, step," reminds me that I've been slacking off. Giving the tree a final pat, I begin to toss slash into piles, so that we'll have a clear trail to drag out the trees still to be cut. Four to six feet long, bristling with the jagged stumps of broken limbs, the slash needs both care and brute strength to move. I toss it downhill, wincing at what I'm crushing—willows, arnica, and beds of lush huckleberry—the bystanders and side-effect casualties of logging. But there is no clear spot of earth where the slash can be harmlessly piled. Vegetation covers the entire forest floor.

Those of us who divide the world into the sentient animal kingdom and the nonsentient plant kingdom might not give a second thought to crushing the undergrowth in this way as a by-product of logging—indeed, would never ascribe such anthropomorphic words as *seeing, hearing,* or *listening* to a lodgepole. By definition, the standing dead, as well as the live plants who inhabit our logging site and are destroyed as we cut skid trails, can't have such faculties or feelings, since they are *nonsentient,* nonfeeling. Investing them with such capabilities, or even the sentience of the animal kingdom, is unscientific. If you are a writer and venture into this territory, you commit what the poet John Ruskin called "the pathetic fallacy."

This division, of course, is one way to understand the world. However, if you spend enough time outside, in landscapes that are quiet enough, you may begin to hear other voices. Listening to the pines respire, the aspens confabulate, and the cottonwoods complain, you begin to wonder whether you are projecting your hopes and desires on the trees among which (whom ?) you walk. Are they mirroring your personality or do they have ones of their own? If, too, the hillsides nod as you walk home after a day's work, saying, "Together we have passed and loved and created another day," if you hear the kindly whisper of grass and the hum of starlight as you fall asleep under the dark sky, if the world starts to speak—and by this I mean not actual words but body language, as dogs and cats and bears have body language that can be read—then it becomes more difficult to apply the term "nonsentient" to all those who are simply not ambulatory. When you let yourself touch the pain and sorrow of live animals and trees as they become food and wood for humans, participating in that great mystery of recombination in which life dies only to bring forth new life . . . when you put your hands up to the elbows into the womb of nature through fishing, farming, hunting, logging, and tenderly caress the place from where life springs, lamenting as well when it departs its current shape . . . then truly is it difficult to reduce the world neatly into the quick and the dead, the knowing and the unconscious.

Granted, I've never heard broccoli scream under my chef's knife, as one of my more sensitive vegetarian friends has, but it has been clear for a long, long time that not only do elk prefer to remain elk instead of becoming each year my flesh and blood, but so too would my potatoes prefer to remain in the ground than go into my microwave, and lodgepoles would prefer to continue thrusting their crowns to the sky instead of supporting my roof. This understory of vegetation, I'm certain, would choose, if it could, not to be converted prematurely into duff under a pile of slash.

For thousands upon thousands of years, other hunter-gatherers saw the plant and mineral kingdoms, not just the animal kingdom, as thus infused with spirit and consciousness. They asked the ash to allow itself to be made into a bow; they inquired of the mountain if it would allow them passage. The sky-centered religions of Judaism, Christianity, and Islam considered these people to be superstitious infidels and lost souls (although why talking to a mountain seems any more superstitious than talking to an invisible God in heaven has never made much sense to me). The Enlightenment, putting its faith in rational man, in progress and perfectibility, continued the disparagement of hunter-gatherers, because these earth-centered people believed in processes that science could not verify with its instruments. We have continued that disparagement, doubting a Bushman who can predict the appearance of an eland or an elephant from over the horizon, because we still have no way to measure what the Bushman does. Only recently, as our recording devices have become more sophisticated—enabling us to hear the long-distance communication of elephants, for instance—have these nomadic people's keenness of observation and their enormous knowledge of the natural world been seen as rivaling or exceeding that of the most experienced field biologist and been given the respect they deserve. But the questions remains, How did they learn so much without radio telemetry, time-lapse photography, sensitive microphones—without even a ruler? The answer is hard for us to embrace. Such cultures differ from ours not in their lack of technology but in their immersion in quiet—a quiet that permits them to hear subtler voices than those which come to our ears. They live among ellipses . . . a state we consider full of omission, a leaving out, and that they see and hear as gravid with information.

Asking lodgepoles to allow themselves to be made into a house before felling them (even standing "dead" ones, for they haven't lost their spirit) is, I guess, my way into the renaissance of that tradition. Perhaps a better word than "living" would be "hearing"—hearing the spirit of the grand and imposing (these lodgepoles) filter down into the meek and innocuous, then turning that hearing into action. A few years ago, I began to put vegetable cuttings outside, and not solely for the utilitarian end of making compost for my garden. It seemed that the salad scraps were happier changing state in the grass around my cabin than in a landfill among unacknowledged trash.

"Wow!" say those who haven't watched the body language of the natural world express how it wishes to be treated. "This is far-fetched homage." Maybe . . . maybe. One can also look at the accretion of these small, heartfelt gestures—saying "Thank you" to the elk who becomes your winter's meat, bidding good-bye and hello to lodgepoles—as a way of moving through the world (what a Christian might call "soul," a New Age practitioner "aura," and a shaman "spirit") . . . a way of moving that is the real reason, not their stature or skin color, that no one mistakes a Sherpa or a Bushman for an American. The reverence that we enforce in our museums, concert halls, and places of worship these people of less compartmentalized cultures give freely to all their surroundings.

When someone from Western culture gives reverence to all in this way, he or she is often judged as slightly touched, certainly maudlin, not grounded. His or her beliefs, if carried out by many, are seen as leading to economic depression, entropy, the end of society as we know it. Again, that's one way to embrace the world. But a person can admit that everything counts, without simultaneously becoming inert. In fact, such an admission can make one more full . . . mindful . . . thoughtful . . . careful . . . which is another way of saying that one grows appreciative of the sacrifices being made to sustain life, and that by appreciating them more, one chooses wisely those sacrifices that must be made. Another word for this state of mind is compassion. Not surprisingly, the consumptive age in which we live is uneasy with the state of mind and heart that such words imply. With only so much space on our biggest hard disks, or in our walk-in closets, can any of us make room for a Father in Heaven or—closer by and more likely to be trampled by our thoughtlessness—the Mother under our feet?

Taking off my gloves, I touch the bank of swarded earth behind me. For a moment—the bell mare's tinkle floating down the mountainside, the thump of Milo's hooves in the soft undergrowth—I feel Her rich beneath us, valleyed and jagged with mountains to be sure, but on the whole curvaceous and breast-smooth, stretching away to the horizons . . . the Earth.

These days, in a return to the animism that informed the cultures that preceded the pagan Greeks and Romans, we have begun to speak to Her: Gaia, Doni, Baba Yaga, Sedna, Mother. She has so many names, holdovers and extrapolations from all those peoples who understood paradise as right here in whatever Mosquito Creek they were logging, not above and not in the future. Myself, I haven't found a name I can truly speak to, though at times like this, when I have my hands resting upon Her understory and put my mouth in Her for a taste—leaf, grass, berry, earth—I hear my voice responding to my stomach with the sound nursing mammals make, "Mmmm." At such a moment, I think of Her as no more and no less than this sound, "Mmmm." First food, first warmth, first name, first mystery . . . our first and last resting place.

Bearded and slight, his blue eyes laughing, Tonio joins me on the skid trail. We wrap chain around a previously bucked log, then send Milo galumphing through the forest. In another moment, Woody appears with his orange chain saw, which all of us respect but dislike for its noise. He pulls the starter cord, and the high-pitched *brrrrr-brrrrr-brrrrr* rips through the forest. Manicuring the path toward the lodgepoles, concerned about the width of the trail needed to get these giant trees out with the two-horse team, he flicks the bar toward the base of a six-foot-high spruce, who has had the misfortune to grow too close to the path we have chosen. He decapitates it neatly at ground level, and before it can fall catches it on the bar while still holding down the trigger. The buzzing chain tosses the sapling aside like a child hit by a car. Without a glance to the spruce, Woody continues to move through the forest, swinging his scythe.

I walk ahead of him, coming at last to the big tree I lingered by. Staring up to where it writes upon the sky, I stretch up an arm and place my palm flat against its trunk. Cone . . . seed . . . tree . . . house.

Woody comes in, makes a wedge-shaped cut on the downhill side, aiming it for the trail we have cleared. Sawdust flies around his knees like wheat from a thresher. He moves to the opposite side of the trunk and makes the felling cut. For what seems like a moment held in amber—the crouching man, the orange saw, the flying sawdust, the white trunk anchored into a pool of sunlight—the tall lodgepole doesn't move. Then it starts its slow silent arc through the canopy. I mark it: there against the sky; there beginning to sway; there swooshing, whooshing, crashing with a mighty breaking of branches and a dull solid thud, bouncing once before coming to rest. Soil to soil . . . earth to earth . . . our brief and lovely shelter. Standing next to the stump, I look up and see a blue hole where a world just stood.

THE HUMAN
CHAUVINIST WITHIN

LAWRENCE E. JOSEPH

Keith Milsap, a third-generation logger working in the original-growth forests of Washington State's Olympic Peninsula, died on the job at the age of twenty. He was a fine, respectful young man, American to the core, and brilliantly good-looking: fair, high-colored from the outdoor life, azure eyes deepset above ruddy cheekbones, a sparse hazel-brown mustache that sooner or later was sure to fill in. The young lumberjack was naturally fit and muscled, health-club bodies seem like forms without purpose, self-conscious approximations, by comparison. Keith had all the sparkling vitality of those actors in milk commercials, with none of the hype. In fact, he had a big glass of cold milk with his inch-thick steak the night I had dinner with him and his fiancée, Kim Richardson, several months before he was killed.

I met the couple in 1988, while on assignment to investigate the spotted-owl controversy. As we talked things over at the Vagabond Inn, in Forks, Washington, the self-proclaimed anti-spotted-owl capital of the world, Milsap made it clear that he was bound and determined "to harvest the crop that God gave us." He felt, as his father had taught him, that God had created those magnificent forests for man to harvest and it would be a sin to let the bounty rot in the field. He spoke of the sadness he felt when a felled tree was dropped or otherwise mishandled and, because of the damage, went to pulp rather than to serve its highest purpose, as fine lumber for someone's home.

Kim, the wit and warmth of that couple, teased her man about how much he loved the forest and hated the big city (Seattle). He protested that he was willing to travel anywhere in the world—anyplace where the fly-fishing was good, that is. Politely, he asked me about my work as a journalist, and I told him that one of the things I loved most about the work was traveling and meeting people and seeing out-of-the-way places. He looked at me with a touch of pity, as a happily married man might look at a bachelor whose greatest romantic joy was not in being with the right person but rather in the search.

It was Kim who called me late one night, after I had returned to New York, to say that Keith had been killed in a head-on collision while driving a loaded logging truck back to the mill. Maybe it was his fault. Probably he died instantly. Kim remembered my snapping their photo as they stood in front of the Vagabond Inn. It was the last picture taken of them together, and she wanted to make copies for herself and for Keith's parents. I managed to dig out the negative.

A moment's grief at the news of Keith's death has prompted me to wonder if the instinct to mourn the passing of another human being is not at odds with what our emotions should be, or are in the process of becoming. Instinct links us to other human beings for no other reason than that they are members of the same species. The power of that bond is largely projective. Most of us feel far deeper grief for the death of an individual than, say, for the destruction of an ecosystem. Yet in terms of what's good for us, for humanity and the rest of life on Earth, the fewer human beings the better. Doesn't it follow, therefore, that the death of a human being—particularly of someone like Keith, whose work was especially inimical to the magnificent and endangered original-growth forests of the Olympic Peninsula—should be a joy to the rest of us?

Try as we might to be ecologically correct in our emotions, many of us are still stuck in the old homocentric paradigm, in which birth is good and death is bad. Fortunately, there is a vanguard among us so highly evolved as to manage indifference, or even a touch of spite, at the story of Keith's demise. For example, the editors at the outdoorsy magazine for which I was on assignment declined to publish anything about the logger's passing, even when I offered them the story for free. Ditto a high-gloss publication devoted to praising the grandeur of the Pacific Northwest. These visionaries knew that running such a story might move some readers to sympathize unduly with the embattled logging culture that Keith held so dear. On the other hand, bewailing the plight of the rubber tappers and other endangered rain forest cultures is eco-O.K. The premature plucking of one mammalian weed from the swelling *Homo sapiens* mass—how tragic is it, really? Isn't the worth of human beings ultimately determined by the laws of supply and demand? Today we have pushed past the five-and-a-half billion mark and should hit double-digit billions before the youngest among us expire. More disturbing, the relentless increase in global median life span has multiplied the cumulative number of person-years that the planet is forced to endure. The average human being, for most of history an economic asset, is now a liability—particularly when the cost of waste disposal (including that of the carcass itself) is factored in. That means that each individual's value, young loggers included, is dropping like a stone.

How often enlightenment is preceded by momentary blindness! Having affirmed that the state of the planet is our utmost priority, and dedicated to the proposition that the next decade will be crucial to the survival of the race, we must fight against those impulses—seemingly charitable but actually born of our own fears and longings—that impel us toward erroneous sympathy. Let us never forget that emotions are fundamentally biochemical, and that however "genuine" they may feel, they can, with the proper self-discipline and/or pharmacology, be reconfigured to serve the greater ecological good.

Who knows? Perhaps the tropical rain forests will one day yield the perfect mind-altering drug. But I say, Let's try to do it cold turkey. After admitting there is a problem, we can take the first step on the path to reform, which is to challenge our widely held delusion about the sacredness of human life. Take, for example, the much-vaunted Mother Teresa.

What good are all her mercy missions if she refuses to support population-control measures to ensure that such squalor will never occur again? What folly the charitable dalliances of Omaha investor Warren Buffett, recently named America's richest man by *Forbes* magazine, who plans to leave his more than eight-billion-dollar fortune to fight world hunger! After people have a few good meals, the next thing they do is reproduce. Perhaps we should confiscate his estate, in the name of environmental action.

As the purpose of this collection of essays is to advance the cause of nature, I would like to propose a simple, novel, and self-sufficient program created not just to address the ecological problems plaguing our planet but to restore the value and integrity of personhood. The name of this program is Dynamic Demise.

Dynamic Demise (DD) is founded on the principle that suicide can be an act of ecological heroism. As such, it should be encouraged, and practiced, by those in power. When committed without coercion and conducted in a medically and environmentally responsible manner, Self-Initiated Departure (SID) should be seen as an expression of selfless love for Mother Earth, and therefore be rewarded handsomely. For the first time, everyone will have a chance to be a war hero, a champion in the struggle to preserve the planet.

The Dynamic Demise program is designed to dispel any initial resistance there might be to SID, given the residual negative associations that linger from the old "life for life's sake" mind-set. Who could disagree that death seems anticlimactic under the current involuntary system. For most of us, the end will come after months or even years of enfeeblement, the distinction between vivacious and moribund as gray as the hair and skin of those hanging on. But under Dynamic Demise, death will be the culmination, the pinnacle, the parting dramatic gesture, rather than a protracted and (to be blunt) less than entertaining withering-away.

What if, instead of grief, we felt joy at the positive, triumphant—indeed, glorious—act of a person offering up his or her life for the greater ecological good. Are not Christians, Muslims, and many other religionists taught that the greatest joy in life lies in the hereafter? The doctrine of Dynamic Demise says, Joy to those who bestow upon the rest of us the ecological blessing of relinquishing their claim to air, water, fuel, and other resources! Joy, and perhaps cash to their next of kin, in proportion to the amount of waste they won't emit and to the resources they won't consume, given their expected life span, general consumption habits, and so forth. Let there be a bonus, paid to the ecocharity of choice, for each kinsperson who joins in. Even the elderly, though they would have used up much of their life span, still have valuable and expensive end-of-life medical treatment to forfeit, and their SID will merit our heartiest applause.

For those wishing to leave a parting message, we propose the Farewell Channel. This twenty-four-hour cable service would carry the volunteers' good-byes, with prime-time programming devoted to youthful and celebrity departees, and might even prove a ratings challenge to MTV. The right to depart from scenic spots, such as San Francisco's Golden Gate (where the freedom to commit suicide is currently abridged), could be auctioned off to the highest bidder. Or awarded to those who demonstrate superior abilities in diving, gymnastic flips, dramatic recitation, and the like. Imagine, for a moment, the farewell routines of a series of world-class gymnasts, each performing flips, splits, somersaults all the way down the hundred and ten stories of the World Trade Center, to a spot dead-center in the Plaza. Nothing in the Olympics, with its ground-bound events, could come close to this ultimate competition.

A Cold Feet Assistance Squad (CFAS) will be helpful in exhorting those who, having committed themselves to voluntary departure and having reaped the benefits accrued thereby, hesitate. We propose that the Kevorkian Prize for Excellence in Suicide Assistance be awarded annually to the counselor who best exemplifies the can-do spirit of the legendary Michigan euthanatist. Indeed, CFAS presents an employment opportunity ideally suited to the aggressive lifestyles of today's inner-city youth. Special incentives, such as priority in choice of departure site, television coverage, and farewell-party facilities, will be offered to CFAS workers who go on to choose SID for themselves.

America can and must lead the way. While it is true that our population is not the largest, the densest, or the fastest-growing in the world, we are the undisputed leader in terms of per-capita consumption and waste production: a population of two hundred and fifty million inhabitants, but, judging by our collective mess, two and a half billion slobs. (A cruel irony indeed that those who waste the most—generally, the residents of affluent high-consumption societies, such as the United States, the European Community, and Japan—also tend to live the longest. To understand the twin crises of overpopulation and overconsumption from the planet's point of view, imagine having to lodge several times as many uninvited houseguests as ever before, and that instead of staying for only a couple of days the biggest slobs hung around for weeks!)

The time for change is now. I hereby dedicate myself to Dynamic Demise until every last detail of this program is fully implemented, not only as national policy but also as a ratified amendment to our Constitution.

Ask not what your planet can do for you but what you can do for your planet! Eco-activists of the world, unite! You have nothing to lose but your chains! Let us break the bonds of species affinity, smash the life-for-life's-sake dogma, and conquer the human chauvinist within. If for no other reason than that the alternative—caring for and respecting decent people like Keith Milsap, regardless of their beliefs—is utterly inconvenient.

THE CREATIVE SPIRIT
IN ART AND LITERATURE

JOHN HAINES

In the movement of trees, I find my own agitation.

> —*Wallace Stevens,*
> Opus Posthumous

*I asked myself whether the higher forms of the esthetic emotion
do not consist merely in a supreme understanding of creation. A
day will come when men will discover an alphabet in the eyes of
chalcedonies, in the markings of a moth; and will learn in aston-
ishment that every spotted snail has always been a poem.*

> —*Alejo Carpentier,*
> The Lost Steps

Creativity is a continuous and visible process inherent in existence, a
capacity latent in all living things, well described in a phrase by the
naturalist John Burroughs as "the vitality of connections." What we understand and appreciate in the creative process originated in a close re-

---

This essay was originally given as a paper at a conference on creativity at Ohio University, in
April 1990, and subsequently revised.

lation to and observation of nature and its processes; there is no creative intelligence apart from that.

Three years ago, while at home in Alaska, I was sitting at the desk in my small study in the woods one early summer morning, and looking out the window at a birch tree just beginning to bud. The dark branches mounting at intervals up the trunk were in sharp contrast to the pale, papery bark. It was a scene I had watched many times in the past. And as I was watching, I saw a small bird, a warbler, flitting from branch to branch, from twig to twig, up and down the tree in search of insects. The image of that bird in relation to the tree and its branches was arresting—in the constant movements, and then in their sudden significance. For it struck me that here, in a single and astonishing impression, might be seen an early stage of musical notation, with the bars and notes ascending and descending in scale.

For many years, I made the better part of my living from the wilderness of the far north, in Alaska. That is, I hunted and fished, and gathered food from the countryside. In doing so, I learned (in what I think of as a true sense) to read and interpret the country: the ground underfoot, the coming and going of creatures, the arrival and departure of birds, the seasonal flowering and fading of plant life. These things— the physical evidence of them—constitute a language, a grammar, and a syntax; they represent in some way the original perception we may have acquired of a fundamental order in things, in their relationships and significant connections. And by this I mean (among other things) story, narrative, the thread of sequence and consequence.

There is a close connection between reading signs in the snow—the imprint of a bird's wing or the scattering of leaves and seeds over the surface—and reading words on a page; the same inherent order and process is at work in both of these. And as the spring sun erases the snow and all of its signs and evidence, so do we from time to time find it necessary to erase what we have written and begin over, for the sake of a clearer definition and understanding.

The secret of creativity, of creative imagination, is not to be discovered in a laboratory, or in abstract theory, or in any dissection of the brain or the nervous system, or in computer models of intelligence—thinking machines and mechanical pseudopods—but in attention to the world; for me, that means mainly attention to the natural world—to such vital relationships as we may perceive there.

For when we begin looking—and I mean really looking, with an attention cleared of formulations and preconceptions—we begin to see combinations and possibilities, order and beauty, anywhere. Seeing the reflections of trees in standing pools, the light of the sun on leaves and water, the shapes of buildings and houses, the textures of stonework and pavement, the movement of clouds over the landscape: here, under our feet and close at hand, can be found those primary patterns of creative order.

Early in our history, we read the course and meaning of events from signs in nature: a prophecy in the flight of birds and the seasonal behavior of animals, in the metamorphosis of insects, in the waning and flaring of the planets. And there was in this first perception, surely, nothing either foolish or merely incidental. The capacity for observation and evaluation on which we depend in so many ways originated in that first attention to natural details.

From looking at the world, the details and events of forest and field, came the sense of balance and fitness—of economy and order, of esthetic rightness—that we value not only in the arts but in all activities and pursuits. The model for what we attempt exists in nature, and without it—without nature's example of how a thing can be, or ought to be—we may lose our sense of relation and proportion, and imperceptibly substitute for it some less reliable imitation of our own devising, thereby losing, little by little, that primary relation to the immediate and original object.

I have been strongly moved to see in Egyptian hieroglyphics the images of birds and insects: how hawk and ibis stand not only for themselves but for certain concepts; how the scarab beetle, in a particular configuration, is born of the lotus under the eye of the sun. Once, long ago, someone watched an insect warmed by the sun crawl out of a flower, and to that person this signified birth and creation. All things are connected in this fertile process: water, bird, insect, plant, and light—the great sun-given cycle of life.

Our sense of order, of proportion, of right relation, of what we call beauty—that which provides us with a certain practical and esthetic satisfaction—must have its source somewhere in an original model given us by natural forms, patterns, and the like. And among natural forms I include the human face and figure, the primary subject of sculpture.

For thousands of years, before high cultures evolved, people observed nature as a matter of survival, learned and imitated patterns in the world around them. It follows from this that an imprint has remained, a deep and irradicable understanding that certain arrangements are right and have prevailed, while others are faulty and less satisfying. We may not always be able to say just why this is so, but we do feel it. It is the one principle on which we can base judgment of a given act or piece of work.

We can see this fundamental relationship in many instances—in the way that an insect, for example, is put together, the way in which it functions. To anyone who has looked closely at a piece of machinery, the resemblance is obvious, and children will often see this.

Every artistic creation, whether it is a poem, a painting, a dance figure, a temple, or a musical composition, is an attempt to recover something of that original sense of order, of right proportion. Our capacity for wonder, for awe, our sense of the magical and the sacred, too, has its source here—in what we can call a state of grace, and which I take to mean a certain psychic equilibrium. I suppose that what we refer to as sacred is so because of some primal relation between ourselves and the world. We feel that a part of our being is hallowed or blessed by this, that some acts of ours enhance this feeling, while others violate it.

I suspect that in the interrelatedness of things—the world of shapes, colors, forms, patterns, and so forth—lies the origin not only of art but of religious emotion, of what Wordsworth thought of as his "moral being." In this perception of a fundamental order lies the entire notion of an ideal social order that we seem to aspire to but have never attained.

The ordering, the unifying or harmonizing, of scattered and apparently unrelated material is the very essence of the creative impulse. And this activity is everywhere much the same, whether it means ordering the characters and events in a story, the placing of objects and figures upon the ground of a painting, the arranging of objects in a room to make a pleasing and habitable space, or the placing of certain words and sequences of words in a metrical structure we call verse, or in a paragraphic order we know as prose. And one would have to say, too, that this basic description applies to systems of thought, to political and economic systems, and to all systems of social and hierarchical order.

This is what I understand as the creative process. What we refer to as artistic vision is an ability on the part of certain individuals—poets, artists, thinkers—to grasp and present to us, in words and in visual imagery, a kind of totality of relationships which represents the greater totality of existence. We may call this capacity *vision*—both in the sense of *seeing* and in the sense of *insight* into the fundamental mystery of life.

Implicit here is the element of play, the delight in fantasy that originates in the play of light and shadow, in the multiplicity of changing forms in the natural world—the interplay of things that suggest infinite combinations. Carpentier, in a passage from *The Lost Steps,* refers vividly to the action of the wind in tall reeds, a clump of bamboo, or slender trees, suggesting that in that waving and tossing, that bending and shaking, can be seen the origin of dance. This perception speaks as well for our delight in ideas, in organizing forms and spaces into a momentary coherence. The writing of a poem, the making of a book, are variations on an essential ability, born of necessity and latent in the human spirit everywhere.

I referred at the beginning of this essay to the restless, fleeting image of a bird in a birch tree. In conclusion, I am led directly to another image, that of the Cumaean Sibyl, the oracle consulted by the hero of Virgil's *Aeneid,* whose replies to the questions put to her were written upon leaves that almost immediately blew away in the wind. This compelling classical figure reappears in the final canto of Dante's *Paradiso:*

So is the snow unsealed beneath the sun,
  And so the Sibyl's prophecy was lost
  Among the light leaves scattered to the wind.

And the resolution toward which Dante's verse and his vision seems inevitably to be borne is this concluding figure of eternity:

Within its depths I saw, bound together
  By love into one volume,
  All the open pages of the universe:
Substance and accident and their functions
  Seemed intermingled in such a way
  That what I speak of is one simple light.
I think I saw the universal shape of things,
  Because in saying this
  I have the feeling of a greater joy.

It may be that the creative impulse can be defined as an eternal search, both actual and symbolic, for those lost leaves and the answers written upon them.

THE COLOR OF A BIRD'S EGG

BERND HEINRICH

The four tiny eggs that were cradled on feathers in a nest of moss, lichens, and spiderwebs were more beautiful than anything I had ever seen. They were greenish blue, marked with purple and lavender blotches and black scratchy squiggles. The cascading songs of a chaffinch rang exuberantly from the forest on that beautiful spring morning, and I knew I had discovered paradise.

I was eight years old, and with Papa's bedtime stories of his adventures collecting the eggs of rare waterbirds in the swamps of the Danube delta inflaming my mind, I was hooked. I became obsessed with finding the nests and eggs of more and more species. Each one was a triumph, and a lesson in ornithology, because each species has its own intricate and individual behavior that must be learned before you can find its nest.

Later, in grammar school and high school in Maine, I continued to search out birds' nests. My pleasure was so great that it did not seem that it could be morally right, and my carefully tended collection remained hidden under the floorboards of an abandoned shed. Now, close to half a century later, this collection of ninety-six species of Maine land-bird eggs with their nests is still in excellent condition, but it is housed in the museum and teaching collections of the University of Vermont. I long ago stopped collecting birds' eggs in the wild, but my fascination and enthusiasm have not waned. Instead, they have grown to encompass all living things. I grew up to be a biologist.

I still treasure these jewels, but now I do not arrange them in glass-covered boxes. Instead, I file their essence in my mind, and sometimes in scientific journals. The filing system I use is based on evolution, and it reveals levels of reality and beauty that were never imagined by Papa, or me. I now see the beauty of the eggs not only in nests in the field but also in the analyses of dedicated researchers.

First, you see the diversity. The eggs of the scarlet tanager, in a cup of loose twigs lined with dark rootlets, are sky blue and spotted with light brown in a ring at the larger end. Crows' and ravens' eggs are olive green with gray and black splotches and dots. The eggs of the eastern peewee are a light cream, with a wreath of reddish-brown and lavender spots about the larger end. These colors are set against a round nest-cup decorated with gray-green lichens. Woodpecker and kingfisher eggs—from holes excavated in trees and sandbanks, respectively—are translucent white and without any trace of markings. The different colors, or lack of them, are all products of evolution. How did they come to be? What were the selective pressures that generated them?

The combinations of markings and colors on birds' eggs may seem like creativity gone berserk. Why should the color of an eggshell matter? Why, indeed, have any color at all? There must have been reasons to add the color, or else specialized glands to apply color would not have evolved after the reptile ancestors of birds no longer buried or covered their eggs. So why are catbirds' eggs a bright, almost luminescent, blue, flickers' eggs pure white, and the loons' eggs a dark olive green?

Birds' eggs are marked by pigments secreted from the walls of the oviduct. They are uncolored before being laid and become painted when traversing the uterus; the pressure of the egg squeezes pigment out of the uterine glands onto the eggshell, and the motion of the egg affects the color patterns. It is as if innumerable brushes hold still while the canvas moves. If the egg remains still, there are spots, and if it moves while the glands continue secreting, then lines, scrawls, and squiggles result.

There is considerable genetic plasticity in egg color. Some strains of domestic chickens have the familiar white and brown eggs. Others have been bred that lay eggs tinted blue, green, or olive.

It is not surprising that Charles Darwin, with his wide-ranging interests, also thought about the adaptive significance of the coloration of birds' eggs. Since coloration is generally absent in the eggs of hole nesters—for example, woodpeckers, parrots, kingfishers, barbets, and honeyguides—he supposed that the pigmentation on the eggs of open nesters acts as a sunscreen to protect the embryo. The British ornithologist David Lack, in turn, believed the white coloration of eggs of most hole nesters allowed the birds to see their eggs in the dark. Yet even if it is advantageous for birds to see their eggs in the dark (which I doubt), we still have to explain the tremendous differences in colors and patterns, especially in the species that do *not* nest in holes. Why isn't one sunscreen best? And if one is, why don't all use it? And why are some hole nesters' eggs spotted? Perhaps, as Austin L. Rand, the former chief curator of zoology at the Field Museum in Chicago, has said, "Like some of the specific differences in nest building, variations in egg color are simply expressions of the general tendency of birds toward diversity." This idea, too, might be right, but if so it is only a small part of the elephant that the proverbial blind men try to describe by touch.

Nobody who has seen the drab buff, black-blotched eggs of a killdeer on a sandbar or the olive-green eggs of a snipe in a sedge meadow, or who has walked the tundra and flushed the semipalmated sandpiper and golden plover out of their nest, will doubt that one function of egg color is camouflage.

Experiments confirm that the color of some birds' eggs conceals them from predators. In one famous experiment, the Dutch Nobel laureate and ethologist Niko Tinbergen distributed equal numbers of naturally spotted eggs of black-headed gulls, uniformly khaki-colored eggs, and white eggs near a gull colony and then recorded the predation by carrion crows and herring gulls on these unguarded eggs. The spotted eggs suffered the least predation.

We might reasonably assume that the darkly blotched and spotted markings of snipe, killdeer, and gull eggs function as camouflage, and that they evolved under selective pressure from visually oriented egg predators. But why then do other ground-nesting birds, such as most ducks and many grouse, have *unmarked* eggs—eggs that cannot be considered camouflaged by any stretch of the imagination? Perhaps part of the answer is that most of these birds hide their nests in dense vegetation, and the incubating female's own body is camouflaged, and she sits on them or buries them with nest lining.

A pet mallard hen gave me the suggestion that this was so. The downy mallard chicks had been an Easter present for my daughter Erica, and they soon grew into ducks. The hen built a nest by scraping leaves together under a bush by the front window. Being well fed, she laid enormous clutches of creamy pale-green eggs. But I never saw the eggs uncovered. Each morning before she left, after laying an egg, she used her bill to pull leaves from around the nest to cover the eggs completely. The leaves were better camouflage than spots on the eggs could ever be. Years later, when my nephew Charlie and I made a canoe trip down the Naotak River, in Alaska, I found several willow ptarmigan nests, their numerous eggs heavily blotched and marbled with blackish-brown markings. I predicted that such camouflage indicated that the eggs would not be covered up during the week or more it takes to accumulate a full clutch, before incubation can begin. What a thrill it was to find that this was so! The nests were always in scrapes of pebbles and debris, where there was no material (such as leaves or grass) to cover them.

Many birds with nests that have no loose material with which to cover the eggs also have unmarked, uncamouflaged eggs. They include hummingbirds, pigeons, and doves. But these birds lay only two eggs per clutch, and they incubate as soon as the *first* egg is laid. Perhaps because none of their eggs is normally left uncovered for long, there has been no need to color them for camouflage.

This is probably the best explanation for the lack of color and markings on hole nesters' eggs and those of birds that lay small clutches: there was no need for color, so none evolved. Yet some birds—such as chickadees, nuthatches, and wrens—nest in holes yet still lay spotted eggs. (True hole nesters excavate their own holes and lay white eggs without adding any nest material.) I suspect, therefore, that the spots on the eggs of these birds are evolutionary baggage. They tell us that these species were previously open nesters who switched to hole nesting, or to building nests with a roof, in more recent evolutionary time. They retained the habit of building nests, as well as the coloration of their eggs, because there was no great selective pressure for change.

While the coloring and markings of birds' eggs function primarily as camouflage, they can also have the opposite function. On our Atlantic and Pacific coasts, on adjacent islands, and in Europe, murres nest on ledges and sea cliffs in colonies of hundreds of thousands. Several species of colonial cliff-nesting murres (as was also true of the extinct great auk) have eggs that vary widely in color and markings. The ground color of the eggs may be creamy, white, reddish, warm ocher, pale blue, or even deep greenish blue. The markings upon this ground color may be blotches, spots, or intricate interlacing lines of yellowish brown, bright red, dark brown, or black. Some eggs are unmarked. When a murre loses its one egg—its entire clutch—it lays another, and this one is colored like the first. In contrast, the closely related auklets of various species nest in burrows or rock crevices; the nest entrance serves to identify a bird's clutch of eggs, and so the individual eggs need no markings to be identified in the vast assemblage of others.

Chester A. Reed, an oologist during the heyday of egg collecting, in the last century, says of the murres: "The eggs are laid as closely as possible on the ledges where the incubating birds sit upright, in long rows like an army on guard. As long as each bird succeeds in finding an egg to cover on its return home, it is doubtful if the bird either knows, or cares, whether it is its own or not." Thanks to experiments by the biologist Beat Tschantz, of the Zoological Institute of the University of Bern, we know that Reed was wrong. Murres no more incubate one another's eggs than lobstermen tend one another's traps. Both use color markings to identify their property. Tschantz switched eggs and found that if an egg of a different color or marking pattern was substituted for the bird's own egg, that egg was rejected, but another egg with a similar pattern was accepted. However, the birds don't know *a priori* what color egg they produce. Egg color is learned. For example, if a murre's first egg is marked with white feces in small increments, the bird learns that color pattern and will reject eggs of its own pattern. This acute ability of murres to differentiate eggs by their color stands in strong contrast to the behavior of some birds—herring gulls, for example—which accept almost anything even remotely resembling an egg, of any color.

Reproductive success in murres is enhanced if the females can pick out their own uniquely colored eggs. In contrast, under the selective pressure of brood parasitism (the laying of eggs in the nest of another), a bird's reproductive success is enhanced if it can recognize the eggs of other birds in its clutch and then discard them. The possibility of parasitism would place selective pressure on the host bird to detect the odd-colored eggs. This would, in turn, put pressure on the parasite to produce eggs resembling those of its host.

Several species of cuckoo may have evolved the most sophisticated egg-color matching. The European cuckoo, for example, never builds a nest of its own. Among the various birds it victimizes are wagtails, which have white eggs densely spotted with gray; bramblings, whose pale-blue eggs have reddish spots; and European redstarts, which have blue, un-spotted eggs. The cuckoo eggs found in these nests usually match closely those of their hosts. The accuracy of the imitations is sometimes so good that even the human eye has difficulty in distinguishing the eggs of the parasite from those of the host.

It was long a mystery how such color matching could occur, for surely cuckoos do not control the pigment glands in their ovaries in order to match their eggs to those of their intended victims. The real answer, however, is almost as bizarre: In any given area, the cuckoos are thought to be made up of reproductively isolated subgroups called "gentes," whose females restrict their parasitism to particular hosts. Two or more gentes may occupy the same area, each parasitizing its own host. A given female always lays eggs of the same color, as will her daughters after her. She must identify the proper host, and this means that an adult female cuckoo will parasitize a bird like her foster parents.

In European passerine birds heavily parasitized by cuckoos, there has been potent selective pressure to foil the parasitism. Hosts have developed a strong attention to the egg color code, abandoning many nests with cuckoo eggs or throwing these eggs out. This puts stronger pressure on the cuckoos to produce even better egg mimicry. Only the well-matched eggs are accepted, and even then not all of them.

Parasitism in North America is no less severe, but the principal parasite of songbirds, the brown-headed cowbird, thus far has not evolved egg-color mimicry. Nevertheless, the cowbird is a highly successful parasite. It is one of the most common of our native passerine birds, and it is also one of the most widely distributed. According to Herbert Friedmann, a longtime student of avian brood parasitism, the cowbird—unlike a cuckoo gente, which is restricted to only one or a very few species of hosts—parasitizes more than three hundred and fifty species and sub-species of birds. Some species suffer heavily. Up to 78 percent of all song-sparrow nests in some areas have been victimized by this parasite. The cowbird, however, also occasionally lays eggs in the nests of such unlikely potential hosts as the spotted sandpiper and the ruby-crowned kinglet, where its eggs get damaged or evicted. Thus, there are both advantages and disadvantages to its nonselectivity, but the balance depends on the acceptance behavior of the birds it comes in contact with.

The cowbird was formerly known as the "buffalo bird" and is partial to open habitat. It has spread east from short-grass prairies in the Midwest only within the last two hundred years. In the Midwest, its former range, there is the beginning of color matching between some hosts and the cowbirds' eggs. Apparently some hosts are evolving rejection behavior. But in the East, which the cowbird invaded after the creation of open pastures, it still wreaks havoc among songbirds. In a recent study, Scott K. Robinson, of the Center for Wildlife Ecology, in Illinois, found that 90 percent of ninety-two wood-thrush nests were parasitized with an average of three cowbird eggs.

At this point in the evolutionary race, only some of the potential victims of the brown-headed cowbird have evolved appropriate egg-rejection responses. Stephen I. Rothstein, of the University of California at Santa Barbara, determined this by making plaster-of-Paris eggs and painting them to mimic cowbird eggs. He deposited these in a total of six hundred and forty nests of forty-three species. He found that two-thirds of the passerine birds accepted the parasite eggs, while only one-fourth consistently rejected them. Some birds, such as the red-winged blackbird, the yellow warbler, the phoebe, and the barn swallow, consistently accepted both fake and real parasite eggs, while others, such as the catbird, the robin, and the kingbird, consistently rejected them. Since the birds were either consistent "accepters" or "rejecters," he speculated that once the rejection behavior was genetically coded, it was of such great advantage that it spread rapidly and became fixed. We usually think of natural selection occurring over eons. Will wood thrushes and the threatened Kirtland's warbler (which most authorities believe would be extinct now if it were not for cowbird-control programs in its breeding area) genetically encode rejection behavior in time and be saved from extinction? As with all threatened species, a large population base is necessary for a source of genetic variability to draw from, but once present, the trait will spread most quickly in a small population.

Since a key component of defense against parasitism involves egg recognition, you would predict that means of detecting foreign eggs would evolve. For example, it would be easier to recognize a stranger's egg if all one's own eggs within a clutch were similar. Does this help explain that songbirds subject to parasitism have *uniform* egg coloring in the eggs of one clutch, while birds such as hawks, ravens, and crows, which are not plagued by egg parasites, have a variety of egg colorations in their clutches?

There are at least three models for a mechanism of rejection behavior. The bird could either innately recognize its own uniquely colored eggs, or it could innately discriminate against all "odd" eggs, or it could learn what its first egg looks like (like the murre), and then discriminate against all others. (It would then also have to evolve the behavior to abandon its nest or to remove the offending egg.) The last hypothesis is the most likely. Some sixty years ago, Bernhard Rensch, studying mimicry of cuckoo eggs in Germany, experimented by replacing the first three eggs in a nest of the garden warbler with lesser white-throat eggs. The warbler then ejected its *own* fourth egg! Rensch concluded that egg rejection was not on the basis of recognition of a bird's own eggs but on the basis of the discordance in appearance relative to the other eggs in the nest. But recent experiments by Rothstein show that, like the murres studied by Tschantz, some songbirds also learn to recognize the appearance of their own eggs, becoming imprinted with the image of the first egg they see in the nest. In an experiment that showed this most clearly, Rothstein removed all eggs in a catbird nest each day as they were laid, replacing them with cowbird eggs. Although catbirds normally reject cowbird eggs placed with their own, this catbird accepted a whole clutch of cowbird eggs. When Rothstein added a single catbird egg to the nest with cowbird eggs, the catbird rejected its own egg.

Why don't more birds practice the art of parasitism? As with many historical questions, we don't have an ironclad answer, but we may identify some of the selective processes at work. One possibility is that after a parasite has become established, and through millions of years improved its strategy, the hosts will have such good methods of egg detection that another bird just starting out would have no success. For example, the brown-headed cowbird could not likely become established in Europe, because the European birds, already under selective pressure to detect strange eggs because of the cuckoo, have evolved such a sophisticated egg-recognition system that they would not be fooled by the crude tactics of the cowbird. Analogies with the immune system—or for that matter political systems—come to mind.

There is another important implication of parasitism—one that affects the *variety* of egg colors among species. We can go from the premise that a parasite would have a great advantage if it could utilize a variety of hosts. And multiple parasitism would be easy if all of the parasite's potential victims had similar eggs. Any bird lucky enough to have *distinctively* marked eggs will most easily spot and reject a parasite's eggs. For example, brown-headed cowbird eggs are spotted brown, as are song-sparrow eggs. Song sparrows rarely reject cowbird eggs. But robins and catbirds, both of which have blue eggs, almost always do. Indeed, they reject any egg that contrasts with their own, not just cowbird eggs. For the fun of it, I have for several years painted robins' eggs red, blue, green, and other colors and then replaced them in their nests. The greater the color contrast from their own, the more likely are the robins to reject the "foreign" egg. That is, the robins uniformly throw out red eggs, but they commonly accept green- or blue-painted eggs, which look more like their own. Presumably birds which by chance (random mutation, for example) have purple, green, or pink eggs should also easily become rejectors of white brown-spotted (cowbird) eggs. In other words, to avoid parasitism a bird should have eggs that are different from those whose nests the parasite already uses. This would make for variety of egg color codes among different species but uniformity within the clutches of eggs in a single nest. And in general these are the patterns we see in nature.

Egg parasitism by cowbirds and cuckoos is very costly to the hosts, because the parasite destroys the entire clutch of the host; the young parasite hogs all the food, or pushes the foster parents' babies out of the nest. However, there is another, more subtle parasitism—that of birds laying their eggs in the nests of others of their own kind. For example, Harry Powers, of Rutgers University, has recently found that more than a third of European starling nests may contain at least one parasite egg of the same species. Starlings (which nest in holes) are unable to detect a stranger's eggs, and for "insurance" against such parasitism the birds lay no more than five eggs in a clutch, rather than six. Powers notes that, "If you start with five and pick up a parasite egg, you can handle it, but if you start with six, and get an extra one, you'll fall off the edge, because you won't have the resources to raise the clutch. Then *all* suffer." Chickens also routinely dump their eggs into any chicken nest they find, thus abrogating parental responsibility. Sociobiologist Paul Sherman at Cornell University has noticed such "egg dumping" in wood ducks. The behavior has been most observed in waterbirds under relatively crowded conditions or conditions of limited nest sites. It is probably especially likely in colonial birds and in birds whose eggs are hidden from view. Charles R. Brown, of Yale University, found that cliff swallows regularly deposit their eggs in neighboring nests whenever the opportunity affords. Recently, Charles Trost, of Idaho State University, found eggs of pinyon jays and magpies he had marked in one nest appearing in others of the same species, suggesting that the birds actually carried their own eggs to another nest. Perhaps there is, after all, an evolutionary reason for the "general tendency of birds toward diversity." Catbirds' eggs, by being blue, may be less camouflaged, but they may gain by providing a sharp contrast, so that a parasite's egg can be detected and evicted.

It would be strange indeed if birds had not evolved counterstrategies to reduce this perhaps most pervasive parasitism of all—that of laying eggs in nests of members of one's own species. Egg coloration could again play a major role, as it does in interspecific parasitism. If any individual bird had eggs of a different color from those of its neighbors and potential exploiters, then it would have a means of detecting their deceptions. It cannot mark its own eggs with initials, but unique markings would be equivalent. Few such studies are available, in part because egg collectors were impressed with the astounding differences among species and so collected only one or a very few sets of eggs thought characteristic of a particular species.

But within species, differences exist. Dr. Elsie C. Collias, of the University of California at Los Angeles, has found from a study of over a thousand eggs from thirty-four individuals, of a captive colony of African village weaverbirds that different females consistently laid differently colored eggs. Furthermore, her colleague Dr. J. K. Victoria went on to demonstrate that these females recognize their own eggs, because they reject from their nests those of other females that are marked differently from their own. A recent study by Wendy Jackson at the University of Washington showed that as many as a third of the African weaverbird nests in any one colony contain a parasite egg from another weaver. But females eject the odd-colored eggs. Presumably a female takes a chance that her egg will match those in another nest. Normally, a weaver can rear only three chicks at a time, so a fourth egg in its own nest is wasted, and the gamble to lay an "extra" egg in another nest has a potential pay-off.

It will likely not be possible ever to say with any degree of precision why a robin's egg is blue or a kingbird's egg is white and splotched with dark brown and purple. However, the diversity of patterns shows that there are different selective pressures at work. The coloration of birds' eggs reflects a long interplay of evolutionary forces, in the face of randomness and chance. This, in turn, "colors" the mind as well as the eye, and gives eggs an additional beauty that no person's brush could ever impart.

ELECTRON-MICROSCOPY: A CLOSER LOOK AT NATURE

GREGORY S. PAULSON AND CHRISTINE DAVITT

There is inherent beauty common to all organisms that share the planet Earth. Sometimes nature's spectacles are shamelessly blatant, such as the delicacy and grace of a butterfly in flight, or the ethereal beauty of the sun filtering through the canopy of a rain forest. But often the beauty is more subtle—for example, the proportion and symmetry of a spiraling snail shell. Perhaps it is all just a matter of perspective, and one of the most interesting perspectives you can have is provided by the high-level magnification of an electron microscope. Magnified several hundred times, even the grossest maggot or the slimiest slug reveals a hidden world of unimagined beauty.

There are two basic types of electron microscope: the transmission electron microscope (TEM) and the scanning electron microscope (SEM). Both of them use a beam of electrons generated by running an electrical current through a filament of metal, often tungsten, much like that in a lightbulb. As current passes through the filament, electrons are accelerated by a high-voltage potential (up to a hundred thousand volts) to form an electron beam. The beam is controlled by electromagnetic lenses, which work like the lenses of a camera, controlling the diameter, direction, and focus of the beam. Because the beam of electrons travels at a much smaller wavelength than a beam of light, electron microscopes have greater resolving power than standard light microscopes and can therefore be used to attain much greater detail of a specimen at high magnification.

In a TEM, the beam passes through an extremely thin slice, or section, of a specially prepared specimen. The specimen is viewed on a fluorescent screen. The TEM is typically used to examine internal structures of a specimen and magnifies up to around a hundred thousand times, while the SEM is usually used to study the external features of a specimen, typically at lower magnifications. In an SEM, the beam of electrons scans across and interacts with the sample, which reflects electrons to a collector, enabling the specimen to be viewed on a televisionlike cathode ray tube. The pictures in this layout, technically called electron micrographs, were all taken with an SEM.

Prior to being examined with the SEM, the specimens were dehydrated by soaking them in progressively stronger concentrations of ethyl alcohol. The specimens were then dried using an apparatus called a critical-point dryer. Drying a specimen at critical point prevents distortion and damage of the sample. After drying, the specimens were affixed to a specimen holder and coated with an extremely thin coat (less than one micron, or 0.00004 inches thick) of gold, using an instrument called a sputter coater. The gold coating grounds the specimen to the holder, preventing the specimen from "charging up" while exposed to the electron beam of the SEM.

Honeybees have several adaptations that facilitate the collection of pollen; perhaps one of the most intriguing is this pollen comb. Located on the foreleg, it is used by the bee to clean pollen off of its antennae. Photograph magnification 110. *Photograph by Gregory S. Paulson.*

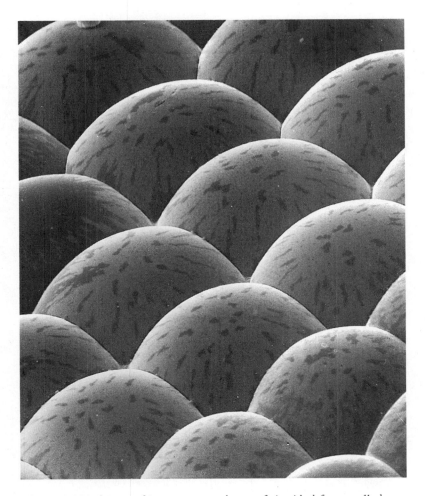

The compound eyes of insects are made up of six-sided facets called ommatidia. Some insects will have hundreds of ommatidia in each eye. From the side, the facets of this robber fly's (Diptera: Asilidae) eye look more like mounds than part of an eye. Photograph magnification 1110. *Photograph by Gregory S. Paulson.*

These "empty barrels" are actually the hatched eggs of a true bug (Hemiptera). The small protuberances around the opening are micropyles—conduits for gas exchange between the embryo and the atmosphere. Photograph magnification 50. *Photograph by Gregory S. Paulson.*

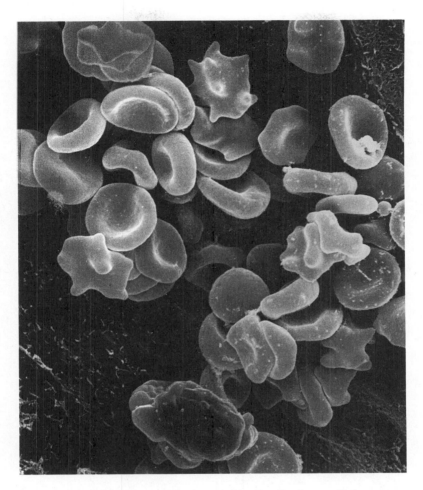

Red blood cells of a mouse. Like human blood cells, these cells have a characteristic concave shape. The oddly shaped cells are deformities caused by the preparation of the specimen. Photograph magnification 150. *Photograph by Christine Davitt.*

This fearsome creature is a water bear (Tardigrada), a tiny organism
(less than ⅟₃₂ inch, or 0.5 mm, long) that lives in mosses and lichens. These
animals have an incredible ability to survive drying and can lose up to 90
percent of their body weight through water loss. Photograph magnification
3500. *Photograph by Christine Davitt.*

The Mind's Eye

From a Novel

—⌇—

EDWARD HOAGLAND

I find that if I hike up the sidehill for about thirty minutes the soft mushy ground near the bottom, webbed with alder roots and half a foot of dead poplar leaves and big fountaining ferns like ostrich plumes as high as my chest, gives way to drier soil, with birch trees and maples. I can't see up as high as the leaves, but the white birch bark beckons me, and I know maple bark by its feel.

I am becoming crepuscular because of my failing eyesight. In the dusky or early light, my vision is best, and the white-skinned trees, like bright spots, are comforting. Along the small watercourses running almost straight down, through furrows in the hillside ten or twenty feet deep, I'll find firs and spruces—none very tall, because there's not much sun or rooting space for them between the rocks. A family of red squirrels will be quarreling, and a family of veerys *veery*ing. The wood sorrel under my feet is in pink-lilac flower, and the ground gradually gets so stonily steep that along with the return of some mosses and small ferns that suit a thin soil, we get little waterfalls, seven or eight or a dozen feet high. Nothing spectacular, if you were to stand back critically—but of course I don't; I'm grateful for them. I rest next to them, sometimes with my face at ground level to make them majestical—almost Niagaral—as if for the purpose of fortifying as well as entertaining myself. As the water runs blindly forever off jumps, into catch pools, and out to Jack Brook and the Athol River, so will I.

The delicate skin of green moss on the rocks is so lovely—or lush and thick like a coverlet, too, at other places where the species are different—that the black and white water, hiding in shadows or glinting with sun, is beautifully set off, and one is reminded of why there is such a division among photographers as to which people like color and which do not. The grainy veined boulders are purply brown, the canopy of branches and boughs are dappled with yellow sunshine where they don't close tight overhead. As you descend again, the brook spreads more generously over red and white pebbles, creates yard-size islands, scoots through a slot between rocks and goes underground for a bit, comes thocketting out, before hitting a kind of a raceway bedded in sand, then blocked by a log, with a pool beyond with shiners and fingerling trout. Old oaks over it. A flat, leaf-mold woods.

I love Jack Brook. Carol and I swim there, above where it cuts through my property, at a stretch that we call The Tubs, because they're like a series of scoops in a flooring of rock—potholes, I think my prep-school geology teacher would have called them, if I remember my field trips right.

You will wonder who Carol is. She's the daughter-in-law of the people I eat with, but she and their son have separated, and by encouraging her to work for me I suppose they're hoping to get rid of her, clear her out of a house they regard as theirs—though, with two kids, a court would no doubt give it to her. Randy works only sometimes, in the manner here. Canada is fifteen miles away, so not much is available anyhow—dairy farming, cottage industries, and the swamp and the woods. Rupert and Mae Curley, my hosts at lunch, have a farm, and I walk a mile or so to eat with them most noons. Carol comes over after that for a few hours. Makes supper, cleans, brings the boys—twins, almost three—which cheers me up. Carol is what you might call a hippie. She married Randy at a commune that is also located on this road, Ten Mile Road.

The hippies in northern New England are survivors of many years. Since the late sixties, they've been huddling by their woodstoves, almost as winter-proof as the Curleys are. They've seen the local kids abandon the military-style, redneck crewcut in favor of their own shaggy hairdos and take up smoking pot, and if they're not as good as a local boy like Randy is at going down in the swamp and "niggering out" logs for pulpwood for the paper company, they can do better by growing pot, because their heart's really in *that*. Carol, who straddles both worlds, says they're better at marketing pot too, because of course if Randy and his pals have ever been to a big city like Boston or New York at all, it's been when they've delivered a load of Christmas trees, dumping them off in midtown at a street corner prearranged on the phone and pocketing some currency and heading nonstop for home. They don't just truck Christmas wreaths and maple syrup and stuff like that to the city; they've figured out that flower shops need peat moss and fern fronds and dried flowers. They'll bring them down, with bushels of apples, turnips, tomatoes, brussels sprouts, or whatever they have, and if they've picked up an antique quilt or a spinning wheel, so much the better. But the notion of dickering over price with a bunch of pistol-packing drug dealers in a tenement house in the Roxbury section of Boston or a black housing project on the Lower East Side would flummox them. Even peddling the stuff to college kids on a campus would be beyond them; they'd have to split with a middleman.

You'll wonder if my "pathological myopia," as the ophthalmologists call it, has me going native—if I've lost my footing entirely. No, I still mix a decorous martini in the evening and I have let it be known that I want no marijuana planted on my land (the communards don't plant it on theirs because of the searches the state police do; they prefer paper-company land). But I do let Carol smoke a toke as I have my martini, because that means she may stay for supper, keeping me company, putting her little boys to bed for a couple of hours, while we listen to tapes we can both tolerate—not Mozart, not rock, but somebody like Joan Baez or Judy Collins, where our tastes coincide.

Carol is pale, with straight hair and a deceptively passive air. I call her the Coal Miner's Daughter, because she grew up in coal country in Pennsylvania, though she has since crewed on sailboats in the Caribbean and wintered in Belize and done other nice things that such people do.

The Curleys, my dinner mates—lunch is, of course, "dinner" here—are foursquare, blue-ribbon traditionalists, on the other hand. Have never been in an airplane, or to our nearest city, which is Montreal. They have the Bible instead of *I Ching* and Carlos Castenada in the house, and never speak of having indulged in even the usual Ten Mile Road and Ten Mile Swamp forms of outlawry—namely, moonshining and hooch smuggling across the line, though the wider Curley clan did specialize in these. Rupert Curley is highway commissioner, but in an old town like this one, where nothing ever happens, you don't live down your outlaw relatives by plowing roads for a generation or two. My own doggedness in turning up here at my summer place when I ought to be down in the city buying myself dark glasses and a white cane makes him feel friendly. He's a man who walks around half the day with a milking stool strapped to his ass (leaves your hands free) and practical living is what appeals to him. But he prods me to tell him what France is like. "I've heard about France," he says. I tell him French children drink wine instead of milk, and he says that's O.K. as long as they don't do it here.

We adjoin French Canada, so it's the French families here, like the Deveraux, that may still do some smuggling; and there's a hunter named Karl Swinnerton who lives at the end of the road who Rupert says has shot more deer than he's ever seen. Rupert will shoot out his window—he even got a bear that way once—but he claims that a good farmer only farms, does nothing else, and that the job of highway commissioner, which a couple of them fight over every March 1st at town meeting, is too much of a distraction as it is.

At least farmers keep all their fingers, he says. Randy, his son, who works in the woods, lost two to a chain saw soon after Carol gave him the boot. And his dog, who was with him at the time, quickly ate them.

"Then you can't never get rid of the dog. I've seen that three times," says Rupert. "Three people whose dog ate their fingers, and after that they feel they have to keep him until the day that dog dies. Of course he doesn't know what he's eating. Randy used to throw bits of sandwich to him, so any piece of meat that flies at him, he grabs it out of the air just like ham and cheese and gulps it down. You can't shoot the creature, as if you blamed him. But he's got your fingers in him, so you can't give him away to somebody else either."

I ramble over there for lunch. Mashed potatoes, cow meat that Mae's run through the grinder, gravy, and whatever root vegetable she's decided on. She gets five bucks each day from me for feeding me (she set the price: like milking an extra Jersey cow), and afterward Rupert and I and whichever "boy" is there from among his sons, nephews, cousins' sons, play pool on the sunporch. Or we've been known to go down to the stream and "drown a worm." But not Rupert; he goes to his barn. He believes that if he once went fishing he'd never stop, his productive life would come to an end, and as it is, work will barely break you out even. By his "boys," I include in-laws, who in the country add bulk to a family like this—add numbers of bodies that can be mustered for a quarrel with neighbors, or a vote at town meeting, or assembled at haying time or corn-chopping season, or for milking if somebody gets sick, or for fighting a snowstorm or clearing trees off the road after a wind if Rupert does win that vote at town meeting. His father died of a heart attack on the road as road commissioner, so he feels he should have a lock on the job.

And he's felt chest pains, too. "Milk sixty-five cows and then go out and plow roads all night after ten inches come down, until it's time to milk cows again, and the phone ringing all the time from people you haven't gotten to yet." (Cows are "keeyows" in the accent here.)

Mae is also a distant cousin, as she will repeatedly tell you with humorous emphasis; and they operate as "two dictatorships," she says, one inside the house and one out. Hers is for stockinged feet and cats and canaries, and while she doesn't regard Rupert as simply a necessary evil accompanying the main business of mothering children, she doesn't mind him calling her "the War Department," either, because she says it "keeps him respectful." In the traditional manner here, he inherited the entire farm, his sisters and brothers being just about totally left out of the will, once his father had made up his mind that Rupert was the one that could carry it on.

The big swamp below us is lozenge-shaped on a map but it doesn't feel like a comfy little lozenge when you go into it. Except for the railroad roadbed that runs through, there's nothing there till you get next to Canada, so this is the place where a good many of the town's kids play out their rituals of passage—whether it's poaching a goose out of season or skinny-dipping with your girlfriend in the river or trying to catch enough coonskins before Christmas so your mother can have a coat made. Mae Curley has one of these. She says she looks out the window and can see the apple trees that grew the fur that's keeping her warm.

In early June I heard a horn honk, and when I went outside I found a carful of kids in the drive, with somebody's mother accompanying them, who was one of those slender, shy, doelike women in a cotton turtleneck who live around here, who are both quite elusive-looking and as tough as nails, I have no doubt. Can ride all day with the snow-machine club, sitting behind their husbands in just a windbreaker and jeans.

"We could have gone in without asking your permission, but I wanted to set a good example to them," she said.

"Good."

"It's prom time. We want some orchids. Three boys. So three orchids."

I was confused.

"Corsages," she said.

"Oh! Sounds like fun. Can I see where they are?"

"I guess you can if you don't pick any—even though you bought the land." She laughed.

"How do you know what's my land? Did you grow up here?"

"I guess everybody knows who bought whose land. No, I grew up over the drugstore."

She had brought along, besides the three graduating senior boys, three younger children so they could see where the orchids were found. "Not all mine, thank heavens. No, I wouldn't have wanted to live on your land. My friend in school did, and every time we'd get a horse that we both could ride and keep in the pasture here, her father would sell it to the mink farm in Chelsea for drinking money—sooner or later. It was a hundred dollars just walking around to him. Oh, how we cried; it happened twice. One time we were standing out in the schoolyard, and here goes this mink-farm truck coming by and *our horse* is riding in the back of it! We shrieked—you would have thought he had run over us—and he knew why. His daughter was in school with us. But he didn't stop."

We all took the little path toward Jack Brook, but turned off on a path I hadn't noticed before, to a sort of lush sinkhole eventually, where the grass was different. And there were the lady's slippers, sure enough. Seven plants in full, pink bloom.

"My grandmother's orchid came from here," she said. "And my mother's too. And mine. If you graduate from high school you can have one for the dance, but not if you don't, and never take more than half."

She had scissors, rubber bands, a roll of wax paper, and a shopping bag. Each boy chose one flower for his date, and then she added some fern leaves and blossoms from the less conspicuous flowering plants that were growing nearby and practically completed the corsages as we watched.

"You can't sell flowers to the mink farm, so that's why he never ripped these up," she said.

When we got to the house, Carol had come—was lying in the hammock on the porch in a blue pullover and white shorts—and my new friend nodded to her, piled all the kids in the car, and left without my ever learning her name.

With pathological myopia diminishing my vision, I'm rediscovering my nose and ears. Just as small children lift things to their noses to smell, so do I. When I cook, I bring the pot to my nostrils for the crucial calculation of when the unseen dish is done. I cross the street with my ears pricked to tell me if the coast is clear. My bare feet inform me when the carpet needs vacuuming. And I recognize my friends more by their voices than by their faces now.

By adulthood we become responsible for what's in our minds—the character of the memories there, the music that we're familiar with, the store of books we have read, the scenery that we know and love, the people whom we can call. And you do find what's in your head when your eyes go bad. You can either recognize a mourning dove's whistling wings or not, and the wild geese calling overhead in the fall, and a winter wren, and the towhees' and indigo buntings' songs. When I'm crossing a schoolyard lot, I remember from experience where the kids will be running if they're playing baseball, soccer, football, though unfamiliar sports like Frisbee and archery throw me off.

In fancy restaurants, I can sometimes guess what the specials are without reading the blackboard—red snapper, duck, prawns, spinach salad. In a taxi at the airport, I can't really read the meter, but know how to pretend to do so to avoid being cheated. "What does it say?" I inquire, as I plumb my wallet; then glance confidently up and toward it as the cabbie turns around. Hugging becomes intensely important these days, and walking is such a puzzle as to be either exciting or tearful. So much of life that had been simple, habitual—supermarkets, small jaunts and visits—has become a riddle, a challenge, and in the case of driving, must be scrupulously renounced. At the market, I do remember how the food is organized, in what packages and colors and associations—coffee near the ketchup, bread close to the beer, and so on. I know, too, how to stroll into a bar, speak tellingly to grown-ups on occasion or calm a child, attempt to combat fatigue and insomnia, and manage my money. I know a bit about the cycles of life, the needs of my own sex and of the opposite one. However, my mind's eye is becoming my main eye now. And my sixth sense is my fifth sense, after my ears, nose, taste, and touch—which are all getting better.

I think it's worse to go gradually blind in the city. You lose the street signs, the store signs, the swarming intrigue of city faces, without the immensity of the sky and the trees to take up the slack for at least a good while. Nor can you walk around peering at everything through field glasses like me. Carol has the faculty of entering other people's enthusiasms, and she will point out a band of mauve in the clouds for me to focus on, or a goldfinch on a dandelion. It can be a joke, how constantly I'm shifting the lenses to spot a redstart out the window, changing from my telescope to binoculars, and how close I must lean to see her face. She teases me by testing my vision, making a joke between us of what is otherwise a sad thing by holding up a certain number of fingers to see if I can tell her how many. That way, she also figures out how far I can see for our swimming—taking off her clothes upstream from me and bathing in another "tub" with her kids.

What you have when you lose your sight is whatever body of knowledge you had before. Blue jays' various calls; a crow's caw versus a fox's bark (which is like a caw)—summer-camp stuff, but either you know it or don't.

An eagle can make out the shape of a mouse at a mile; and I can't. But neither can you.

Drunk on Honey: Seeing Ourselves in Nature

Chet Raymo

It's been a bumper year for Indian pipes. I can't recall another time when I've seen so many. As I write, in late September, they are common in the pine-oak woods, pushing up through leaf litter on the forest floor: covens of waxy-white wildflowers, ghostly, bewitching, vaguely demonic.

Corpse plant, ghost flower, ice plant: other names for Indian pipe convey that same spooky, cold-as-death impression. No gaudy petals, not a tinge of green, the Indian pipe simply doesn't fit our idea of what a wildflower should be. But a wildflower it is, a true, seed-producing, vascular plant, almost unique among our common plants in that it has no chlorophyll. Colorless in every part, or perhaps with just a hint of pink in the flower head, Indian pipe lacks the green pigment that enables other wildflowers to absorb energy from sunlight. It must therefore live off food produced by other plants. Like a mushroom, it derives its sustenance from decaying vegetable matter on the forest floor.

These spectral, parasitic flowers have inspired in their beholders a dark range of sentiments. In her wildflower guide published early in this century, naturalist and nature writer Neltje Blanchan draws a turgid moral tale. The plant stands branded as a sinner, she writes: "Doubtless its ancestors were industrious, honest creatures, seeking their food in the soil, and digesting it with the help of leaves filled with good green matter on which virtuous vegetative life depends; but some ancestral knave elected to live by piracy, to drain the already-food of its neighbors." Blanchan finds only one thing to admire in Indian pipe: "When the minute, innumerable seeds begin to form, it proudly raises its head erect, as if conscious that it had performed the one righteous act of its life."

Early nature writers like Neltje Blanchan cast their nets of likeness wide. Nature writers today are more sparing of allegory. We resist drawing moral lessons from flora and fauna. We are hesitant to stray too far from the aseptic, impersonal prose of science, fearful that we'll squander our credibility, afraid of not being taken seriously. But why? Nature writers are not scientists. We are writers. Scientists know by dissection; their method is reductive, analytic, single-visioned. Writers know by weaving such a web of likeness that the world is seen whole again. Nature writers should not feel beholden to science; our aim is esthetic, moral, synthetic. Anthropomorphic prose can serve our purpose.

I was raised on nature writing of the allegorical sort. In our family library when I was a kid were the fulsome works of Jean-Henri Fabre and Maurice Maeterlinck, astute observers of nature and masters of an-thropomorphic prose. Here is Fabre on the nuptial stroll of a scorpion pair:

With their tails prettily curled, the couple stroll with measured steps along the pane. The male is ahead and walks backwards, without jolt or jerk, without any resistance to overcome. The female follows obediently, clasped by her finger-tips and face to face with her leader. The stroll is interrupted by halts that do not affect the method of conjunction; it is resumed, now here, now there, from end to end of the enclosure. Nothing shows the object which the strollers have in view. They loiter, they dawdle, they most certainly exchange ogling glances. Even so in my village, on Sundays, after vespers, do the youth of both sexes saunter along the hedges, every Jack with his Jill.

And here is a passage from Maeterlinck's *The Life of the Bee,* describing the queen bee's nuptial flight: "Around the virgin queen, and dwelling with her in the hive, are hundreds of exuberant males, forever drunk on honey; the sole reason for their existence being one act of love." Even now, in these more explicit times, Maeterlinck's gushy prose makes us blush. What Hollywood scriptwriter ever wrote a steamier copulatory scene than this:

> She, drunk with her wings, obeying the magnificent law of the race that chooses her lover . . . rises still; and, for the first time in her life, the blue morning air rushes into her stigmata, singing its song, like the blood of heaven. . . . She summons her wings for one final effort; and now the chosen of incomprehensible forces has reached her, and seized her, and bounding aloft with united impetus, the ascending spiral of their inter-twined flight whirls for one second in the hostile madness of love.

These early nature writers drew more honey from the sex lives of birds and bees than any bee ever drew from a blossom, and if they projected onto creatures something of their own libidos, well, it has been commonplace since Aesop to endow animals with human traits. Modern naturalists report their observations in less fervid language, but they still, perhaps, project. An article in *The American Naturalist* titled "Marriage Entrapment by 'Solitary Mothers': A Study on Male Deception by Female Pied Flycatchers" uses words like "fool" and "trap" to describe how female birds, artificially widowed by researchers, trick male flycatchers into think-ing that they are the father of the female's brood. The voluptuous language of early naturalists may make us blush, but at least they drew their morals explicitly.

Earlier this year, tree swallows came to nest in bluebird boxes on conservation land near my home. The boxes weren't meant for swallows, but it was spring and first come, first served. The blue-green birds zipped across the meadow with strike-out speed, quicker than the eye could follow. Then, one Saturday in May, new boxes went up. The next morning a pair of bluebirds was in residence, the essence of quiet domesticity.

Male and female, they perched on the roof of their new home and surveyed the meadow. But the tree swallows would not leave them alone. Diving and darting, the swallows harried their new neighbors, sent the bluebirds fluttering from their box, disrupted their repose. As I watched this fractious scene, anthropomorphic metaphors came to mind. The swallows were feathered in "Brylcreem-slicked, sweptback blue." They darted with "zipgun speed." They flung themselves into the air like "sky-smart, speed-crazed teenagers cruising for trouble." Of course, the luckless bluebirds were "innocent victims."

What is this compulsion to anthropomorphize? Why can't I just let the swallows and bluebirds be? It's an old habit, deeply ingrained in our race, to see ourselves in nature. Aesop did it. Philosophers and theologians of the Middle Ages did it. Victorian naturalists did it unblushingly, and the tradition has been carried right into our own century. Disney created cultural icons by projecting human characteristics onto animals. And why not? Have we so fallen under the sway of scientific prose that we cannot take note of moral threads that stitch the world together? I am not talking here about some sort of metaphorical imperialism. We do not subvert nature by finding among the creatures likenesses to ourselves.

Here is Neltje Blanchan again, describing the house wren:

> If you fancy that Jenny Wren, who is patiently sitting on the little pinkish, chocolate-spotted eggs in the center of her feather bed, is a demure, angelic creature, you have never seen her attack the sparrow, nearly twice her size, that dares put his impudent head inside her door. Oh, how she flies at him! How she chatters and scolds! What a plucky little shrew she is, after all.

In another bird handbook from early in this century, Mabel Osgood Wright describes the American crow as a "feathered Uriah Heep" and the jay as a "robber baron." The bluebird is the "color-bearer of the spring brigade" and the song sparrow is "the bugler." One of my favorite anthropomorphic metaphors is F. Schuyler Mathews's description of the meadowlark's song as the first two bars of Alfredo's aria in *La Traviata*, "sung with charming accuracy." It is a charming metaphor, and instructive. It tells us something about the meadowlark, and something about our-selves. Mathews was another of the ornithologists who instructed our grandparents in nature's moral lessons.

All gone now. Anthropomorphic references in nature handbooks are proscribed. Nature writers go out of their way *not* to impose themselves upon the things they describe (as if it were possible not to). The human-izing metaphors of Maeterlinck, Fabre, and the rest are dismissed as forced, phony, homocentric. We no longer see ourselves in the animals and plants. We are too sophisticated for that.

But even as nature writers turn their backs on anthropomorphic prose, sociobiologists are suggesting that there may have been something there all along. They look to our affinity with other animals to explain not only our physical frame but also our moral and intellectual behaviors. Harvard University's E. O. Wilson, the father of sociobiology, places human intellectual qualities squarely on the evolutionary continuum. He writes: "The brain exists because it promotes the survival and multipli-cation of the genes that direct its assembly. The human mind is a device for survival and reproduction, and reason is just one of its various tech-niques." Thus, we look into our brain stems for shadows of reptilian ancestors. We examine the anthill for the origins of human societies. We study gorillas and chimps in the wild to discover the roots of human aggression and sexuality. Even our ethical systems and religions are part of our evolutionary heritage, say sociobiologists.

The world is in pieces, shattered by scientists. They have taken it apart in their successful search for subliminal laws. And when we have decided that nothing is truly real except the dissected fragments, then that is exactly what we get. Anthropomorphic metaphors may seem hokey, but at least they bind us to nature by moral likeness, and—according to sociobiologists—the likeness may be more than metaphor. In other words, it is not so much that the crow is a "feathered Uriah Heep" as that we are crows. It is not so much that jays are "robber barons" as that human robber barons share an evolutionary inheritance with jays.

Aesop and sociobiologists share a conviction that our common cause with animals is more than limbs, gullets, and genitals. For Aesop—as for early nature writers—animals symbolize human virtues and vices. For sociobiologists, humans embody animal characteristics through the agency of shared genes and evolution. Even the spooky Indian pipe is part of a web that includes ourselves, a web of shared chemistry and evolution. In anthropomorphizing plants and animals, we express something about the wholeness and interdependence of life. These metaphors are not empty; they embody truth.

Our metaphors, of course, will change with the times. For instance, I would be disinclined to admit that Indian pipe deserves its reputation as grave robber and spook. The plant is no more or less ghoulish than any other wildflower parasite—pinesap, beechdrops, broomrape, or dodder—and considerably prettier than most. In this day, when the recycling of waste and the frugal use of resources are considered honorable (indeed, imperative) activities, Indian pipe cannot be faulted for squeezing a modest living out of the squandered residue of summer. ("In summer, greenness is cheap," said Thoreau.) Plants with chlorophyll can afford to be spendthrifts; Indian pipe pinches pennies.

The poet Muriel Rukeyser wrote: "The universe is made of stories, not atoms." Telling stories is the writer's business. Stories bind. Contemporary nature writers can learn from the likes of Blanchan, Maeterlinck, and Fabre. We should decline no device that will help make nature whole again.

KISS AND TELL

⌢

JUDITH STONE

Until an infant sea lion kissed my foot, I had no real plan for saving the planet.

But that ticklish reinitiation into the animal kingdom gave me notions. They didn't sort themselves out, though, until some time after the encounter on a serene beach in the far Galapagos, the chain of fifteen large and six small volcanic islands slung along the world's waist six hundred miles west of Ecuador.

Here, astonishingly, wild creatures—some of the rarest and most richly varied—don't flee humankind, despite a long history of betrayal to the brink of extinction. In the mere three decades since this place has been covered by the laws protecting paradises, all seems to have been forgiven.

What a treat it was not to strike terror into the hearts of other living things! I could spend hours regarding rubbery black marine iguanas sunning in sloppy, chummy piles like discarded dime-store dinosaurs; instead of bolting, they simply grinned and dozed. A six-hundred-pound tortoise, who may well have lived a century and a half, regally extended his leathery neck for me to stroke. And, most thrilling of all, that curious month-old sea lion told me with a whisper of whiskers that I wasn't the enemy.

Madly anthropomorphizing on the strand, I regarded the pup's probing as a smooch and an invitation. Swimming with its sleek clan, I attempted to mimic their dipping and looping; they looked back as if to say, "You poor, pale, porky fish! Can't you manage any tricks?" I had never frolicked with wild things before, unless a New York City subway ride counts. It was almost more bliss than I could bear.

Back in the city, I recalled at odd moments the pup's huge eyes, its goofy, touching cry—a cross between a lamb's bleat and a car alarm. At the grocery store, offered a choice between a paper bag and a plastic one, I would try to calculate the ultimate benefits of each to sea lion and company. Haunted by the vision of a tiny, tender nose sliced by some discarded can tumbled from an overstuffed rogue garbage barge, I got tough with my landlord, who is haphazard about recycling, despite city ordinances. I hate such confrontations. But the pup made me do it.

I wasted less. I made donations to organizations dedicated to saving our seas. After looking at photographs of small creatures suffocated in oil, I eschewed a certain gasoline credit card, in spite of the inconvenience. I didn't do nearly enough, of course, but I was becoming a less lazy and more careful citizen of Earth. A princess was being transformed; that kiss had awakened sleeping duty.

The more I traveled, the more I had to think about besides the pup. A moist, fern-fringed forest at the top of California, for example, and the feel of a particular seventeen-hundred-year-old redwood already ancient when Marco Polo met Kublai Khan on his travels. Or the mouth of a cave in India's Thar Desert, where, at the final moment of sunset, a thousand swallows swooped through the new dark, grazing my hair, to shelter for the night.

There were people, too: Azucena, a ten-year-old coffee picker I met while touring a collective in the cool mountains of Nicaragua; Kho Tan, an inspired guide through the ancient Burmese capital of Pagan, by the shore of the Irrawaddy; he'd led us among the town's two thousand temples shaped like bells and beehives and corncobs, and worried that his "unhandsome" salary wouldn't pay for the arthritis treatment his father needed; Solveig, who grows plums and cherries in the Norwegian village of Lofthus, on the Sørfjord; Costas, a fisherman on the tiny Greek island of Kastellorizon, who chatted with me while he mended his nets, holding the yellow strands with his toes as he wove.

Because of these people and places, I can no longer ignore certain stories in the newspaper, damn it: A tanker sinks off Greece. Costas's catch! Acid rain from the factories of North America and Western Europe is showing up in the streams and soil of the Norwegian mountains. Solveig's plums! The repressive military regime cracks down again in Myanmar. Can Kho Tan survive? Congress is stalling on an aid package to Nicaragua. Will Azucena ever have the chance to go to school? Believe me, I want to turn the page and get to the Bloomingdale's ads. But all these people and trees and fish I've met have been nagging at me, changing the way I read and shop and donate and vote.

Travel isn't just broadening, I've realized, but burdening, too. I now carry these lives and places with me. But I'm grateful for the ballast; it's keeping me from tipping into total complacency. Call it benevolent narcissism: Once I've been to a place, I care more about it. I'm grateful to the pup for the reconnection; I should have kissed *its* feet. And I hope to keep doing better, thanks to the Greek (and Norwegian and Burmese and Nicaraguan) chorus in my head.

And what if, I recently mused, people with power to do more were similarly affected? What if the folks with the whole world in their hands carried the whole world in their heads and hearts? I'm thinking especially of the corrupt and the careless, the shortsighted and the self-serving, the architects of human disasters and the violators of the wild.

So here's my plan: I want to sentence these people—the profligate, the polluters—to . . . travel. In far, wild places.

Would those anxious to drill for oil in the Arctic National Wildlife Refuge be quite so interested once they'd waltzed with wolves there? Could the head of a waste-disposal company so readily approve a plan to dump lethal toxic sludge in an African village after playing tag with its children? If he'd spent a few weeks in a rain forest, with the wet, silvery web of life filigreed on his face, would former United States Secretary of the Interior Manuel Lujan have been so quick to ask in 1990, "Do we have to save *every* subspecies?"

It's easy to ignore or hate or hurt an abstraction, not so easy when a person or a place is specific and real to you. My scheme would make the world more specific, real, intimate.

Though I highly recommend it, these ecologically backward types I'm talking about needn't submit to a sea lion's kiss; I realize enforced bussing is highly controversial. There are only a couple of rules: They must break bread with people in the places where those people live, and they must look them in the eye. The regions they roam must be remote, lovely, and in peril.

"Oh, we get it," you're saying, winking broadly and nudging one another in the ribs. "If the CEO of Exxon had frolicked with an otter in Alaska's Prince William Sound, he'd have been so concerned with the critter's welfare that he'd have insisted that more care be taken in overseeing the company's shipping subsidiary, thus avoiding a mishap that caused several billion dollar's worth of damage, the deaths of tens of thousands of animals, and damage to shoreline and tidal zones that will persist well into the new millennium?" Yup. That's what I'm saying.

As a young naturalist, Charles Darwin was inspired by the variety of wildlife in the Galapagos Islands to formulate his theory of evolution by natural selection. He found thirteen species of finch, identical except for tiny differences precisely suiting them to the islands on which they lived. Birds living among flowers had long slender beaks for sipping nectar; those surrounded by seeds instead of blossoms had thick, tough beaks that worked as nutcrackers. Darwin reasoned that the animals changed over time, passing on characteristics that helped them successfully adapt to their surroundings.

The Galapagos has inspired me to formulate the Sea Lion Theory of Global Salvation: Send the right people on an adventure vacation, and fast! As soon as possible, our species needs to evolve beaks capable of sipping this planet's nectar before its sweetness is forever lost.

A GATHERING OF BIRDS

^

KAREN PRYOR

I have been studying animals and their behavior all my life. I spent my childhood summers catching butterflies and hunting minnows in Connecticut. I have since then floated over coral reefs to see what the fish are doing. I have dived among wild dolphins and watched mothers nursing calves and rival males fighting. I have seen flamingos feeding in freezing salt lakes in the high Andes. I have exchanged remarks with a signing chimpanzee. I have gone to school and published papers and books about behavior.

While the behavior I watch might be interesting, even thrilling, it has seldom been inexplicable; courting, fighting, feeding, tending babies, communicating—these are activities common to many sorts of living things. The first truly baffling piece of animal behavior I ever saw occurred in the yard of a house I rented one summer in Vermont. I had been living in New York for some years, earning a living as a writer and occasional scientific consultant. One spring day I took a walk, noticed a buttercup blooming in a vacant lot, and felt my eyes fill with tears. I thought about that, and decided I was homesick for the New England countryside of my childhood. I wanted fields, brooks, woods, ponds, dappled sunlight on dirt roads, cicadas buzzing, Queen Anne's lace.

I was working on a book on learning and behavior and the central chapter was giving me unexpected difficulties. New and quiet surroundings might help. So I made a foray to Vermont and rented the house of a schoolteacher who planned to be away for the summer. The house stood on a dirt road, surrounded by lawn, then hay fields and woods. There was a brook across the road. Buttercups in the grass. Cicadas and Queen Anne's lace would surely come in August. Perfect.

I packed up the cat and my typewriter, drove north, and moved into my new territory just as the birds were moving into theirs. While I wrote, they sang.

When I finished my work each day, I would wander around in the fields and woods looking for wildlife. I saw a mother and baby porcupine. I saw a businesslike red fox trot off to work across the fields in the afternoon. I saw a pine marten, a rare and thrilling sight to me, trying and failing to raid the nest of a pair of kestrels in the top of a huge maple behind the barn. (The clamor of the parents drew my binoculars to the event, and also succeeded in driving off the marten.)

I located, I thought, all the nesting birds on the premises: A pair of flickers in an old butternut tree in the pasture; the red-winged blackbird, with his three wives, down the road in a patch of cattails; the catbird, robin, and warbler families in the underbrush; and several other species.

There were bluebirds raising a family in a nest box put out for them by the schoolteacher, and they showed me something I'd never heard of or read about, though no doubt it is old news to ornithologists: bluebirds can catch grasshoppers in their wings. Here's the technique: spotting a grasshopper in the lawn, the bluebird spreads its wings and stalls out, as it were, fluttering vertically down onto the grass like a falling leaf. The grasshopper doesn't read this as an attack, at first. When it does jump, it's a moment too late. The grasshopper thumps into the inside of a spread wing, from whence the bluebird, by ducking its head, neatly snaps it up. I watched the bluebirds doing this from the kitchen window, and so did the cat, making *k-k-k-k-* hunting sounds and lashing her tail.

The Vermont sojourn was good for my country nostalgia and good for my work, too; after a couple of weeks of false starts I found the tone I wanted and began making real progress on the book. But being alone in the country was not really good for me. I became profoundly, ferociously lonely—lonely, it seemed to me, not for any one person but for my own familiar cluster of humanity, my neighborhood.

My fourth-floor corner apartment in Manhattan overlooked two small but busy streets in Greenwich Village. From my window, I could see what kind of sandwich Reuben was making in his delicatessen, and for whom. If my upstairs neighbor, the wine critic, came out of the butcher's with a large package, I knew he was giving a dinner party. I saw the cops whooping their patrol-car sirens at their girlfriends. I saw old ladies walk their dogs, and often I knew the name of both the walker and the dog.

All these people knew me, too. We were not social friends, but we recognized each other—we were all part of the neighborhood. If some event of interest occurred, we all took part in it. For example, there was the day Duke caught the mugger. Duke was an elderly harlequin Great Dane belonging to the antique shop in my block. Like a lot of big dogs, he had hip trouble, and rarely moved more than he had to; mostly, he lay in the shop doorway. He was always polite to customers. He never needed a leash.

One day, I heard screams—real screams—coming from the street. I rushed to the window in time to see a smallish person in white running down the sidewalk, carrying a big black purse. The screamer was a woman at the far end of the block, presumably the owner of the purse. The thief, hotly pursued by a plump bearded gentleman who was losing ground, reached the street corner just as gimpy old Duke, walking beside his owner, reached the corner from the other side of the building. Surprised to see someone running, Duke gamboled forward in play (it was probably the first time in years he had done anything so energetic). The mugger, terrified, attempted to change direction in midair and fell to the sidewalk, kicking. Duke, now looking confused and a little worried, put his big mouth carefully over one of those kicking legs, whereupon the mugger became still as a statue, enabling the bearded gentleman to catch up. He very sensibly sat down on the mugger.

A small crowd gathered, a crowd in which I could see several familiar people. Duke sat by his owner. Reuben came out of the deli and gave Duke a pound or so of pastrami, which he ate. Bob the butcher came out of his shop and gave the dog a steak, and he ate that, too. The cops drove up and took the mugger away, and the crowd dispersed. Later, someone in my building who had been in the crowd told me one thing I'd missed from the window: the mugger was a woman.

In our city neighborhood, this was an entertaining rather than an alarming event. Petty crimes exist, and our neighborhood had put a complete stop to this one. Just so, some country event, such as the butchering of a hog, might be traumatic to an urban person, while being only mildly interesting to locals.

Now, in the country silence, I missed not only the eventful life of the city but also having those many familiar people all around me. The quiet countryside seemed dangerous without my neighbors. The result was acute insomnia. I couldn't get to sleep, I couldn't stay asleep, I couldn't even nap without starting awake at every sound. Alcohol made it worse, exercise made no difference, and I knew better than to try pills.

One morning, I woke up about 4:00 A.M.—too late to go back to sleep, too early to start writing. In a mood of irritable despair, I made a cup of tea and took it outdoors. I sat down on the lawn on the east side of my rented house—the side facing the road—to watch the sunrise. It was a part of the yard I ordinarily avoided, since sitting there might entail talking to the occasional stranger passing by on that narrow dirt road, and I felt unwilling to do that. But dawn was just breaking and passersby seemed unlikely at dawn.

At the edge of the lawn, about twenty feet from me, was a little dead tree hardly bigger than a sapling, the only leafless tree in the yard. By and by, I noticed that there was a bird in the tree—a veery. I often saw two veeries feeding along the road. As I watched, a catbird flew in from the thickets, where I knew it had its nest. With it came two of its fledglings. Then a red-winged blackbird landed in the upper branches, presumably the male from the patch of cattails down the road. I was surprised; he seldom strayed this far from his own premises. Next, into the little tree's bare branches came a male Canadian warbler, with his tidy necklace of black spots on yellow vest showing up in the increasing daylight: perhaps the very one who was nesting in the bushes down by the brook.

Then I saw the male flicker sail in from the butternut tree in the pasture. The flicker landed on the trunk of the sapling, hanging on vertically as woodpeckers do, right next to the warbler. They weren't six inches apart. A flicker is quite a big bird, almost pigeon-size, and I myself would be a bit nervous that close to its wicked woodpecking bill; but the warbler, not much bigger than a golf ball, didn't move. This was getting incredible; why were these diverse species gathering in one tree? Why were they being so sociable? They were not feeding, they were making no sounds, they were just gathering.

For that matter, what birds, nesting on this old farm, were *not* in this one little tree? Robins, I thought, and sure enough, here came both the male and the female robin, with their disheveled, noisy fledglings. And then a bluebird. What *was* going on here?

Then from the sky, fluttering onto the lawn at the foot of the little dead tree, came a scrap of black and white and shocking pink; it was a rose-breasted grosbeak, a bird I had not seen since childhood and did not know was nesting on the place. (I later realized why I'd overlooked him; I was locating nests by the birds' songs, and the grosbeak's song was so similar to the robin's that I never trained my binoculars on him, assuming that I already knew who he was.)

The whole thing—this little tree at daybreak, cluttered at final count with one or more each of eight species of birds—was incomprehensible, and the grosbeak somehow was the last straw. I got up and took my teacup indoors, shutting this bizarre sight out of my mind for the time being.

That fall, however, when I got back to New York, I went out to the zoology department at Rutgers University in Newark, where I knew some top-notch young naturalists (nowadays called behavioral ecologists). I described this gathering of birds to them and asked them what was going on. They believed that I had seen what I said I saw—and I was glad, because some professors would not have—but they had no idea what the birds were doing. One mentioned something about migration. The others simply shrugged. It would be four years before I found out for myself what was happening—and the solution would come six thousand miles away.

The following summer, I married an old friend (the decisions and changes involved in this step may have contributed to that Vermont insomnia, I now suspect). My husband's business as an aquaculture consultant took him to southern Chile several times a year; on some trips, I went along.

We spent a lot of our time in Chile in remote rural areas, usually as guests of the owner or manager of a fish farm. My husband worked all day, and I often had a lot of time on my hands. Luckily for me, a dolphin researcher I know who had spent a lot of time in Chile had lent me his rare copies of Johnson and Goodall's *Birds of Chile*. A. W. Johnson was an English mining engineer who spent much of his adult life as a businessman in Santiago. His real life's work, however, was birding, and he accomplished many years of fieldwork. In 1946, with his friend, J. B. Goodall, an amateur painter, he published in Spanish two volumes covering every species of bird in that Andes-isolated land. An updated English-language version came out in 1967. *Birds of Chile* is distinguished by Goodall's delightful, naïve watercolors and Johnson's even more delightful (and very sophisticated) behavioral observations.

I had never before seen any of the species of birds in Chile, except English sparrows and some migratory shorebirds. So Johnson and Goodall became my constant companions. When I was tired of reading novels or practicing my ersatz Spanish, I went out into the woods and fields and looked for birds.

In the south, along the windy, lonely shores of Seno Ultima Esperanza (Last Hope Cove), I saw Chilean flamingos and flightless "steamer" ducks—so-called because they flee by running across the water, beating with both wings like a paddle-wheeled steamer; several spectacular species of Andean sheldgeese; and black-necked swans with their babies riding on their backs. In the vast and unpeopled national park, Torres del Paine, we saw condors, Darwin's rheas, the huge Magellanic woodpecker, and

wild parrots. In tumultuous Andean rivers, we saw torrent ducks calmly
bathing themselves in the seething rapids. In the villages and towns of
the coastal islands, I learned the names of the common songbirds in
people's gardens—gardens very like those of home, with roses and cab-
bages and apple trees—but with other birds standing in for New England's
robins and blackbirds.

On our fifth or sixth trip, we spent part of the Christmas holidays in
the lake district of Chile, staying at the lakeside vacation house of one
of my husband's fish-farming clients. The client's family had preserved a
nice patch of native forest behind their house, in what was otherwise
largely farmland; this made for splendid birding. I saw the big wine-
colored native pigeon there for the first time. I spent numerous hours in
the woods, crouching near a stream trying to spot the *chucao,* a sort of
waterbird. The *chucao* has a magnificently loud gobbling song, which, alas,
it can throw like a ventriloquist, making it impossible to spot the bird,
though one is being deafened by his racket.

One morning, I got tired of this fruitless hunt and instead went out
across the lawn to the rail fence along the bluff, to look for ducks on the
lake below. The acres-wide mowed lawn was not usually a good place for
birds, except for the omnipresent *queltehue,* a big ploverlike bird that
lives in open fields in pairs, and rises with a flash of white-banded wings
and a loud clamor when disturbed. (The *queltehue* is such a noisy alarmist
that Chilean farmers have been known to pinion them and keep them in
the farmyard as watchbirds.)

I stopped by the fence next to a six-foot clump of kila grass, a relative
of bamboo, left by some gardener's whim to stick up from the well-
mowed verge of the bluff on the other side of the fence. I looked out
over the beautiful lake, Lago Llanquihue, with its highly ornamental snow-
covered volcano, Osorno, on the far shore. It is a famous view; our host's
house and every other summer villa on the lake is oriented to take in
the sight of the lake and Osorno's snowy cone.

Great scenery. No ducks. Gradually, however, I became aware that
there were some little birds very close to me in the kila grass; three or

four *jilgueros,* little yellow sparrowlike birds. Then here came a *diuca,* the gray singing finch that in Chilean gardens occupies an ecological niche similar to that of the song sparrow in North America.

Then a couple of *zorzals,* the austral version of our robin, flew into the kila clump, followed by a handsome little red and black *cometocino.* All of them sat in the kila thicket, saying nothing, doing nothing, and amazingly close together. I looked over my shoulder to see that even the suspicious *queltehues* had tiptoed within ten yards of me, although when I looked back they hurried away, pretending they weren't involved.

As a finale, a little fire-crowned hummingbird landed in the topmost twig of the kila grass and glared about with the typical hostile stare of male hummingbirds, raising his spiky crest so that he looked like a furious version of the bird in the "Peanuts" cartoon. With the vast blue lake and the snowcapped cone of Osorno for a background, the clump of kila grass, crammed with a dozen species of birds, looked like a bad museum display: "Songbirds of Chile."

I realized that I was looking at just what I had seen in Vermont: a gathering of birds. It was summertime below the equator, and just as in Vermont this gathering consisted of the males, with some females and young, of small territorial birds all nesting on our host's property. This time, however, the birds were only two yards away, the sun was shining, I was rested and wide-awake, and it was obvious what the birds were doing. They were looking at me.

I was a novelty. Men pushing lawnmowers, they knew about. The property owners, coming and going in cars, no doubt with children and dogs, they knew about. But presumably nobody ever strayed down to the lawn's edge for no reason. That was new. And while I of course cannot pinpoint exactly what was especially novel about me to the birds, they appeared to be looking most particularly at the object hanging from my neck—my binoculars. I had drawn a crowd. It was just like the day on Tenth Street when Duke caught the mugger and neighbors gathered to see the interesting sight, except that this was a neighborhood of birds.

That is also, of course, what the birds in Vermont had been doing:

gawking. Their neighborhood Person was in the wrong place, at the wrong time of day, with the wrong object—a teacup—in hand (the Vermont birds presumably *expected* my binoculars). So they came to see what was going on. Here I had been feeling so isolated and alone, and yet I had been a well-observed member of a neighborhood after all.

The phenomenon called mobbing, in which various species of small birds join forces to attack a predator such as a hawk or owl, is well known, but aggression is gaudy and obvious behavior and has been the focus of much behavioral research. The phenomenon of neighborliness, however, has I think been rather overlooked. In both Vermont and Chile, I am sure, it was not just any small birds that came to gawk at my odd doings; it was those specific birds in that specific neighborhood. Being territorial defenders, each one would have driven off any member of its own species that tried to set up housekeeping nearby, but they didn't mind other species. Just so, Reuben the delicatessen owner on Tenth Street probably felt no animosity toward Bob the butcher or Sam the dry cleaner but might have been distinctly upset if another delicatessen had opened on his block.

I was witness to the fact that these birds shared neighborhood duties and events easily. From the relaxed behavior and physical closeness of the birds, I judged that they knew each other by sight, maybe even as individuals; in my experience, even in the close quarters of a cage small songbirds usually avoid sitting with birds they don't know. Maybe these birds were drawing comfort from each other's familiarity: oh, that's just "our" flicker, "our" catbird, "our" red-winged blackbird, "our" *diuca;* I know him. Would a stranger, a bird from another farm or field, have caused consternation in the kila-grass gathering? Maybe so.

The day after I saw the gathering of Chilean birds, I went out with a camera at the same hour, hoping to photograph my audience. The birds were having none of it; they'd already checked me out and lost interest. Not a single bird showed up. But I was elated, anyway, to have solved my mystery. The bird gathering fixed itself in my mind as an example of a strong evolutionary phenomenon across many species—a phenomenon that I think is almost completely overlooked, at present, by science: by physical ecologists, by ethologists or behavioral biologists, and by experimental psychologists. We don't even have a technical term for this phenomenon, so I can give it only anthropomorphic names: Neighborliness, friendship. It would be a good area for serious investigation, though; the seeds of social peace might be in it.

SWIMS WITH FROGS

ROGER B. SWAIN

The best approach to frogs is on their own level. Leave the meadow its milkweed and August asters, and instead belly up to the pond's bank in an inner tube. Half submerged, legs spread, arms dangling, you can scan the shore—the sedges, the ferns, the colonizing alders—and count each pair of bulging eyes. Where the sphagnum moss curls down over the pond's lip is where the bullfrogs crouch, looking like fat, clenched fists.

It is futile to stalk them on foot; they'll jump at your approach. But drift up to them slowly, staying low in the water yourself, and you can get close enough to look into their eyes, the black horizontal pupils with their encircling rings of gold. And if you hold your arm so that it's underwater, you may even be able to reach out and briefly finger a soft mottled-white chin. Then, with the suddenness of a kingfisher's cry, the frog will shriek and leap out over your head, sometimes slapping two or three times across the water like a skipped stone before diving and burying itself in the mud at the bottom. Scull to where it disappeared and cup your eyes against the surface glare, and you can see where it is hiding, down past the long amber-flecked cords of pondweed, down where the shafts of sunlight converge.

This tiny blue chip on the United States Geological Survey map is our investment in frogs, though we didn't know that twenty years ago when we built the pond. At the time, we were simply taking the Soil

Conservation Service up on its offer to help landowners construct farm ponds. The Soil Conservation Service was intent on the advantages of such ponds for flood control, for watering crops and livestock, for fighting fires. We, on the other hand, were thinking of swimming. Nobody was planning for frogs.

Two hired bulldozers did the excavating, uprooting the stumps of the trees we had felled, pushing the topsoil and rocks aside, and scraping the underlying material into a two-hundred-foot-long crescent-shaped earthen dam. The engineers had designed the dam to raise the water to a depth of only four feet, so, in the interests of swimming, we sent the machines deeper still, until we were looking down on the tops of the twin earthmovers, their bright yellow flanks caked with the gray mud of freshly exposed glacial till.

It took a week before the operators were finished digging and shaping the pond's contours. Their last act was to breach a temporary dike they had constructed to divert water coming from the spring that bubbles out of the ground among witch hazels and royal ferns a short way above the pond. But other springs within the pond were already filling it. So were the frogs. Scarcely had the last bulldozer rumbled back up the hill toward the road than the first frogs appeared, staking their claims at the edges of the muddy, oil-speckled pools.

By the time the water reached the level of the overflow, the pond was fourteen feet deep and a third of an acre across. It took a winter for the water to clear. And it took a few years more for vegetation to cover up the last of the machinery scars. Today, though, a meadow of wildflowers covers the dam. Daisies, orange hawkweed, black-eyed Susans, goldenrod, pearly everlasting, and vetch have taken the high ground. Closer to the water are clumps of turtlehead, gentians, and the round-leaved sundews, whose sticky red hairs slowly digest passing ants. Were we to stop our annual mowings, the surrounding white pines, gray birches, and red maples that are mirrored in the water's surface would soon press their offspring right up to the shore.

We like to boast that we swim here nine months of the year, and we have pictures to prove it—one of us grinning manically at the camera after going in on a dare on the tenth of March, posing naked and barefoot on a sheet of ice. But most years it's not human swimmers but frogs that take the first plunge. The seven species of frogs and two species of toads that occur in this part of New Hampshire all lay their eggs in freshwater. To them the fact that this pool is unchlorinated is even more attractive than it is to us.

The wood frogs—diminutive frogs with dark-brown raccoonlike masks—hibernate under forest debris and swarm to the shore when there is still some ice on the pond. After a few days of frenzied mating and egg laying, they disappear again, back to the privacy of the woods. It is easy to miss the emergence of the wood frogs, but there is no mistaking the spring peepers. You may not see the tiny frogs themselves, but their high-pitched clear calls, massed like the incessant jingle of tiny bells, can be heard a quarter of a mile away. Their nightly nuptial chorus goes on for weeks, the males calling from wet hillocks of grass or the stems of shrubs at the water's edge. It is as much the signature of spring as the cicadas' song is of summer.

We are not privy to all the amphibian mating that goes on along our pond's banks, but we can certainly spy the consequences. On the mornings after, we find the shallows littered with eggs, some in gelatinous clusters, some loose on the bottom, others attached to submerged stems or bound in long jellied ropes. They aren't all frogs' eggs, or even toads', for we also have salamanders, the blue-spotted and yellow-spotted ones, and the red-spotted newt.

The mating and egg laying pass quickly. By the time we have finished planting the garden, it's not eggs we see but tadpoles—or, rather, pollywogs, as we say in New England. Their appearance coincides with our own annual return to the water.

There are many attractions to a farm pond. It's not the exercise, for there is enough of that on the land. But a swim is a chance to soak one's black-fly bites, a way of washing up without the inconvenience of a formal bath, a break from the endless cycle of work. But in a pond like this what is even more alluring are the tadpoles. They are the reason we linger, after the requisite swim to the other side and back, after the lathering up with the bar of soap and the one last plunge. There is something endlessly fascinating about frogs-in-the-making, and kitchen strainers were made for scooping up tadpoles. There in the bottom of the mesh basket, you can check each fat, shiny wriggler for signs of legs. Our own prenatal growth is visible only through fiber-optic lenses and ultrasound, whereas the metamorphosis of frogs takes place in full view. So we begin every summer by scouting the shallows, scooping up tadpoles ahead of the spreading cloud of silt, performing our well-baby-frog checks.

By August, however, the nursery has largely emptied out. The frogs we spy as we drift in our inner tubes are chiefly bullfrogs and green frogs. There's no mistaking the bullfrog's call, its distinctive "jug o' rum, more rum," which it continued to repeat all the way through Prohibition. The green frogs don't grow to be as large, but you can't tell the two species apart by size alone. You have to get close enough to look for the lengthwise fold of skin that runs along each side of the green frog's back. The leopard and pickerel frogs at this time of year have gone farther inland to forage. We regularly surprise them as we pick beans in the garden—athletic-looking frogs with lines of dark spots or squarish blotches down their backs, jumping across the rows of peppers, taking refuge beneath the potato vines. But like the warty toads that patiently share the garden, too, they have come from the water and to it they will eventually return.

Some of our summer visitors, joining us for a swim, are less appreciative of our pond's wildlife, and a few are downright hostile. We have one friend who insists on always wearing a bathing suit—for protection. He dives from the dock rather than risk wading in and encountering something along the bank. Other newcomers take the opposite tack and ask whether we have stocked this pond with fish. Or they tell us that they have just seen a fish break the surface out in the middle. We say it was probably a turtle surfacing or a dragonfly laying eggs. When they insist on showing us the fish, we take a look ourselves and patiently explain that it's a newt or one of the slow-maturing bullfrog tadpoles, which take two or three winters to become frogs.

Our certainty that our pond has no fish in it comes not from any fisherman's frustration, nor from the fact that we have swum here so many times that we know the pond's waters cold. Rather, it comes from the way that the pond is constructed. A vertical pipe, two feet in diameter (big enough, the engineers say, to handle all but the hundred-year flood) rises to the surface under the dock. Water flowing over its lip drops three feet to a concrete pad before exiting sideways through a pipe that runs through the heart of the dam. Over the years I have on more than one occasion cursed this design; for example, when beavers exploring up-stream neatly packed it full of branches, mud, and moss. Since then, we have enclosed the pipe's mouth with a chain-link fence, and covered it with the dock.

There are those who say that piped spillways are inherently bad designs—that sooner or later they always get plugged up or leak. But at the moment we have come to see this spillway as something special. Yes, its maintenance is an added chore. But it serves to keep fish out of the pond. Even the most gung-ho trout will not be able to fling itself up the vertical section of the overflow. And this very fishlessness of our pond, far from being a disadvantage, is what has given us our abundance of frogs.

On the face of it, you might think that any pond big enough to support fish ought to have them—that they would complete the diversity of pond life. But, in fact, fish are such extraordinarily efficient predators of am-phibians that their presence actually decreases diversity. They snap up tadpoles with enough thoroughness to extirpate entire species.

We didn't discover this for ourselves, because, despite the repeated encouragement of friends, we've never set about to stock this pond. Instead, the insight comes from Owen Sexton, a professor of biology at Washington University in St. Louis. *Signals from the Heartland,* a recent book by Tony Fitzpatrick that profiles the ecology of Illinois and Missouri, contains a chapter describing Sexton and the remarkable story of his inadvertent experiment with frogs and fish. The bare facts are contained in a 1986 paper in the *Transactions, Missouri Academy of Sciences,* titled "A Qualitative Study of Fish-Amphibian Interactions in 3 Missouri Ponds," but that makes it sound like a dry tale.

In layman's terms, what occurred was that a series of three artificial ponds were constructed at Washington University's Tyson Research Center, located in western St. Louis County. The largest of these ponds, the so-called Railroad Pond, is, like the others, filled only by runoff water. It is situated some two hundred yards from an intermittent creek that runs to the Meramec River. Repeated sampling of the pond by Sexton and his students in the years after its excavation in 1970 found eleven species of amphibians using it for some stage of their life cycle.

On April 11, 1979, nearly five inches of rain fell in one hour, and the overflow from Railroad Pond created a short-term connection between it and the stream, and on December 8, 1982, heavy flooding of the Meramec River sent it high enough to flood the pond's outlet directly. Both events introduced fish. Fathead minnows, green sunfish, and golden shiners were the first species found; later they were joined by black bullheads, bluegills, and largemouth bass. In the years since these two invasions, amphibians have continued to be abundant in the vicinity of Railroad Pond. And in fact, their abundance hasn't changed in the one pond that wasn't flooded. But the number of amphibian species found in Railroad Pond itself has plummeted. From a preinvasion species count of eleven, censuses in the years since—with seines, dip nets, drift fences, and pit traps—have never yielded more than two. The only consistent species has been the bullfrog, whose tadpoles are not only the largest, and thus the hardest to swallow, but also have distasteful skin. For all the others, however, Railroad Pond has become a lethal nursery.

You don't have to be a herpetologist to be aware that frogs and other amphibians are facing hard times—not just in ponds that have been intentionally or unintentionally stocked with fish, but all over the world. Since the 1970s, and especially in the last decade, researchers have noticed dramatic drops in amphibian populations in a wide variety of habitats in Europe, Asia, Africa, and Australia, as well as in North and South America. And what is most disturbing is that some of these declines, like that of the golden toad in Monteverde, Costa Rica, have occurred in seemingly pristine locations.

The dependence of most amphibians on freshwater for reproduction has, of course, made them especially vulnerable to urbanization and its accompanying draining or filling of wetlands. Water pollution from chemicals, pesticides, and acid rain have all been implicated in the decline. Even the increase in ultraviolet radiation as a result of ozone depletion may be part of the problem. And frogs under stress may have become vulnerable to epidemics, such as the red-leg disease that has recently been suggested as a proximate cause in *Froglog,* the publication of the Declining Amphibian Populations Task Force.

In the wake of his paper's publication, Owen Sexton says that he has received a number of letters from pond owners around the country not only reporting similar results when they introduced fish but also saying that now they were sorry they had done it. I, for one, am cheered by the news, the word that our investment in frogs has proved to be the right one. In a world that is already well stocked with anglers and fish hatcheries, what we need are more frog hatcheries—places where the water is fresh and clean and fish-free. Some will be temporary pools—seasonal accumulations of runoff, whose short duration precludes any possibility of fish. But others will be permanent bodies of water, like this pond, that by design or historical accident have never been colonized by fish. Whether created by glacier or bulldozer, these are special waters, attracting many voices. We who swim with frogs need to add our own.

VOYAGEURS

SCOTT RUSSELL SANDERS

for Olivia Ladd Gilliam

In morning mist on a northern river, a slab of stone tumbled from a boulder into the water, where it came to life and floated, turning into a sleek black head that swam in circles dragging a V of ripples behind it. A beaver, I thought, as I watched from shore. But no sooner had I named it than the creature bobbed up and then dove, exposing a long neck and humped back and pointed tail. Not a beaver, I realized, but an otter. I was pleased to find a label for this animate scrap, as though by pinning the right word on the shape-shifter I could hold it still.

Presently a second otter, then a third and fourth broke free of the boulder and slithered down into the mercury sheen of the river. They dove without a splash, their tails flipping up to gleam like wands in the early sunlight, and they surfaced so buoyantly that their forepaws and narrow shoulders lifted well out of the water. Then one after another they clambered back onto the rock and dove again, over and over, like tireless children taking turns on a playground slide.

My daughter Eva came to stand beside me, the hood of her parka drawn up against the cool of this July morning here in the north woods, on the boundary between Minnesota and Ontario. We passed her binoculars back and forth, marveling at these sleek, exuberant animals.

"Wouldn't you love to swim with them?" she whispered.

"I'd love to sit on that boulder and let them do the swimming," I answered.

"If only they'd let us!"

Always quick to notice the flicker of life, Eva had spent the past two summers studying birds with a research team, and now, halfway through college, she had become a disciplined as well as a passionate observer. Science had complicated her vision without lessening her delight in other creatures.

"What do you suppose they're doing?" I asked.

"The technical term for it," she said, "is goofing around."

"I suppose you've got some data to back that up."

"I'll show you the graphs when we get home."

Drawn by our whispers and watchfulness, the others from our camp soon joined us on the granite bluff, some bearing mugs of coffee, some with plates of steaming blueberry pancakes. We had been canoeing in the Boundary Waters Wilderness for several days, long enough for the men's faces to stubble with beards, for the women's faces to burnish from wind and sun. When all ten of us were gathered there beside the river, intently watching, suddenly the otters quit diving, swiveled their snouts in our direction, then ducked into hiding beneath some lily pads. After a couple of minutes, as though having mulled over what to do about this intrusion, they sallied out again and resumed their romping, chasing one another, bobbing and plunging, but farther and farther away, until they disappeared around the next bend.

If our scent or voices had not spooked them, then our upright silhouettes, breaking the glacier-smoothed outline of the shore, must have signaled danger to the otters. There was no way of knowing what else, if anything, we meant to them. What did the otters mean to us? What held us there while our pancakes cooled, while acres of mist rode the current past our feet, while the sun rose above a jagged fringe of trees and poured creamy light onto the river? What did we want from these elegant swimmers?

Or, to put the question in the only form I can hope to answer, what did *I* want? Not their hides, as the native people of this territory, the Chippewa, or the old French voyageurs might have wanted; not their souls or meat. I did not even want their photograph, although I found them surpassingly beautiful. I wanted their company. I desired their instruction, as if, by watching them, I might learn to belong somewhere as they so thoroughly belonged here. I yearned to slip out of my skin and into theirs, to feel the world for a spell through their senses, to think otter thoughts, and then to slide back into myself, a bit wiser for the journey.

In tales of shamans the world over, men and women make just such leaps, into hawks or snakes or bears, and then back into human shape, their vision enlarged, their sympathy deepened. I am a poor sort of shaman. My shape never changes, except, year by year, to wrinkle and sag. I did not become an otter, even for an instant. But the yearning to leap across the distance, the reaching out in imagination to a fellow creature, seems to me a worthy impulse, perhaps the most encouraging and distinctive one we have. It is the same impulse that moves us to reach out to one another across differences of race or gender, age or class. What I desired from the otters was also what I most wanted from my daughter and from the friends with whom we were canoeing, and it is what I have always desired from neighbors and strangers. I wanted their blessing. I wanted to dwell alongside them with understanding and grace. I wanted them to acknowledge my presence and go about their lives as though I were kin to them, no matter how much I might differ from them outwardly.

The root of *wild* means "shaggy hair," and *wilderness* means an unruly place where shaggy creatures roam. I became shaggier during our stay in the Boundary Waters, for I had left my razor at home in Indiana, as I had left behind my watch, calendar, and books. Because of limited cargo space in the canoes, and because every item would have to be portaged many times, each of us was allotted for personal gear a bag the size of a grocery sack. Packing for the trip, Eva and I whittled away and whittled away, aiming to carry only the essentials.

Discovering the essentials, after all, is reason enough for going to the wilderness. When everything that you will use for a week must ride on your back or on the back of a friend, you think hard about what you truly need. With twice the cargo space, I still would not have carried a calendar or a watch, not even a book, my favorite tool. I wished to unplug myself from all our ingenious grids; to withdraw from print, from telephones, mailboxes, computers, from radio and television. There were the earth and sky to read, sun and belly for keeping time. As for the razor, my whiskers would grow without any tending.

I decided not to shave on the morning of our departure. By the next morning, when we reached our putting-in spot on Fall Lake, near Ely, Minnesota, I looked like a bum, according to Eva.

"If you wrapped yourself in a greasy blanket," she told me, "you could beg for spare change."

I rasped a palm along my jaw, but I would not see the bristles until my return home, for I avoided mirrors in truck-stop restrooms on the drive to and from the Boundary Waters. As we slid our canoes into Fall Lake shortly after dawn, the surface was calm enough to mirror the shore, and I could have studied my reflection by gazing straight down. Yet I felt no desire to see my face, not then, not once all week. I meant to leave behind whatever I could that had the word *my* attached to it.

On that first day, Eva and I paddled together, she in the bow and I in the stern. We were out of practice, and so, while the other four canoes in our party pulled straight across the water, we traced a zigzag path. As the day wore on, however, and we wore down, shoulders beginning to ache, we stopped trying so hard and eventually found our rhythm. For minutes at a stretch, I forgot the canoe, forgot myself. Breathing and paddling and seeing became a single motion, a gliding meditation. Then a rock would loom before us, a gust of wind would jostle us, a hawk would call or a muscle twitch, and suddenly I would be yanked back into myself. There were my hands gripping the paddle, there were the boxy green packs leaning together over the middle thwart, there was Eva with ponytail swaying beneath her plum-colored hat, there was the gulf once more between seer and seen.

What I saw hemming the water on all sides was a low-slung landscape that had been scoured down to bedrock by glaciers, had been thronged with pine and spruce and aspen and birch over the next ten thousand years, had been stripped again to bedrock by loggers, and was now being slowly reclaimed by forest. Here and there the spiky green humps of islands broke through the gray plane of water. On the portages between lakes, staggering beneath the weight of canoes or rucksacks over trails worn down through mud and roots to stone, we could see how thin the soil was, how precarious the hold of life.

After one of those portages, as we started the long pull down Pipestone Bay, the wind picked up and blew somber clouds from the north. We could see the rain coming, like a translucent scrim wafting toward us over the water. By the time Eva and I put on our slickers, the squall had blown past, and we found ourselves sweating in sunlight. So we peeled off the slickers, only to see another curtain of rain approaching, and behind it another dose of sun. After three or four cloudbursts, wet from without and within, we gave up on rain gear and paddled on through whatever the sky delivered.

"How're you doing?" I asked Eva during a lull between showers.

"So far so good," she answered. "Those years of ballet may have messed up my feet, but they've given me stamina."

"You're not chilled, are you?"

"I'm fine, Daddy."

"Maybe take some extra vitamin C tonight."

From the bow came a sigh, then silence. At twenty, Eva was the youngest in our group, and I was the oldest at forty-seven. She was the only one who had a parent along, a fact that annoyed her whenever I reminded her of it by some fatherly gesture. She was also annoyed when any of our companions seemed to coddle her—by urging her to carry a lighter pack on the portages, for example, or by offering her the first food at a meal.

I have called those companions friends, because that is what they became by journey's end; but at the beginning I scarcely knew these four women and four men. Our friendship came about less through the sharing of a landscape than through the sharing of good work. From dawn until dusk, we lifted, carried, paddled, hiked, packed and unpacked, sawed, cooked, and scrubbed. The work was good because every bit of it served an obvious need—to move, to eat, to shelter, to keep warm—and because all of us joined in willingly, taking up whatever job was there to be done, helping one another without being asked. Only when the chores were finished did we swim or sing or pick berries or stretch out on sun-warmed stone and talk.

We camped that first night within earshot of Basswood Falls, and as I lay in the tent, the thrum of water made me feel as though I were still afloat. Waiting for sleep, I heard from muscles and joints I had not thought of for a long time.

I woke in darkness to the wacky sound of loons, a pair of them wailing back and forth like two blues singers demented by love. Listening, I felt the tug of desires I could not name.

Before setting out again, we changed canoeing partners. I knew that Eva would be glad not to have me looking over her shoulder as we paddled. Out from under my gaze, her own gaze grew keener. She was the first to spy a bald eagle perched on a dead tree, as she was the first to spy blueberries and raspberries on our portages, the first to notice the swoop of a peregrine falcon and the pale blue sprays of harebells on shoreline rocks. Since her birth, she had been restoring to me lost pieces of the world or disclosing pieces I had never known.

From its perch the eagle followed our slow progress, the great white head turning. What did it see? Not food, surely, and not much of a threat, or it would have flown. Did it see us as fellow creatures? Or merely as drifting shapes, no more consequential than clouds? Exchanging stares with this great bird, I dimly recalled a passage from *Walden* that I would look up after my return to the company of books:

> What distant and different beings in the various mansions of the universe
> are contemplating the same one at the same moment! Nature and human

life are as various as our several constitutions. Who shall say what prospect life offers to another? Could a greater miracle take place than for us to look through each other's eyes for an instant?

Neuroscience may one day pull off that miracle, giving us access to other eyes, other minds. For the present, however, we must rely on our native sight, on patient observation, on hunches and empathy. By empathy I do not mean the projecting of human films onto nature's screen, turning grizzly bears into teddy bears, crickets into choristers, grass into lawns; I mean the shaman's leap, a going out of oneself into the inwardness of other beings.

The longing I heard in the cries of the loons was not just a feathered version of mine, but neither was it wholly alien. It is risky to speak of courting birds as blues singers, of diving otters as children taking turns on a slide. But it is even riskier to pretend we have nothing in common with the rest of nature, as though we alone, the chosen species, were centers of feeling and thought. We cannot speak of that common ground without casting threads of metaphor outward from what we know to what we do not know.

An eagle is *other,* but it is also alive, bright with sensation, attuned to the world, and we respond to that vitality wherever we find it, in bird or beetle, in moose or lowly moss. Edward O. Wilson has given this impulse a lovely name, biophilia, which he defines as the urge "to explore and affiliate with life." Of course, like the coupled dragonflies that skimmed past our canoes or like ospreys hunting fish, we seek other creatures for survival. Yet even if biophilia is an evolutionary gift, like the kangaroo's leap or the peacock's tail, our fascination with living things carries us beyond the requirements of eating and mating. In that excess, that free curiosity, there may be a healing power. The urge to explore has scattered humans over the whole earth, to the peril of many species, including our own; perhaps the other dimension of biophilia, the desire to affiliate with life, could lead us to honor the entire fabric and repair what has been torn.

If you know where to look, you can find ancient tokens of biophilia in the Boundary Waters. Downriver from the eagle's perch, we came to a granite cliff that was splotched with iron stains and encrusted with lichens. Paddling close and holding our position against the current, we could make out faint red figures on the rock, paintings that had begun to weather long before the first Europeans straggled through here in search of pelts. The pigment of ocher and fish oil had faded to the color of rouge, barely distinguishable from the rusty iron smears.

"There's a moose," Eva called, pointing at a blurry shape.

The rest of us agreed that the figure might be a moose, and we also agreed in discerning a bear, a bird, a beaver, a man or woman, a canoe, and, clearest of all, the prints of hands. What those pictures meant to their makers we could only guess. Perhaps they were hunters' icons, for worship and meditation. Perhaps they told stories or marked boundaries. Perhaps they were doodles. Without discounting other meanings, what I saw in the faint red figures was a group portrait, a way of declaring: Here are the people of this place, those that fly and those that go on four legs and those that go on two. The artists identified our human tribe by the upright stance, by the canoe, and by the imprint not of a foot, as for any other beast, but of a hand, that tool capable of fashioning canoes and drawings.

If one could paint such an elusive trait, our kind might also be identified by the urge that kept ten members of the human tribe paddling there below the cliff, studying those hazy shapes, trying to read our ancestors' minds, casting threads of meaning from our lives to theirs. Whether our interpretations were right or wrong matters less than the impulse that led us to make them. With nearly six billion of us now on the planet, and the web of life unraveling under the burden of our appetites, we need to foster in every way we can this countervailing urge to weave, to stitch, to bind.

It may be my craving for a source of hope that persuades me to see in the pictographs evidence of biophilia. Certainly I felt a kinship with those vanished artists, even as I sensed in their drawings their own feeling of kinship with bear and beaver and moose. If I were to mix red clay with fish oil and daub pictures on the granite cliff, I would begin with an otter and a loon, and when I came to represent the human tribe I would draw two figures, side by side, a father and a daughter.

Although the pictographs are ancient by human measure, they are brand-new by comparison with the rock on which they were painted. As dark as charred bones, as gray as concrete, in places a dull rose, smoky pink, or crystalline white, the bedrock in this portion of the Boundary Waters was formed between two and three billion years ago, which makes it half as old as the earth and a thousand times older than *Homo sapiens.* How, standing barefooted on such venerable stone, and diving into the river for a swim, can one reach back through the abyss of time without losing hold of the icy, exhilarating present?

I swam each day of the trip, and each day the first dive was daunting. This was July, I kept reminding myself, and the otters frolicked here in January. Once I made the plunge, I stayed under as long as I could, eyes open to glimpse the otter's realm, mouth closed to protect myself from disease. Until a few years ago, travelers here could safely drink straight from the streams. But now acid rain has fouled even these remote waters, leading to the growth of *Giardia*, an intestinal parasite, and so we filtered every drop we drank and we sealed our lips as we swam. Once the initial shock of cold wore off, it felt good to rinse away the day's sweat. The water cleansed me through and through. After the swim, back in camp, where Eva and the other women brushed their long damp hair by the fire, I tingled for hours.

The day we paddled up the Horse River, several of us found ourselves swimming with our clothes on. The water was high from rains that had swollen the Missouri and Mississippi Rivers with five-hundred-year floods. Throughout much of its length, the channel spread out lazily into marshes of cattails and willows, but wherever it was pinched in by rock the current surged. The only way of maneuvering a canoe through the fiercest rapids was for one of the paddlers to climb out, grope for footing among the slippery stones, and push or pull the canoe upstream.

As I slogged through the first few riffles, I wore my life vest; but eventually I became so hot from the effort and from the midday sun that

I decided to take it off, and I noticed the other waders doing the same. And so it happened that none of us was wearing a vest when we came to the last and worst of the rapids. Eva was in the bow of the lead canoe, and the man in the stern, the strongest paddler in our group, thought they could dig their way up through the central chute without wading. They made one hard run, then another and another, but each time they were stalled in white water and shoved back downstream.

At last Eva decided to climb out and tug from the front while her partner paddled. The canoe inched forward, foam brimming around Eva's knees, then her thighs, her waist, and when she lurched into the narrowest place, where the water pounded between boulders, suddenly her feet were swept from under her and she fell, barely keeping her chin above water by clutching the gunnel with one hand. The canoe spun crossways to the current and wedged against the boulders, and there Eva dangled, her face jammed against the upstream side of the canoe, her booted feet bobbing up uselessly on the downstream side. Watching her, I had the slow-motion sense from nightmare that something horrible was about to happen, and that I was powerless to intervene. I saw my daughter being sucked under and battered against rocks and tumbled down past me through the bruising rapids.

I *saw* it happen; but it did not happen. While voices all around me shouted advice, Eva clung to the canoe with one hand, worked the other hand free to seize the gunnel, then dragged herself across the roiling water and hauled out onto a ledge. Only the top of her head was dry. When I saw her safe, I realized that I had been holding my breath. I opened my throat, letting out stale air, but for a long while I could not speak.

Much later, after miles of winding through fragrant water lilies and gliding past the tranquil gaze of basking turtles, their domed shells gleaming in the sun like hubcaps, we arrived at a campsite on Horse Lake. Eva and I were to cook supper that night, and while she was unpacking the food and I was building the fire, she asked me if I had been worried by her dunking.

"I was terrified," I told her. "Weren't you?"

"No," she said. "It was kind of fun."

"What if you had gone under?"

"I didn't go under."

"But what if you had?"

"I would have washed up again sooner or later."

Recalling those fierce waters, those indifferent rocks, again I lost my voice. Eva frowned at her alarmist father, and we both returned to our chores.

Near the fire pit, where I knelt to fan the flames, stood a wild-cherry tree whose bark had been raked by claws and whose branches, glinting with purple fruit, had been twisted and smashed. Black hair dangled in tufts from twigs and paw prints gouged the dirt below. We had been instructed to bang pans or shout if we spotted a bear. We never spotted one, but if we had, I might not have been able to make a sound, any more than I could cry out when I saw the river snatch my daughter.

There were dangers enough in the Boundary Waters. A few years ago, a father and son were pulling to shore when a black bear came rushing at them, seized the father, and began mauling him; the son beat the bear with a paddle until the father wriggled free, then father and son escaped in their canoe. More recently, two men sleeping in a tent during a thunderstorm were electrocuted when lightning struck nearby and the juice flowed through roots under their sleeping bags; two other men in the same tent were only dazed. The week before our trip, a woman canoeing alone was killed when a tree felled by a beaver crashed down on her as she passed by.

We had not gone seeking danger in the wilderness, as sky divers go to the treacherous air or climbers to steep rock, but we had stumbled into danger anyway. We knew the risks of broken bones and drowning, the hazards from leeches and ticks. In the wilds, risk is the underside of beauty. To be a creature is to be vulnerable, to bruise, and sooner or later to break. Unlike most dangers in our cities, where guns or bombs or drunken drivers or heedless sex might kill us, what could harm us in the Boundary Waters had no will behind it, no malign intention.

The Horse River did not mean to hurt Eva, did not mean to frighten me, did not mean anything. Whether the browsing bear meant to wound the cherry tree is a harder question, but I suspect the answer is no. Whether the original world itself—the one that precedes and upholds our human world as ancient stone upholds the pictographs—means anything, whether it has a purpose or direction, is an even harder question, perhaps the most difficult of all. I do not pretend to know the answer, nor how one might be found, yet I find myself living as if the answer were yes. Arising out of a dead universe, evolving from simplicity toward unimaginable complexity, life does seem to be an immense journey, as Loren Eiseley described it, but not one with a human destination. We are not the goal of evolution, nor are we competent guides, despite our tinkering with DNA. If we are voyageurs, then so are the otters and eagles, locusts and spiders, lichens and pines, along with countless species that have gone down into the earth.

While the Horse River was roaring through its boulder-strewn trough, the Mississippi River was drowning dozens of towns and thousands of farms. Headlines described the Mississippi as rampaging, brutal, cruel, the same words we use for street gangs or packs of feral dogs. After we had spent so many dollars and decades to control it, how could the river turn on us this way? the commentators asked. How could it defy our levees, our concrete and steel? Cancers and hurricanes, earthquakes and the AIDS virus are often described in the same outraged tone, as if by shattering the walls of our houses or our cells they were violating some covenant between us and nature.

In defining wilderness as an unruly place where shaggy creatures roam, our language betrays an uneasiness about our own hairy origins and a regret that the world does not dance to our music. Beyond our campfires, beyond our tents, beyond our makeshift structures, the whole universe is wild, from quarks to quasars, from black bears to black holes, but far from being disorderly, it follows intricate, exquisite rules that we have only begun to decipher. They are not *our* rules, however, no matter how fervently we may desire to legislate.

Even such a remnant of wilderness as the Boundary Waters reminds us, at every turn, that we are not running the show. On our last evening there, the sky was clear, so Eva and I and two others gathered on a stony point beside the lake to wait for stars. Mosquitos came droning in as usual at dusk, and the calls of night birds picked up as the calls of day birds dwindled away. A V of ripples caught the ruddy light of sunset, this time from a beaver, which carried in its jaws a stick the size of a baseball bat. The ripples arrowed straight toward us, and the beaver climbed out just below our point, so close that we could see its wet fur slicked back like a greaser's hairdo, and hear the scrape of teeth on wood as it gnawed bark from the stick.

I glanced at Eva, to share with her a conspiratorial grin. But she was lost in looking, and soon I was, too. By and by, disturbed perhaps by our feet stamping the rock and our hands flailing at mosquitos, the beaver nosed away into the lake, gave the water a resounding smack with its tail, and dove. Moments later, it emerged again on the opposite side of our point, even closer to us, the wood still clenched in its jaws. One end of the stick was pale and shining, the other end, unchewed, still gray with bark. After a spell of gnawing, the beaver nosed away from shore again, smacked the water, dove, climbed out once more, gnawed, then reversed the procedure several more times, until we lost its movements in the gloom and lost its sounds in the stir of wind. Only then did we remember the stars, and we looked up to find that the sky had been covered by a quilt of cloud.

The next afternoon, we slid our canoes out of Fall Lake onto the same landing from which we had launched them, closing the circle of our journey. Before getting on the bus, I picked up a palm-size chunk of rosy granite, the edges sharp enough for scraping hides, and I stuffed it into my pack. I have often reached for the stone while writing these pages, turning and turning it, never quite able to make the hard angles fit my hand.

From inside, the shell of the bus seemed flimsy, the floor unsteady, the windows deceitful. My weariness alone made sense. Eva squinted across the aisle at me and said, "More and more like a bum. Now you could beg for change without a greasy blanket."

I stroked my beard, which had begun to feel like fur. "What do you think? Should I let it grow?"

"Sure," Eva said, "if you want to look like Father Time."

After a week away from clocks, I was beginning to hear time again in the whir of the tires, beginning to see it in the mile markers along the road. To keep time at bay a while longer, I hummed the melody from a song we had sung while paddling, and I shut my eyes. When I opened them again, rain was drumming on the roof and mist from an open window was falling on my face and lightning was cracking the pitch-black sky.

I was still watching the storm as we cruised through Chicago, the expressways deserted this Sunday morning, the streetlamps a bleary yellow. The bus pulled in for a rest stop at a hamburger franchise near the Indiana border, and I made the mistake of going inside. The light and noise were painful, the surfaces too shiny, the smells too coarse. Everywhere I looked, mirrors multiplied the garish colors, the harsh lights, the feeding faces. Televisions suspended from the ceiling played cartoons, and at the tables beneath them diners shoveled in fatty food and sucked sweet liquids. Another day, I might have sat at one of those tables myself, might have shoveled and slurped; but this day, this thundery morning, I backed away feeling sick.

Another day, I might have stayed there to admire the people, in all their shades and shapes; I might have listened to their accents and tried to guess where they were from. This was Chicago, after all—my mother's polyglot city, where my Assyrian grandfather practiced medicine among poor immigrants from dozens of lands. But so soon after returning from the original world, I was not ready to see the human world as enough, not even in Chicago. Of course we should celebrate our own diversity. But we flatter ourselves if we think our rainbow of races, our preferences in making love, our flags, our ways of cooking and speaking and praying, our X or Y chromosomes make us more various, more mysterious, than all the rest of nature.

Back on the bus, Eva told me she had dreamed of looking out the window to see a great blue bird flying along beside us, a mighty beast with the crooked neck of a heron, the body of an eagle, and the fur of a lion. Mythology teems with such composite beasts. Eva's dream animal, in fact, sounds like a near relative of the griffin. While banishing griffins and centaurs and sphinxes from our textbooks, biologists have revealed that we ourselves are composite creatures, built up over millions of years from ancestral species, part lemur and part lizard, with bacteria in our bellies and mitochondria in our cells. Mountain and lowland gorillas differ genetically from each other more than we differ from chimpanzees. Does that make us indistinguishable from apes? No, but our genetic heritage does make us kin not only with apes and otters but with frogs and ferns and fritillaries—indeed, with every organism on earth.

The fellowship of all creatures is more than a handsome metaphor; it is a fact entwined in our DNA. The appetite for discovering such connections is also entwined in our DNA. Science articulates in formal terms affinities that humans have sensed for ages in direct encounters with wildness. Even while we slight or slaughter members of our own species, and while we push other species toward extinction, we slowly, painstakingly, acquire knowledge that could enable us and inspire us to change our ways. Only if that knowledge begins to exert a pressure in us, and we come to feel the fellowship of all beings as potently as we feel hunger or fear, will we have any hope of creating a truly just and tolerant society, one that cherishes the land and our wild companions along with our brothers and sisters.

In America lately, we have been carrying on two parallel conversations: one about respecting human diversity, the other about preserving natural diversity. Unless we merge those two conversations, both will be futile. Our effort to honor human differences cannot succeed apart from our effort to honor the buzzing, blooming, bewildering variety of life on earth. All life rises from the same source, and so does all fellow feeling, whether the fellows move on two legs or four, on scaly bellies or feathered wings. If we care only for human needs, we betray the land; if we care only for the earth and its wild offspring, we betray our own kind. The profusion of creatures and cultures is the most remarkable fact about our planet, and the study and stewardship of that profusion seems to me our fundamental task.

While Eva and I were sorting the week's laundry in the basement at home, the good smell of mud rising from our jeans, she recalled her dream as one of the most powerful events of the week, and so I recall it now. Accounts of wilderness sojourns, like the sojourners themselves, often turn their backs on the human realm. Here is pristine nature, these accounts imply, and over there is corrupt society. Likewise, many who write about social problems, about poverty or prejudice or war, turn their backs on nature, as though we were acting out our destiny on a bare stage. But the stage is crowded with life, the stage is teeming—indeed, the stage is the main story. The only durable community is the one that embraces the whole planet, wild and tame. We need to find ways of speaking about that great community without drawing lines between nature and society, for such boundaries are just as illusory as the one between Canada and the United States, over which we paddled time and again during our trip without so much as a bump.

At any rate, that is what I am trying to find, a way of writing and thinking about the whole of life, human as well as nonhuman, in all its dazzling array. Although I am caught much of the time in ego's shiny jar, distracted by my own reflections, there were moments during our wilderness sojourn when I slipped out of that small self and entered, however briefly, into the great community. Those are the moments worth telling.

Empty at the Heart of the World

CHRISTOPHER SHAW

You reach the carry at the western end of Low's Lake by skirting a large floating bog and threading your canoe through eight or ten acres of drowned timber and gnarled stumps, known locally as "floodwood." The place has a terminal quality, like an edge or a dead end, and is ringed by low forested hills. On clear days, the water reflects the sky's hard blue and the bright green of maples near shore. On dull, leaden afternoons, the landscape has an altogether different aspect, the bleached and weather-polished floodwood trunks, like photo negatives of living trees, triggering grim correspondences in the heart.

State Surveyor Verplanck Colvin searched for a reputed "lost lake" near here in the autumn of 1872. Colvin, twenty-five, remembered the place, then called Mud Lake, as "lonely and doleful water," in his first official report to the New York State Legislature, in 1873. His perceptions were clouded by the observations of previous writers, notably S. H. Hammond and Alfred Billings Street, who found the whole region around Mud Lake so depressing that they vowed never to return. Few places in Adirondack wilderness annals have drawn such complex emotions from their visitors.

By the time Bob Marshall explored the area as a forestry student,

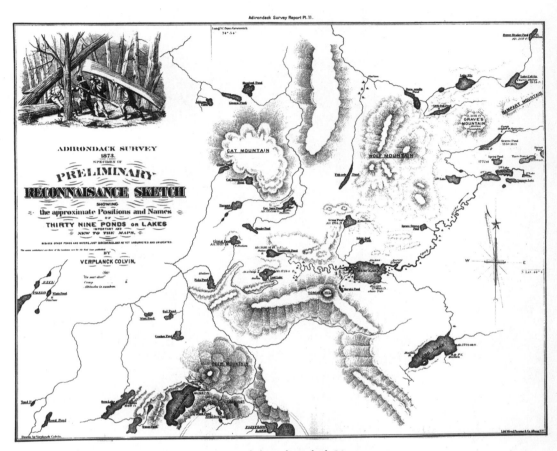

Map courtesy of the Adirondack Museum.

exactly fifty years later, it had been ravaged by lumbering and a decade of apocalyptic forest fires. Standing on the summit of Graves Mountain, a moderate peak northeast of Low's Lake, in the summer of 1923, Marshall wrote, "It was not hard to understand why the early writers called this the gloomiest region of the Adirondacks." Marshall had devoured Colvin's narratives as a boy. Later, as he rowed a guideboat up Mud Lake on his way to the junction of St. Lawrence, Hamilton, and Herkimer counties, he once again remembered that those writers "were unanimous in calling it the wildest and gloomiest place in the Adirondacks. So I let my imagination carry me back sixty years to the days when the wolf, moose and panther were of daily occurrence, while man was almost unknown in the region."

For Colvin, the season and the company of his rough-cut guides and porters certainly intensified the loneliness of that trip. It was late October, daylight at a premium. A group of surly market hunters were camped there ahead of them. The seasonal derangement of the color scheme was over, leaving the hills stark, the color of pewter and storms. He found wolf tracks in the mud at the head of the lake. His crew resented the low wages he paid—though the money often came from his own pocket—and his prohibition of alcohol. He may have felt outnumbered and surrounded.

It was then a true wilderness by every definition of the time, untrammeled and unmoderated. A few years later, in the 1890s, a man named Abbot Augustus Low acquired forty thousand acres of the Bog River drainage, including Bog Lake and Mud Lake. Low, whose fortune came from the China tea trade, was a latecomer among industrialists who had bought extensive tracts in the area—the railroad Webbs, Durants, and Whitneys—but not to be outdone. Low built a hobby empire in the woods, damming the Bog River ten miles downstream from the head of Mud Lake for a small hydroelectric plant. The dam raised the level of the Bog River and flooded the land around Mud Lake. It backed up the channels of Grass Pond and Bog Lake. The floating bog at the western end of Low's Lake is the shore of the original Mud Lake, Colvin's "broad, soft, peat marsh." Mr. Low named the huge deadwater after himself.

Low's summer neighbor, a few miles south on Lake Lila, William Seward Webb, ran a railroad spur through the area in the 1890s, to facilitate the removal of hardwood logs too dense for river drives. The line later became part of the New York Central system. Around the turn of the century, the NYC shunted its obsolete coal burners to the Adirondacks. The engines lacked smokestack guards, and cinders sparked numerous fires in the timber slash along the right-of-way. In the dry August of 1908, according to one account, Low counted at least twenty fires caused by locomotives.

That fall, fires swept over tens of thousands of acres in the big country between Cranberry and Long lakes, and north of Raquette Lake, burning the soil down to bedrock. One burned from near Low's camp on Lake Marian all the way west to a ridge overlooking Cranberry Lake, where residents read newspapers by its light at midnight. On September 27, the fire crowned out and swept over Long Lake West, a logging hamlet near Low's dam on the Bog, destroying the railroad station, school, and post office, stores, lumberyards, freight cars, houses, and the Wilderness Inn, a renowned brothel esteemed by lumbermen for its queen-size French-Canadian whores. The town was never rebuilt.

When Bob Marshall stayed at the summer quarters of the New York State Forestry College, on Cranberry Lake, in 1923, he found traces of the fires and continuing bad logging practices in the surrounding woods. He found other things, which astonished him. The first was a roadless area of a size unparalleled in his long experience in the Adirondacks. The second was an expanse of first-growth eastern white pine and black spruce of nearly fifty thousand acres, in a remote area south of Cranberry Lake which had been acquired from Webb as part of State Forest Preserve legislation in 1886 (passed under pressure from Verplanck Colvin, among others). It remains the largest stand of such primary forest in the northeast.

It humbled Marshall, who wrote, "It was . . . pleasant, as we layed [sic] down to reflect, that we were in the heart of a tract of virgin timber about 40 miles square, absolutely unmaimed by man. And yet, we could not help regretting that there should be so very few of such tracts left."

After the Forest Preserve, the legislature created the Adirondack Park in 1892 ("a six-million acre patchwork of public and private land" etc.) and passed the "forever wild" clause of the state constitution in 1894, which prohibited lumbering on state land. Private lands in the park were unregulated, however, until the Adirondack Park Agency Act was passed in 1969. (Private land makes up about 55 percent of the park.) The APA Act also created the State Land Master Plan, designating seventeen separate areas, totaling one million acres, as "wilderness." According to the plan's definition, wilderness areas required a minimum of ten thousand acres, which would be managed to "achieve and perpetuate a natural plant and animal community where man's influence is not apparent."

In the 1970s, New York acquired Lake Lila from Webb's heirs. It is now designated a Primitive Area (essentially, wilderness), surrounded by private timberlands and reached by a long dirt road from Route 30.

In 1966, A. A. Low's widow sold her land to the Boy Scouts, who turned over Low's Lake and nine thousand acres to the state in 1985. The land abutted the Five Ponds Wilderness on the west. Lake Lila was a short carry over private land to the south.

A controversial commission appointed by Governor Mario Cuomo in 1990 recommended that the state consolidate its holdings with existing private parcels in the vast forested reach bounded approximately by the Adirondack Park boundary (the Blue Line) on the west, state Routes 3 and 30 on the north and east, and Raquette Lake and the Fulton Chain on the south, calling it the Oswegatchie Great Wilderness (or Oswegatchie–Bob Marshall Great Wilderness). The necessary private tracts would be acquired slowly over time. When complete, the area would contain more than four hundred thousand acres, or six hundred and twenty-five square miles—a postage stamp by Alaskan or Amazonian standards, but huge for the East, where it would be the largest designated wilderness area north of the Everglades. An environmental bond act that would have funded the first necessary acquisitions was defeated that fall. Few of the commission's recommendations have been acted on at this writing.

The area contains hundreds of ponds and lakes, hundreds of miles of navigable waterways at the headwaters of five rivers, three existing wilderness areas, and the greatest variety and concentration of native species in the state, including the spruce grouse and pine marten, both rare. Where mammals are concerned, it is remembered for its many "lasts": the last moose shot in the Adirondacks, the last cougar, the last wolf. The moose went first, by the 1860s. As Paul Jamieson, author of *Adirondack Canoe Routes: The North Flow,* put it, "the last moose was killed many times there." The other two held out somewhat longer, by dint of reticence and intractability. The last wolf hide was brought in for bounty in 1899. Tradition says that Colvin himself shot the last known cougar in 1896, though one source claims a hide was submitted for bounty in the 1920s.

The northwestern Adirondacks remained a refuge for big mammals, big timber, and Civil War deserters—terra incognita in an industrialized state—for many reasons. It was remote from major timber markets, poor in minerals. It lacked the Wagnerian scenery of the High Peaks and lake country to the east, and the spa culture of Lake George and Saratoga. It was, for the East, big, diffuse, amorphous. Scary.

Sparsely settled, it was traveled intermittently. Oneidas and Mohawks from the south and Algonquins from the north hunted and lived there for centuries. In the colonial era, Iroquois from La Preséntation, a Jesuit mission at present-day Ogdensburg, used the Oswegatchie River on their treks between the St. Lawrence and the longhouse country to the south. The "Albany Road" ran between Ogdensburg and William Johnson's Fish House on the Sacandaga River during the colonial wars. In living memory, remnants of the road were said to have made up sections of the "Red Horse Trail" from the Five Ponds south to Beaver River.

In 1771, land speculators using the names of two investors, Totten and Crossfield, acquired more than one million acres from Mohawk representatives, the largest purchase of its kind until then. They paid a little more than a thousand pounds. The following year, a survey crew ran blazes along the northern line, and the owners drew a hypothetical grid of lots and "townships" on the highly inaccurate map. (The survey crew, moving west to east, quit marking the line at the summit of Graves Mountain, where, according to tradition, their rum gave out.) Typically, their grid disregarded topography. After the War of Independence, the land reverted to New York State. The exact location of the northern line was one of Colvin's preoccupations. It cut through Mud Lake and approximated the northern border of Herkimer and Hamilton counties and the southern border of St. Lawrence County.

In 1792, another speculator, Alexander McComb, bought four million acres to the north from the cash-strapped state for eight cents an acre. A few years later McComb went bankrupt, and creditors seized the property to parcel it off. The state slowly reacquired some of these parcels as the Adirondack Park took shape in the 1890s, including the old-growth pine and spruce of Five Ponds.

Timber companies arrived around the same time as Colvin. As they had elsewhere in the Adirondacks, they stripped the forests and let the state reclaim the land for unpaid taxes. Colvin based his pitch to the legislature for an official Adirondack survey on the need to know exactly where these parcels lay. To establish legal boundaries, he proposed starting from fixed points and comparing the blazes and landmarks mentioned in colonial patents and deeds. The area involved was approximately the size of Vermont. It was "an undertaking of the greatest magnitude," Colvin wrote, one which his friends advised him to forgo: it required a huge labor force, to be coördinated over hundreds of miles; expensive equipment; unlimited energy; and, as it turned out, thirty years of his life.

In the spring of 1872, with a paltry handout from the state, Colvin headed north, intending to fix baselines from a federal geodetic survey taking place on Lake Champlain. In one incredibly productive season, using giant reflectors erected on mountain summits for triangulation, and barometric altitude computations, he scaled, surveyed, and measured twenty-two summits in the High Peaks and Saranac lakes. In the fall, he traveled west and up the Bog River from Tupper Lake, intending to complete the work he'd outlined for the year. With a few more years' experience, he would probably have quit for the season.

The only child of a prominent lawyer and legislator, Colvin grew up in Albany steeped in the literature of exploration. His reports to the legislature for the years from 1873 to 1898 are neglected master-pieces of the genre, echoing accounts by Lewis and Clark, Henry Morton Stanley, John Wesley Powell, and Charles Darwin. As a surveyor he was self-taught. His narratives routinely chronicled triumphs of the will over obstacles placed by nature in the path of science. His view of the Adirondack wilderness was essentially nostalgic and romantic. The 1873 account of his work in the High Peaks is written with breathless élan.

At the headwaters of the Bog, though, with the vastness of low gray hills and uncut forests confronting him, his prose turns brooding and gloomy. He becomes momentarily fixated on discovering the "lost" lake, a cliché and banal archetype of exploratory romances, revealing a youthful penchant for melancholy and fantasy behind the empirical façade, the desire for an illusion of encompassing mystery close to home, some un-redeemed blankness in the state's encircling frontier.

Late October on the Adirondack plateau can fill the sunniest dispo-sition with spleen. At Mud Lake, Colvin's luck petered out. Things fell apart, especially the weather. Labor relations deteriorated. Food ran out. ("We had food for reflection, but little else.") The party wandered aim-lessly west of Mud Lake. It stumbled on Lost Lake unexpectedly soon, became lost itself on the return, and was taken in by a solitary wolf trapper—another archetype—who lived on Nick's Lake. Colvin hired the trapper to guide him west over the divide from the Oswegatchie head-waters to the Beaver River, "against all hazards," then hired as additional porters the entire crew of surly market hunters camped at Mud Lake.

Before heading south to the Beaver, the crew lingered another day in this oddly compelling though "dubious" region, while Colvin deter-mined the location of the St. Lawrence, Herkimer, and Hamilton county corner. It was exactly where he expected it to be.

On November 1, 1872, the party embarked from Mud Lake "directly westward into an unknown region of dismal wilderness," with one bag of flour. Conditions deteriorated further. On November 4, having found old blazes marking St. Lawrence County, Colvin wrote, "Our affairs began to look gloomy." There follows a harrowing narrative of cold, error, low rations, stove boats and near disaster, as the party worked its way south from the Five Ponds to Beaver River, measuring and surveying numerous "unknown" ponds, lakes, and minor summits. On reaching the Beaver, with snow deepening by the hour, he paid his porters and his guide—presumably in cash—and watched them turn back the way they had come. He then struck out east with his original crew toward Long Lake, thirty miles through the "winterbound wilderness." Despite the conditions, he took time to pursue a cougar that crossed his path. The party eventually emerged at Long Lake on November 21, "none the worst for our trials," as he blithely put it.

Colvin had inadvertently circumnavigated most of the area that in 1990 would be proposed as the Oswegatchie Great Wilderness. With a good deal of backtracking, survey work, and immense baggage, it took him more than a month. (In 1878, he returned and marked the northwestern corner of the Totten and Crossfield Purchase, in the Red Horse Chain.) His route, still blanketed in undeveloped timberland, can be reproduced today, though not without trespassing on private lands.

Colvin's reports and lectures helped establish the State Forest Preserve, the Adirondack Park, and the "forever wild" clause of the state constitution. His personal fortune, as his friends had predicted, bore a sizable cost of the survey, and Colvin was reduced to dunning the legislature in later life. He quit his post in 1900, disgusted with Albany's pettifoggery, his records in disarray and his science in question. He became "a pathetic figure" on Albany streets, according to one writer, muttering in his whiskers about money, and "embittered . . . that politicians in league with the lumber interests belittled his work." His contemporary, the historian Alfred Donaldson, whose own authority has come into question, described Colvin's situation condescendingly: "His office . . . looked more like the dressing room of a sporting club than the repository of valuable records. These, if there at all were apt to be buried beneath a picturesque profusion of snow-shoes, moccasins and pack-baskets." Colvin lived into the 1920s, advising younger "conservationists" of the Progressive stamp, who carried on his dream of a "park" in the Adirondacks.

———

The east-west line separating counties, two big land purchases, and the precolonial northern border of Iroquois territory bisects the area of the Oswegatchie Wilderness like the lea lines of rural England, or the aboriginal songlines of Australia. North of the line, the boreal ecotype prevails; to the south are the mixed pine and deciduous forests more typical of the state.

A picture by Frederic Remington shows a hunter paddling the dark stream of the upper Oswegatchie in a bark canoe, past a metal stake marking the border of St. Lawrence and Herkimer counties, the shaggy gray silhouettes of old-growth pines in the background. An Ogdensburg native, Remington came often to Cranberry Lake in the 1890s. Among other personality deformities, he was known for taking potshots at resting loons from the porch of a tourist hotel.

The same nebulous section of that line west of Low's Lake that drew Verplanck Colvin attracted the young Bob Marshall. Marshall's family had a summer home on Lower Saranac Lake, and by 1923 Marshall had already climbed most of the state's forty-six peaks over four thousand feet. His father, the jurist Louis Marshall, was an early advocate of Progressive conservation laws. In the dedication of his unpublished guidebook, *Weekend Trips in the Cranberry Lake Region,* now in the Moon Library of the New York State College of Environmental Science and Forestry, Marshall wrote, "Just a couple of months before he died, [my father] took a ten-mile walk in the Adirondacks. . . . His love of the outdoors was the purest of anybody I know. His purpose in going to the forest was single: to enjoy the fullness of its beauty."

Along with his prodigious hiking accomplishments, the quest for beauty marked Marshall's own brief, productive career. Writers have cited his record of two hundred day hikes of over thirty miles, fifty-one over forty, and several of up to seventy miles. These figures sound superhuman. In the Cranberry Lake guidebook, he used a rating system for the area's ponds, calling one on the way to Low's Lake "one of the ugliest bodies of water it has been my misfortune to see." ("He was always rating things," a college friend said.) Bog Lake he judged "nothing to rave about."

Marshall put his legs to serious use that summer of 1923, galloping over the terrain from Graves Mountain to Partlow Lake, marking trails (defacing one mountain summit in the process), bushwhacking and exploring. He defined the Cranberry Lake area as extending from the Grass River Railroad on the north (paralleling today's Route 3), the Blue Line on the west, the Beaver River/Oswegatchie divide on the south, and the New York Central line, near Low's, on the east. He visited and described ninety-four ponds in that area. (This represents at least a third of the area covered by Colvin in 1872.) His accounts suggest that he could be a difficult hiking companion. Like Colvin, he was prone to plunge ahead without regard to his backtrail, to lose track of direction and time, to find himself benighted and underprovisioned. More than once he curled up against a rock for the night, in the middle of nowhere. On one trip to the Bog River, he lost his map and went on without it. Another time, he lost his camera and dropped what he was doing to go back and look for it.

Throughout the book, Marshall complains of logging slash and destructive forestry practices. On a long hike south to Lake Lila, he came across remnants of the big burns of 1908, the streambeds all dry, calling it "awful, monotonous country." He valued above everything the presence or illusion of primeval nature. Its destruction angered and depressed him. His standards, conditioned by the High Peaks and Saranac lakes, were exacting. On a pilgrimage to the three-county junction, he camped at Clear Pond, a stone's throw from Big Deer Pond, Colvin's Lost Lake. "It hardly seemed possible," he wrote, "that I was in the crowded Empire State of today. Not a house or a soul was within miles." He found all "as [it] had been when the first pioneer trapper spread his blanket in the uncontaminated country termed . . . the dismal wilderness."

The next day, near Big Deer Pond, he came upon "the first [primeval forest] of any great extent I had encountered in the entire region," though he could not help dismissing Big Deer itself as possessing "mediocre beauty."

Continuing south, Marshall stopped at Gull Lake to meet George Muir, "the last of the great wolf hunters, . . . who had killed 67 of the 108 panthers, and 39 of the 98 wolves killed since 1870." Colvin had encountered wolf packs there. The panther and the wolf were not so long gone from the country that a natural and human continuity with the time of Colvin could not be traced.

The Adirondacks, even in their farthest reaches, tend to constrict the illusion or perception of wilderness. Rivers run into unnavigable thickets or private "parks," like Low's or Whitney's, forcing canoeists to turn back. You may crest one ridge to view an extraordinarily wild valley, while the next will lead to a strip mine or cottage development. From his experience with the High Peaks (now a wilderness area of two hundred thousand acres), Marshall knew the disappointments that could lie beyond the next range. He looked for places that yielded intimidating distances beyond the initial penetration, along with the possibility of being eaten.

The prose and sentiments of *Weekend Trips in the Cranberry Lake Region* show us a young person driven to recover the sense of vastness that recent generations had circumscribed. Marshall wrote that as a child he had suffered "terrible depression" when contemplating his lost opportunities for discovery. (The deprivation inspired some of his least rational expressions.) We can presume that his devotion to wilderness causes sought to balance the perceived loss of some primordial condition. One writer goes so far as to claim that Marshall's perception of wilderness had a Freudian tinge, his hyperactivity fueled by neurosis.

We remember him better, however, for his grand gestures on behalf of the outdoors. After joining the United States Forest Service, Marshall studied forest fires in Montana, explored Alaska's Brooks Range, and served as forestry director in the Office of Indian Affairs. He financed an inventory of roadless areas in the United States of more than three hundred thousand acres, with money from his own pocket. In 1928, Marshall's contemporary Aldo Leopold wrote an article recommending that the Forest Service abandon a road planned for the Gila National Forest, in Arizona, and set aside the region for "wilderness" use. The article widened a breach that already existed in the Forest Service between wilderness and logging factions.

Two years later, Marshall chimed in with an article titled "The Problem of the Wilderness," in which he began refining his definition of wilderness as "the last escape from society." Its balm was in alleviating "the terrible harm caused by repressed desires." A follower of Thorstein Veblen, John Dewey, and democratic socialism, Marshall also wrote a book, *The Peoples' Forests,* which called for the nationalization of the entire United States timber industry. Convinced that commercial forestry interests, having devastated the nation's private lands, were sizing up federal land for the same treatment, he began pushing for the creation of a national wilderness system.

Undoubtedly, the country around Cranberry and Low's lakes contributed to his understanding of wilderness as an area of no less than two hundred thousand acres, untrammeled by man, where a person could wander for two weeks "without crossing his own tracks."

In 1935, Marshall helped found the Wilderness Society, and he continued traveling to the Adirondacks to advise its advocates in the evolving politics of wilderness. In 1939, at the age of thirty-eight, he died inexplicably on a train between Washington, D.C., and New York. He had logged a lot of miles by then. One historian has made a case that he was assassinated by commercial logging interests convinced that his bid for socialized forestry would succeed.

After a federal Wilderness Act was finally passed in 1964, an extensive tract of national forest in the Rocky Mountains of Idaho and Montana was named the Bob Marshall Wilderness.

An Oswegatchie Great Wilderness in the Adirondacks would pay generous tribute to Colvin and Marshall (who viewed it idiosyncratically) and the far-reaching consequences of their experience there. Unfortunately, such hopes are mired in complications too byzantine and mind-numbing for discussion here. They are all too common wherever opposing land-use interests face off. Some recent developments are encouraging, nevertheless. In 1993, New York State passed a bill creating a trust fund for land acquisition and other environmental programs. The fund, though far from adequate, marked a compromise between previously intractable foes and earmarked the fifty-thousand-acre Whitney Park for eventual acquisition, among other parcels. An important piece of the puzzle, the

Whitney property has been managed for commercial forest production for a century, but is otherwise undeveloped. Gifford Pinchot conducted experiments in European-style "scientific" forestry there and on the nearby Webb property. Rising taxes and low timber prices have forced the Whitney family to consider subdividing lakefront or selling the property altogether. The land lies east of Lake Lila and is laced with ponds and streams where the author of *Woodcraft*, George Washington Sears, pen-named "Nessmuk" after his childhood mentor, a Nipmuck Indian, made his historic canoe trips in the 1880s. From a purely recreational standpoint, its reopening to public canoe access, with the addition of the carry between Bog Lake and Lake Lila, would expand existing Adirondack canoe routes to rival Algonquin Park and the Boundary Waters. It would also constitute 15 percent of the total land mass for the proposed new wilderness.*

Since the idea first arose, one of the main goals for an Oswegatchie Wilderness has been the return of the moose, wolf, and cougar. Road-lessness and a land mass such as four hundred thousand acres can provide are among the primary criteria for success, along with a large and diverse prey base. But "social" considerations carry equal or greater weight, in practical terms. Even years after the works of biologist David Mech, and wolf advocates Barry Lopez and Farley Mowat entered the public consciousness, predators like timber wolves, grizzlies, and other indicators of authentic wildness arouse some of our least rational fears. Restoration efforts for other species, furthermore, have proved mixed. Eagles and peregrines are back in strength, but a program that released lynx in the High Peaks was jeopardized when some were killed by cars and another was shot raiding a henhouse two states away. Any mention of cougars or wolves brings rapid and hysterical howls of protest from deer hunters, as well as from dairy and sheep farmers on the fringes of the park.

Yet, to believe reports, all three species have slowly filtered their way back, especially moose. Young bulls have been streaming into the

---

* In November, 1993, the Whitney family ended negotiations with the state to sell the land.

Adirondacks from northern New England for years. A proposal to intro-
duce females for breeding was defeated recently by a local campaign
promulgating fears of the two projected traffic accidents per year an
established moose population would cause, and complaints that the state
wanted to establish an "ecological Disneyland" in the Adirondacks. Cougar sightings are common, especially on the Whitney tract, and a forestry
professor at Paul Smith's College, near Saranac Lake, saw one crossing a
river near my home in the northern Adirondacks in the fall of 1992.
Timber wolves have been reported near Low's Lake by trappers and
hunters experienced enough in Alaska and the West to be able to distinguish them from eastern coyotes (which have usurped the wolf's niche
in many areas). Experts concede that they may have crossed the frozen
St. Lawrence from the Algonquin Park area of Ontario. A technical report
for the governor's 1990 commission said that an Oswegatchie Great Wilderness could support a core population of wolves, and a study by the
United States Fish and Wildlife Service recommended the Adirondack
Park for possible future wolf restorations. It's academic for now. A call
I made to the local office of the state environmental agency to ask about
the possibility brought a typical reponse: "Don't bet on it."

It raises the question of definitions. In Colvin's day, everybody knew
what "wilderness" meant. Much of that meaning was negative but this
was certain: wilderness was real and it had wolves in it. By Marshall's
time, the big scary animals were gone from our temperate wildernesses,
and abstract specifics had become necessary. Marshall spoke of compatible
uses, minimum acreages, and the tonic effect on the human spirit, a social
benefit. Today the poet Gary Snyder defines wilderness as a place where
"the unmediated processes of nature are maximized." Snyder supports
the big animals' return, emphasizing their positive role in local cultures.
Marshall would have, too, though he didn't use them much in his argu-
ments. Aldo Leopold, memorably, watched the "green fire" fade in a
dying wolf's eyes and saw there everything ephemeral and nonrational
that the wild unmediated world contains—the world of our origins, the
world we still live in.

In a 1992 book titled *Forests: The Shadow of Civilization,* Robert Pogue

Harrison writes that in literature, "forests begin to appear early on as the scene for what later comes to be known as the 'unconscious' " (or the "subterranean" consciousness). Early humans made clearings in wild places, he says, "that correspond both literally and figuratively to the purely psychic reality of human consciousness." One was safe, the other the abode of danger and insanity.

For a long time, I was perplexed by this disparity between our perception of wilderness and its reality. I lived deep in the woods, unclear about the meaning of that as a rhetorical position or point of view. Once, I drove south and attended a reading by the poet William Bronk, held in a cinder-block college building in Glens Falls, New York. The poet wore a madras sport coat and green slacks. The poems were flinty and dark, as the Adirondacks can also be. When he read a poem called "The Arts and Death: A Fugue for Sydney Cox" and intoned the lines "World, world, I am scared / and waver in awe before the wilderness / of raw consciousness, because it is all / dark and formlessness; and it is real this passion that we feel for forms," I felt like I knew exactly what he was talking about.

In the last century, we have undergone a radical cognitive shift in our relation to wilderness and geographic vastness. Discounting outer space and the oceans (both compromised), it no longer defines and circumscribes us. We surround *it*. It is no longer "beyond." The global village has become a sprawling megaburb. Tracts of open space where the unmediated processes of nature are left to themselves amount to so many vacant lots. Now the places remotest from civilization are found at the center instead of the fringe.

Outwardly, the biblical process of dominion is complete, yet inwardly we have misgivings, whether we know it or not. We miss the big open. We miss the freedom to migrate, a one-to-one relation with the gods and the land. We miss the adrenaline or endorphin rush just existing in the world induced. The size of our awe is directly related to the size of the vastness, though I admit I speak as an insatiable vastness junkie.

Wilderness isn't supposed to be scary anymore, partly because some of us have accepted our place in the planetary scheme and partly because many of the animals we once considered antagonistic to our presence—the wolves, grizzlies, tigers—have been wiped out or neutralized. Yet the hazards—psychic as well as physical—are real. As Ed Abbey reminded us, a "danger well-known to explorers of both the macro and the microcosmic [is] that of confusing the thing observed from the mind of the observer, of constructing not a picture of external reality, but simply a mirror of the thinker." Bad maps, for instance, resulted. Barry Lopez says that our perceptions of wild land are "colored by preconceptions and desire." Human consciousness has a stake in wilderness. So if it isn't a mirror, it is at least a giant projection screen, and what it shows us is frightening. Our psyches are circumscribed by a darkness. Inside, we still inhabit a plain where carnivores surround us. There exists every possibility of losing the self, of gazing into its heart and being reminded of our ordinariness and eatability, our own marginal importance in the grander design. A desirable consequence, certainly. But there is also the danger of losing sight of the thing itself.

Sheer bigness reduces that possibility. For our wildernesses to attain what the grizzly-bear advocate Doug Peacock calls their "full and former biological glory," they need *depth,* where crossing one range leads to a farther range, and beyond that to another, where bearings fail and the pretense of expertise is ridiculous and all the tugs of civilized comforts and amenities fall away, where the self breaks down into the bits and pieces of its historical prejudices and miscontructions and reconstitutes itself from its basic elements. A place where the eternal caucus meeting in session, unconsciously, in the out-of-the-way boardrooms of the mind, falls silent. Where there is nothing but the presence and the act, and the unmediated unfolding of processes we only dimly comprehend, without justifications of their real, imagined, or contrived use value. A place at the pleasure of which we continue to exist. A place where praise and thanksgiving for the mere existence of its forms and peculiarities whips unceasingly through the pinecones. An offering. A holy and living sacrifice. Wine splashed on the ground.

Colvin and Marshall confronted the amorphous wild between the Oswegatchie and Bog Rivers and were changed. Something in its formlessness mirrored uncertainties that slouched like remnant wildlife through the rational personas they had constructed. One had his feet in the age of conquest; the other tried to evolve a new consciousness and requite a loss. Both were haunted by the existence or memory of vanishing archetypes. Both fought for the wild's perpetuation as for a part of themselves.

The Adirondack Park is still one of the places where our idea of what constitutes wilderness is being worked out (a hazardous undertaking for all involved: the mirror is cracked). For years, its built-in limits frustrated me, until I made the long carry from Low's Lake to the Oswegatchie headwaters one September, a traverse of watersheds which recent acquisitions had made possible. Paddling through the floodwood on Low's Lake, I felt the awe of an approaching vastness, a defining edge, though I knew—at least, hypothetically—what lay beyond. The carry trail wound easily southwest through mixed forest. At the end, I put the canoe down and gazed across acres of alder swamp and beaver dams toward the big pine country of Five Ponds. I had entered a true beyond, the kind of place you might go for reasons more profound than recreation, and knew that if I continued toward the Red Horse country it would yield—instead of a highway, a farm, or the back corner of the mall parking lot—further extents of derangement or enlightenment before I emerged.

Another time I went there to find Colvin and Marshall's "three corners." It suited me as a destination, being hypothetical and therefore imaginary. I also wanted to test the connection between the big empty places in the landscape and the big empty place inside, though I wasn't sure exactly how to conduct the experiment.

I left from Second Pond early one evening, cloud banks floating low and flat on the red sunset, paddled west on the long flow and camped alone on Grass Pond. In the morning, I slipped back down the channel and crossed the flow, leaving my canoe in the shadow of the stark floodwoods that guard the carry. I walked to Big Deer Pond and took a compass bearing west and north. My course took me through a mixed forest of pine and yellow birch, over an easy rolling topography. If any cryptomorphic moose, wolves, or cougars were about, they left no sign that I

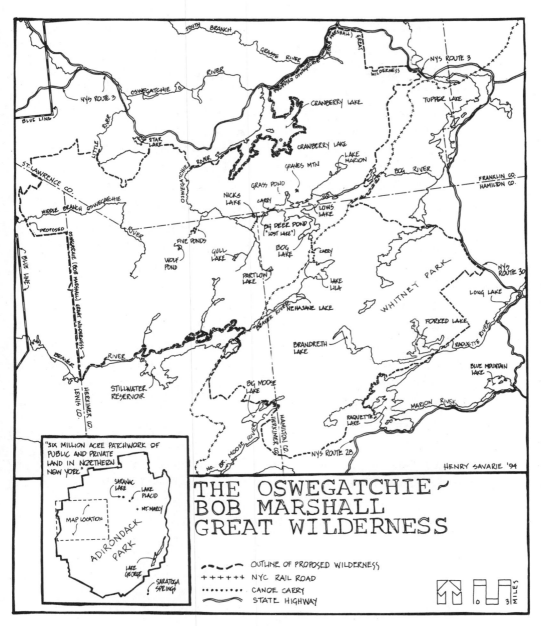

Map by Henry Savarie.

could see, though bears had clawed the beeches and the chocolate kisses of deer lay everywhere in the runs.

After a short hike, I crossed a creek and struck Nick's Lake, where trappers had entertained both Colvin and Marshall. Its shore was deserted. Here I took another bearing, climbing east and a couple of degrees north. A few minutes later, I stood on the edge of a broad flat, under a canopy of mature forest stretching to oblivion. Planes of sunlight with bugs in them transected the shadows. My feet rested on a soft matte of wintergreen, bunchberry, and princess pine. There was no marker, no view, no epiphany, but it was the place. I tried not to think of Colvin with his transit, or Marshall with his loss. I tried to think nothing, in fact—to achieve in this wild heart of the world the resigned acceptance and emptiness of mind that all great teachers tell us is the sole reward and essence of being.

But I couldn't. I was surrounded by wolves. They kept creeping in and crowding the unlit corners of my thoughts like neglected responsibilities, in the dreamy way they do, yellow-eyed and serene, big dogs indifferent to people, patient and unsentimental, as if they had crossed the frozen St. Lawrence of our brief history here and worked their relentless way back where they belonged. In a way, their presence was truer than mine. I was just the vehicle for their lupine reclamation project. I heard a hermit thrush and a white-throated sparrow. A junco rustled in the dead leafage under a tuft of fern. That's all there was, with its implication of everything. Me in my emptiness, surrounded by wolves.

ACKNOWLEDGMENTS

Christopher Shaw wishes to thank The Charles Decker Memorial Fund; the Adirondack Museum; the Adirondack Park Agency; and the Mad River Canoe Company, of Waitsfield, Vermont, for their assistance in this essay.

CONTRIBUTORS TO
The Nature of Nature

————— ∿ —————

DIANE ACKERMAN, poet, essayist, and naturalist, is the author of ten books, including the best-selling *A Natural History of the Senses;* as well as *The Moon by Whale Light; Jaguar of Sweet Laughter: New and Selected Poems;* and, most recently, *A Natural History of Love.*

NATALIE ANGIER, a Pulitzer Prize–winning science reporter for the *New York Times,* is the author of *Natural Obsessions: Striving to Unlock the Deepest Secrets of the Cancer Cell.* Her next book, *The Beauty of the Beastly,* will be published in 1995.

DAVID G. CAMPBELL is the Henry R. Luce Professor in Nations and the Global Environment at Grinnell College and the author of *The Crystal Desert.*

CHRISTINE DAVITT is a research technologist supervisor at Washington State University at Pullman. In 1992, she received an honorable mention in the Polaroid International Photomicrography Competition.

THOMAS EISNER is the Schurman Professor of Biology at Cornell University and director of the Cornell Institute for Research in Chemical Ecology. He has written extensively on science, conservation, and natural history. He is also a filmmaker and a widely published nature photographer.

PETER J. FERRATO is a surgeon and occupational medicine physician, as well as an amateur photographer. He lives in Cleveland.

ROBERT FINCH is the author of *Common Ground; The Primal Place;* and *Outlands: Journeys to the Outer Edges of Cape Cod.* He coedited *The Norton Book of Nature Writing* and is currently writing the Southern New England volume for the *Smithsonian Guide to Natural America.*

DAVID E. FISHER is the director of the Environmental Science Program and a professor of cosmochemistry at the University of Miami. He is the author of nearly a dozen novels (including *The Wrong Man*) and as many science books (including the recent *Fire and Ice* and *Across the Top of the World*). His latest book, *The Scariest Place in the World,* was published in 1994.

AL GORE spent sixteen years in Congress, first in the House of Representatives and then in the Senate, representing the people of Tennessee. On January 20, 1993, he was inaugurated as the 45th Vice-President of the United States. He served as Chairman of the U.S. Senate Delegation to the Earth Summit in 1992, and is the author of the national bestseller *Earth in the Balance: Ecology and the Human Spirit,* which outlines a plan for confronting the global environmental crisis.

JOHN HAINES is a poet and essayist whose works have appeared in many publications, including *Manoa* and the *Ohio Review.* His latest books include a prose work, *The Stars, the Snow, the Fire,* and *New Poems, 1980–88,* the winner of the Lenore Marshall/*Nation* Award for the best book of poems of 1991. He lives in Fairbanks, Alaska.

BERND HEINRICH, a professor of zoology at the University of Vermont, has published extensively on animal physiology, behavior, evolution, and ecology. He is also the author of several books, including, most recently, *A Year in the Maine Woods* (1994).

EDWARD HOAGLAND has published two travel books, *Notes from the Century Before* and *African Calliope,* four novels (including *Cat Man* and *Seven*

Rivers West), and seven collections of essays (including *Red Wolves and Black Bears* and *The Courage of Turtles*). He lives in Vermont.

SUE HUBBELL keeps bees and writes. Her most recent book is *Broadsides from the Other Orders*, published in 1993 by Random House, which in 1995 will publish *Far-Flung Hubbell*, a collection of magazine pieces. She splits her time between rural Missouri, where her bees are, and Washington, D.C., where her husband works.

LAWRENCE E. JOSEPH is the author of *Gaia: The Growth of an Idea* and *Common Sense: Why It's No Longer Common* (1994).

TED KERASOTE has written about nature for a variety of publications, including *Audubon, Outside,* and *Sports Afield,* where his "EcoWatch" column has followed the many issues of wildlife and wilderness preservation. He is the author of *Navigations and Bloodties: Nature, Culture, and the Hunt.*

JANET LEMBKE, a classicist and natural-history essayist, has collaborated on several verse translations of Aeschylus and Euripides. She is the author of four volumes of essays about wildlife and wild places from North Carolina to New Zealand. Her most recent book is *Skinny Dipping.*

PETER MATTHIESSEN is a naturalist and explorer whose acclaimed works of nonfiction include *The Snow Leopard* (winner of the National Book Award); *The Tree Where Man Was Born* (nominated for the National Book Award); *The Cloud Forest; Under the Mountain Wall; Sand Rivers; In the Spirit of Crazy Horse; Indian Country; Nine-Headed Dragon River;* and *Men's Lives.* He is also the author of a book of short stories, *On the River Styx;* the novel *At Play in the Fields of the Lord* (nominated for the National Book Award); and five other novels, including *Far Tortuga* and *Killing Mister Watson.*

BILL MCKIBBEN was a staff writer at the *New Yorker* for four and a half years. He lives in the Adirondacks and is the author of *The End of Nature.*

SUSAN MIDDLETON and DAVID LIITTSCHWAGER have been photographing endangered plants and animals for the past eight years. Their work has been published in two books: *Here Today: Portraits of Our Vanishing Species* and *Witness: Endangered Species of North America.*

SY MONTGOMERY has tracked mountain gorillas in Rwanda, chased giant insects through New Zealand forests, followed orangutans through Indonesian swamps, and been hunted by a swimming tiger in India. She is the author of *Walking with the Great Apes* and *Nature's Everyday Mysteries.* Her third book, *Spell of the Tiger,* will be published by Houghton Mifflin in 1995.

JOHN A. MURRAY teaches English and directs the graduate program in professional writing at the University of Alaska in Fairbanks. He has published over a hundred articles and essays and more than a dozen books, including *A Republic of Rivers: Three Centuries of Nature Writing from Alaska* and *The Islands and the Sea: Five Centuries of Nature Writing from the Caribbean.*

GREGORY S. PAULSON is an assistant professor of biology at Shippensburg University in Pennsylvania. In 1992, he was the grand-prize winner of the Polaroid International Photomicrography Competition. His photographs have appeared in numerous magazines, including *Natural History* and *Discover.* He is the co-author of *Insects did It 1st.*

VICTOR PERERA was born in Guatemala and moved to the United States at the age of twelve. He has written several books, including *Last Lords of Palenque: The Lacandon Mayas of the Mexican Rain Forest; Rites: A Guatemalan Boyhood; Unfinished Conquest: The Guatemalan Tragedy;* and the forthcoming *The Cross and the Pear Tree.* His writing has appeared in the *Nation,* the *New Yorker,* and other publications.

JENNIFER PRICE is an essayist and historian. Her articles have appeared in the *North American Review* and other publications.

KAREN PRYOR is a behavioral biologist and the author of several books on animal and human behavior, including *Lads before the Wind: Diary of a Dolphin Trainer.* Her popular articles have appeared in *New York, Psychology Today,* the *Reader's Digest,* and other publications.

CHET RAYMO teaches physics and astronomy at Stonehill College, in Easton, Massachusetts. He writes a column on science for the *Boston Globe* and is the author of *The Soul of the Night* and *The Virgin and the Mousetrap.*

SCOTT RUSSELL SANDERS is the author of more than a dozen books of fiction and essays set in his home ground of the Ohio Valley, including *The Paradise of Bombs; In Limestone Country; Secrets of the Universe;* and *Staying Put: Making a Home in a Restless World.* In 1995, Indiana University Press will publish his latest collection, *Writing from the Center.*

CHRISTOPHER SHAW is an essayist and fiction writer and a former editor of *Adirondack Life.* His writing has appeared in *Audubon,* the *New York Times,* and other publications. He lives near Saranac Lake, New York, where he is at work on a novel and contributes regular commentaries to North Country Public Radio.

WILLIAM H. SHORE is founder and executive director of Share Our Strength, one of the nation's largest nonprofit hunger relief organizations, based in Washington, D.C. He is the editor of several anthologies of short fiction and science essays whose proceeds benefit Share Our Strength's hunger relief programs.

JUDITH STONE is a contributing editor for *Discover, Health,* and *Glamour* and the author of *Light Elements: Essays on Science from Gravity to Levity.*

ROGER B. SWAIN is the science editor of *Horticulture* and the author of *Earthly Pleasures; Field Days; The Practical Gardener;* and *Saving Graces.* His most recent book is *Groundwork: A Gardener's Ecology.*

DAVID RAINS WALLACE is the author of *The Klamath Knot, Idle Weeds,* and *Bulow Hammock.* His latest book is *The Quetzal and the Macaw: The Story of Costa Rica's National Parks.* He is currently working on a guide to Central American wildlands for the Paseo Pantera Project to coordinate an international nature-conservation system throughout Central America. He lives in California with his wife, Elizabeth Kendall, an artist.

PERMISSIONS